Trickster Lives

Trickster Lives

Culture and Myth in American Fiction

Edited by Jeanne Campbell Reesman

The University of Georgia Press
Athens and London

© 2001 by the University of Georgia Press
Athens, Georgia 30602
All rights reserved
Designed by Sandra Strother Hudson
Set in Berkeley Old Style by G&S Typesetters, Inc.
Printed and bound by McNaughton & Gunn
The paper in this book meets the guidelines for
permanence and durability of the Committee on
Production Guidelines for Book Longevity of
the Council on Library Resources.

Printed in the United States of America
05   04   03   02   01   C   5   4   3   2   1

Library of Congress Cataloging-in-Publication Data
Trickster lives : culture and myth in American fiction / edited by
Jeanne Campbell Reesman.
    p. cm.
Includes bibliographical references (p.   ) and index.
ISBN 0-8203-2214-8 (alk. paper) — ISBN 0-8203-2277-6 (pbk. : alk. paper)
1. American fiction—History and criticism.   2. Tricksters in literature.
3. Indians in literature.   4. Myth in literature.   I. Reesman, Jeanne Campbell.
PS374.T7 T75 2001
813.009′352—dc21   00-030228

British Library Cataloging-in-Publication Data available

Acknowledgments for previously published works appear on page vii.

Contents

Acknowledgments

*T*his book was inspired by the papers presented at the 1997 American Literature Association Symposium on the Trickster, held on Lake Tahoe at the Cal-Neva Lodge, which has the state line painted in gold and silver on its floor, runs its noisy casino all night long, and boasts a tricky past. Photographs of such figures as Frank Sinatra, Marilyn Monroe, and Sam Giancana adorn the walls of the Frank Sinatra Celebrity Showroom, where the papers were delivered. The symposium drew an international, interdisciplinary mix of scholarly perspectives on trickster's many manifestations in American literature and wove them together into a unique set of discourses. For their special contributions to the symposium I wish to thank Alfred Bendixen, Gloria Cronin, Houston A. Baker Jr., Sacvan Bercovitch, Victor Doyno, Lewis Hyde, Jeanne Rosier Smith, McEvoy Layne, and Gail Jones. For insightful comments on the introduction, I am indebted to Guy Bailey. For help in manuscript preparation I thank Roxanne Cuevas and Shannon Cotrell. At the University of Georgia Press, I wish to thank Karen Orchard, Jennifer L. Comeau, and Tammy Oberhausen Rastoder.

An earlier form of Lewis Hyde's essay appears as Appendix II in his book, *Trickster Makes This World* (Farrar, Straus and Giroux, 1998), © Lewis Hyde 1998. Lawrence Berkove's "The Trickster God in *Roughing It*" first appeared in a slightly different form in *Thalia: A Journal of Literary Humor* (Special Issue on the Trickster) 18, nos. 1, 2 (1998): 21–30 and is reprinted here by permission.

Introduction

JEANNE CAMPBELL REESMAN

"*I* was glad when somebody told me, 'You may go and collect Negro folklore.'" Thus begins Zora Neale Hurston's introduction to *Mules and Men* (1935). Though in the next few paragraphs it sounds as though that "somebody" was Franz Boas, Hurston's anthropology professor at Barnard, by the end of the introduction another presence is invoked. "Folklore is not as easy to collect as it sounds," says Hurston, explaining how she had to learn to go home to record the stories and evolve her own identity as tale-teller—having first encountered "some hindrance" as she tried to reenter her hometown of Eatonville, Florida. The introduction then turns to the story of how God made souls for people but didn't give them out:

> "Folks ain't ready for souls yet. De clay ain't dry. It's de strongest thing Ah ever made. Don't aim to waste none thru loose cracks. And then men got to grow strong enough to stand it. De way things is now, if Ah give it out it would tear them shackly bodies to pieces. Bimeby, Ah give it out."
>
> So folks went round thousands of years without no souls. All de time de soul-piece, it was setting 'round covered up wid God's loose raiment. Every now and then de wind would blow and hist up de cover and then de elements would be full of lightning and de winds would talk. So people told one 'nother that God was talking in the mountains.
>
> De white man passed by it way off and he looked but he wouldn't go close enough to touch. De Indian and de Negro, they tipped by cautious too, and all of 'em seen de light of diamonds when de winds shook de cover, and de wind dat passed over it sung songs. De Jew come past and heard de song from de soul-piece then he kept on passin' and all of a sudden he grabbed up de soul-piece and hid it under his clothes, and run off down de road. It burnt him and tore him and throwed him down and lifted him up and toted him across de mountain and he tried to break loose but he couldn't do it. He kept on hollerin' for help but de rest of 'em run hid 'way from him. Way after

while they come out of holes and corners and picked up little chips and pieces that fell back on de ground. So God mixed it up wid feelings and give it out to 'em. 'Way after while when He ketch dat Jew, He's goin' to 'vide things up more ekal'.

Immediately upon the heels of this tale follows a description of how Hurston "rounded Park Lake and came speeding down the straight stretch into Eatonville," with its "three hundred brown skins, . . . plenty guavas, two schools, and no jail-house." She adds almost as an afterthought, "Before I enter the township, I wish to make acknowledgments to Mrs. R. Osgood Mason of New York City. She backed my falling in a hearty way, in a spiritual way, and in addition, financed the whole expedition in the manner of the Great Soul that she is. The world's most gallant woman."[1]

Those familiar with Hurston's discursive style and the difficult relationship between Hurston and her highly directive patroness will not have far to look in this acknowledgment for irony, since Hurston came to realize that patronage—in "falling"—had a heavy price. Mrs. Mason's genuine interest in African American mythology and her personal and financial commitment notwithstanding, it was often difficult for the artists she patronized to account for money in the picayune way she required, accept her control, and realize that the eventual product—research, art—would in a certain sense be the "property" of Mrs. Mason. Hurston's introduction is a subtle but unmistakable warning as to the depths that lie within creative acts undertaken in such hegemonic circumstances; in retaliation it introduces the trope of the trickster (the "Jew" who steals souls) but the author herself also becomes trickster (she tells the story and will have the last word). Mrs. Mason may be like God, handing out the souls, but she is also the thief who wants to keep them all for himself: she is the "Great Soul" in both senses, but of course so is the artist/thief who accompanies and opposes her.

In telling this story Hurston both admires and criticizes the "Great Soul." Poised on the border of "home" and piloting the Chevrolet paid for by Mrs. Mason, Hurston is headed home to find *her* soul by finding the soul of a community, her old one, in order to communicate it to another, her new New York world of writers and scholars. If Mrs. Mason is a thief of words then Hurston is too, with her tape recorder and university education. But, unlike Mrs. Mason, Hurston is part of what she hears, speaker of the Word as well as carrier of the word from Eatonville back to New York. She finds words she does not create, but she also creates words anew. As both anthropologist and artist, outsider and insider, alien and friend, she herself becomes a border of Eatonville that transforms what it touches, a brilliant medium for invention but also an invention itself. Like the Hoodoo priestess she later studied to become, Hurston here serves as an avenue connecting this world and that "other," herself a linguistic invocation of the collective word. Like Eshu, Legba, and other trickster gods of African origin, Hurston is the medium of language between a heaven and earth of her own devising. As such, she is the very model of the American literary artist as trickster.

Mules and Men is a unique study of trickster's presence in black southern folklore. Through its creation myths that explain such phenomena as slavery, marriage, language, ownership of land, and the like, the mingled voices of the store porch and jook joint—those of Big Sweet, High Walker, Good Bread, Joe Wiley, and the rest—are brought together and given written form by Hurston's own retelling. Trickster appears here in every possible place. Once viewed as a rather exotic and even embarrassing rehearsal of cultural difference, *Mules and Men* is now seen as normative, its tricksterism a foundational social reality and source of cultural, artistic, and spiritual strength. Today trickster, that ubiquitous and contradictory figure of play that lives in virtually every culture, has come to be recognized as a key figure not only in fiction based in African American and Native American Indian traditions, but in American fiction in general. American writers have widely recognized the power that taking on some of trickster's personality can give them, and readers have become more conscious of how pervasive an influence trickster really is in American literature.

The most characteristic appearances of trickster in American literature are those that originate in the traditions of Native American Indian and African American literatures, and to a somewhat lesser degree Asian American and Latino writing—such figures as Wakdjunkaga, Iktomi, Coyote, Raven, Esu, Legba, Damballah, Brer Rabbit, John the Slave, Fa Mu Lan, Monkey King, and La Malinche, for example. But "mainstream" writers in many traditions have made trickster an elusive but ever-present character in American literature. Think of Huck Finn, Rinehart, Beloved, the Confidence Man, Simon Suggs, Augie March, the Petrified Man, the Son of the Wolf, the Misfit, Hank Morgan, Sula, Flem Snopes, the Conjure Woman, Westervelt, the King and the Duke, Sut

Lovingood, and Popeye, to name only a few. The essays in this volume present many manifestations of trickster in American fiction. They offer on a broad scale the presence of trickster as an interpretive point of view for writers unlikely to be grouped together in any other context, and they challenge us to read across historical, cultural, and disciplinary divisions. Trickster is ubiquitous in American literature but needs to be seen *as* trickster through new interpretive lenses.

A critical problem of trickster's location in ethnic identity has emerged, specifically whether trickster is a universal figure with a universal voice or culture-specific. Trickster theorists William J. Hynes and William G. Doty have suggested a middle path. They do not view trickster as culture-bound, and unlike Paul Radin, Karl Kerényi, and Carl Jung, they do not argue for archetypal roots in a transcendent human psyche but rather examine "cultural manifestations" with features identifiable across several cultures, including "social functions, psychological mechanisms, literary traces, relationships to religious systems, and ritual transformations." They do not necessarily see the trickster as a constant feature of primitive societies. And what a trickster story "means" must first address its specific, local context and only then move into the broader context offered by the various disciplines of the humanities.[2]

In his classic study of the Winnebago trickster cycle, Paul Radin was heavily influenced by Jung, who generalized the trickster. For him, trickster stories belong "to the oldest expressions of mankind," and they are found in virtually all cultures: "Few other myths have persisted with their fundamental content unchanged." Trickster "possesses no values, moral or social, is at the mercy of his passions and appetites, yet through his actions all values come into being."[3] Jung says in the afterword to Radin's book that, like Hermes, all tricksters confirm "the mythological truth that the wounded wounder is the agent of healing, and that the sufferer takes away suffering."[4] Thus Jung emphasizes the universal healing properties of trickster when he says that "the so-called civilized man has forgotten the trickster. . . . The disastrous idea that everything comes to the human soul from outside and that it is born a tabula rasa is responsible for the erroneous belief that under normal circumstances the individual is in perfect order. He then looks to the State for salvation, and makes society pay for his inefficiency. . . . In this way his code of ethics is replaced by a knowledge of what is permitted or forbidden or ordered."[5] June Singer similarly identifies trickster as a generalized psychoanalytic force: "In dreams the trickster is the one who sets obstacles in our path for his own reasons; he is the one who keeps changing shape and reappearing and disappearing at the oddest moments. He symbolizes that aspect of our own nature which is always nearby, ready to bring us down when we get inflated, or to humanize us when we become pompous. He is the satirist par excellence, whose trenchant wit points out the flaws in our haughty ambitions, and makes us laugh though we feel like crying."[6]

Though they do not deny Jung and Radin's vision of trickster, Hynes and Doty do take pains to elucidate trickster's variations: "plurality, plurivocity, and ambiguity are essential to the trickster Gestalt: this mythological figure encompasses many different social positions, is utilized by different societies to inculcate various types of behavior, and may have manifold modes of appearance even within one culture." Trickster is not "monochromatic."[7] Their definitions celebrate trickster's specificity and variability: "Typical identifications of the Trickster include: Animal-Person (particularly Blue Jay, Coyote, Crow, Fox, Hare, Mink, Rabbit, Raven, Spider, Tortoise), Anti-Hero, Boundary Figure, Bungling Host, Clever Hero, Clown, Culture Hero, Confidence Person, Demiurge, Lord of the Animals, Numskull, Old Man, Picaro, Selfish Buffoon, Selfish Deceiver, Swindler, Transformer."[8] Yet for Hynes and Doty, at the heart of trickster traits is a set of correspondences: "(1) the fundamentally ambiguous and anomalous personality of the trickster. Flowing from this are such features as (2) deceiver/trick-player, (3) shape-shifter, (4) situation-invertor, (5) messenger/imitator of the gods, and (6) sacred/lewd bricoleur."[9] Cristiano Grotannelli supports this dualistic view of trickster's creative consistency-and-irregularity: "Prometheus is the ultimate example of the duplicity of tricksters; criminal and savior, guilty and heroic, impure and sacred, antagonist and mediator."[10] Similarly, Laura Makarius defines trickster as the mythic hero who "transforms nature and sometimes, playing the role of a demiurge, appears as the creator, but at the same time he remains a clown, a buffoon not to be taken seriously. He checks the course of the sun, cleaves monsters asunder, and defies the gods; at the same time he is the protagonist of obscene adventures from which he escapes humiliated and debased." But she stresses trickster as friend to humanity who brings the tools of civilization and as a sacred figure, qualities "that no ridicule or abomination succeeds in effacing."[11]

Margaret Atwood celebrates trickster's sacred outlawry and connects this quality to storytelling itself:

> In every culture that has a trickster god, it's the other gods who have made the various forms of perfection, but it's the trickster who's responsible for the changes—the mistakes, if you will—that have brought about the sometimes deplorable mess and the sometimes joyful muddle of the world as it is. [Trickster] steals fire and burns his fingers. He lives by his wits, yet he falls into traps. He's subversive in that he disrupts conventions and transgressive because he crosses forbidden boundaries, yet he displays no overtly high and solemn purpose about these activities. He's a god, but a god of dirt and mixture and of shameless, unsanctioned sex. He's a teller of lies but of lies without malice. He lies in order to cover up his thefts—thefts made from the motive of simple appetite or simply for the fun of stealing—or merely to fool people or to concoct stories or to stir things up.

For Atwood, one must choose one's god: "If it's a seamless whole you want, pray to Apollo, who sets the limits within which . . . a work [of art] can exist. Tricksters, however, stand where the door swings open on its hinges and the horizon expands; they operate where things are joined together and, thus, can also come apart." Not only does art, with the trickster present, effect such "comings apart," but it also addresses us to very present social concerns, not just supernatural or psychological ones: "What is the 'next world'? It might be the underworld or the world of the imagination, or—in real-life terms—the unobtainable, the denied, the forbidden: other cultures, other nations, other forms of sexuality, other classes and races." [12]

These are basic definitions. Let us examine for a moment the African American and Native American Indian tricksters in particular, since they are especially significant in American culture, and then take note of the most recent theoretical work on tricksters. We may then turn to the essays of *Trickster Lives* with a clear sense of the particular questions they will lead readers to ask about American literature. We will not only be able to understand particular trickster characters but also what it means to interpret entire works from a "tricky" point of view.

Building upon the work of folklorists and anthropologists, Henry Louis Gates Jr. has been the best-known literary scholar of the origins of the African American trickster in African religion; he traces the African American trickster to the divine trickster figure Esu-Elegbara (sometimes spelled "Eshu"), messenger of the gods in Yoruba folklore. Esu's qualities include satire, parody, indeterminacy, double-voicedness, open-endedness, and chance, as well as "disruption and reconciliation, betrayal and loyalty, closure and disclosure, encasement and rupture."[13] Esu and some of his descendants—Legba in Dahomey, Exu in Brazil, Echu-Elegua in Cuba, Papa Legba in Haiti, Papa la Bas in U.S. Hoodoo— are messengers of the gods who interpret the will of the gods for the people and carry the desires of the people to the gods. Gates tells us: "*Esu* is guardian of the crossroads, master of style and the stylus, phallic god of generation and fecundity, master of the mystical barrier that separates the divine from the profane worlds. He is known as the divine linguist, the keeper of *ase* (*logos*)." One of his legs is longer than the other, and he limps because one leg is anchored in the realm of the gods and one on earth.[14] Esu modulates the relations of gods and men, offering escape from social rigidity through the arts of telling the future, of language and fertility. Like other tricksters he is the god of the crossroads, living at the doorway between heaven and earth. As Lewis Hyde notes, Esu is a "shifty mediator" between heaven and earth; he is "the atmosphere itself, shifting, cloudy, full of static and the smoke of human fires."[15] Gates's "Signifying Monkey," the "ironic reversal of a received racist image of the black as simianlike," is a tricky oxymoron "at the margins of discourse, ever punning, ever troping, ever embodying the ambiguities of language."[16] Roger D. Abrahams calls the Monkey's language essentially a "language of implication,"[17] which implies a role for the observer, a response that points to the relationship between trickster and gods or trickster and human beings. The Signifying Monkey, according to Gates, is thus not only a master of technique; he *is* technique, or style.[18] Signifying is a "structure of intertextual revision."[19]

John W. Roberts offers a complementary but different view of the African American trickster; he emphasizes that trickster is in control of his situation, manipulating people at will. Trickster is indifferent to everything but making fools out of people or fellow-animals; yet his is somehow a normative, heroic action. In this sense he is godlike and heroic— bigger than life. African trickster tales emphasize the justifiable importance of creativity and inventiveness in dealing with situations peculiar to the slave-master relationship, for trickster stories embody both the oppression of black people and their feelings of rebelliousness against white culture.[20] Tricksterism was thus a justifiable response to the dehumanizing experience people encountered as slaves.[21] Within a setting of single or multiple cultures, trickster tales assert the right of the individual to contest the irrational authority of religious ritual that benefited those at the top of the social scale while those at the bottom survived through wit. In African cultures, Roberts points out, people were linked together by "a mystical force in the universe that also connected them to nature and the supernatural in a hierarchical and interdependent relationship. Any attempt to manipulate or subvert the force in nature for individual gain . . . threatened not merely the object of such action but the well-being of the entire community, and, by extension, the natural order of the universe itself. . . . While those at the top of the hierarchy could rely on their inherent power—defined in religious and social terms—those at the bottom demonstrated their ability to survive through wit."[22]

As to the Native American Indian trickster, Andrew Wiget points out that trickster "lives best in the ephemeral world of words." Native American Indian stories typically use a word-formula to set the scene for what the audience knows will come:

> "Coyote was going along," the stories usually begin, casually taking for granted the elaborate structure of metaphysical concepts, ethical principles, and social customs that a complex tribal mythology has labored for centuries to articulate. Enter Trickster. Overwhelmed by his own appetites, preoccupied with the orifices of his own and everyone else's bodies, suffering from such severe dissociation that his right hand often indeed does not know what his left hand is doing, proclaiming his irresponsibility in word and deed and relishing it despite all costs, here is a fool fit to discombobulate the self-important servants of status and the status quo. Trotting, skulking, whining, lurking, ranting, leering, laughing, always hungry, never satisfied, he is an animate principle of disruption, about to precipitate chaos and humor through sacrilege, self-indulgence, and scatology. He wanders through the dark field of the liminal imagination until he arrives to summon into play the forces at work in some dimly lit social scene. There for a few moments he exercises his trickery, displays his foolishness, sparks some sure flash of imagination and insight. Then he departs the circled light into the surrounding darkness almost as suddenly as he arrived, still oversexed, underfed, dissatisfied, and on the move.[23]

This version displays some dissimilarities to the African American trickster; this trickster seems to be less in control, and his religious functions are not as clear. But they are certainly present. His ambiguity and his oppositions (fool/hero, selfish/altruistic) horrify and fascinate the audience, teaching important social lessons.[24] Wiget describes the basic pattern: "Trickster the Overreacher" fixes himself on a particular goal, but to get it he will have to transform himself radically or change social norms. He tries several times but fails, and though he may be punished or killed he survives to try again and again. The stories themselves may be simple burlesques, or complex dialogues involving many levels of society, or even lengthy story cycles such as the Winnebago cycle. Generally a discrete cultural scene—a religious ritual or hosting activity—is interrupted by trickster. Trickster exposes institutional power but also suggests by his actions that any attempt to place order upon human behavior is presumptuous and bound to fail. "Trickster functions not so much to call cultural categories into question as to demonstrate the artificiality of culture itself. Thus he makes available for discussion the very basis of social order, individual and communal identity."[25]

Wakdjunkaga, the trickster-hero of the Winnebago, does display a marked social function. After foolishly leaving his "warbundle" feast to cohabit with a woman, Chief Wakdjunkaga is abandoned by his people and left alone with Nature. This desocialized youth wanders around the world far away from the domestications of society, frequently returning to punish his tormentors or occasionally to care for his people, performing actions behind the scenes to help them in times of drought. But Radin identifies Wakdjunkaga's behavior as the mobilization of the shadow in response to suppression of the individual by his society.[26] Yet with Coyote, the emphasis is more upon trickster as a shape-shifter who proclaims his irresponsibility and relishes despite all costs his ability to discombobulate the status quo. Rather than a psychological transformation, he escapes punishment by changing his identity to suit his circumstances. But regardless of which Native American Indian trickster is presented, all of them share a similar sociopsychological function, Wiget believes: "When the weight of culture is felt as a crushing burden on the self, when our heroic sense of all that we ought to be has beaten down our common sense of what we more frequently are, when we feel imprisoned by our own designs, having provided a place for everything in our world except passion, risk, and yes, failure, then at the edge of the imagination, where the all too brightly illuminated present merges into the dark overdetermined future, life twitches in his scruffy tail, and Trickster speaks from some unbeaten part of us, for change and the possibility of a good laugh."[27]

Recent theorists of trickster build upon these past studies and advance the field particularly along two lines: the social impulse behind the "multicultural" context(s) of trickster, and the crucial role he plays in art.

In "A Lifetime of Trouble-Making: Hermes as Trickster" William G. Doty turns to Hermes, the first great trickster in Western tradition. It is striking how much Hermes shares with African American and Native American Indian tricksters, and Hermes' marginal status appeals to postmodern thinking. As patron of roads and travelers, he guides transitions from one place to another, particularly at sunrise and sunset. Hermes' icons, phallic blocks called *herms,* were located at the entrances to houses and rooms or at crossroads. He is messenger of the gods; an old man and a baby; the god of thieves and the prophylaxis against them; masculine and feminine. He is the god of language and speech and the bringer of sleep and dreams, for he enters in at gaps in conversations; people would say, "Hermes has brought us something to talk about." He is at ease on Olympus or in Hades. In his medieval manifestation as Mercurius he appears as both water and fire, Virgin and Lion or Unicorn; he is "both the base alchemical substance, the *prima materia,* and its ultimate perfection, the *lapis philosophorum.*" He is later called *Hermes Triplex* or *Trismegistos* or even *Pammesgistos* and *Multiplex,* all reflecting his inclusive, paradoxical nature.[28]

It is necessary, Doty feels, to avoid the monotheistic tendency to reduce a god like Hermes to a set of clear features. The Greeks had a very different sense of "a divine-human continuum" than did Judaism and Christianity with their sharp differentiations between human and divine: "Greek mythology functioned less to develop theological dogmas than to clarify ethical behavior. It explored our all-too-human existence in the gap between what comes to us through history and fate or *luck* and what we can learn through ethical and cultural training, or *education.*" Yet the most "loving of humankind" of all the gods, Hermes, with his "marginality and paradox, polyvalence and multiplicity," is quite distinct from the "sharp focus" of a Zeus or Hera: "A marginal, border-dwelling figure, Hermes stirs up and initiates. He is not the deity of the singular heroic act, but of the marginal and plural subjectivities of tradition breakers, and metaphor makers."[29]

In his marginalized status, Hermes is peacemaker, patron of youths, flocks, and cooks (he is the original sacrificer). Hermes emphasizes the connections among people, or between humans and gods, as with his association with Eros, "the personified principle of connectedness, betoken phallic expression in its nurturing dimension." But whereas "Eros is 'hot' or 'wild,' his 'generative arrows' wounding even Zeus, Hermes is 'agreeable' and 'good-natured,' and he facilitates but does not force connections." As such, phallic Hermes is peacemaker (caducei), rather than merely a bearer of the spear carried by the other gods.[30]

Hermes' most far-reaching role is as inventor of the various tongues of human communication. To a readerly generation raised on deconstruction, Hermes seems uniquely appropriate as a trickster, for his play with language reflects his sense of play as the essential life force. He is a thief of language like everything else, and he teaches us how to "steal" language too. His traits of deceit, trickery, and thieving often have beneficial results for humans; in carnival, such hermetic transgressions as sexual license and pickpocketing are to be permitted as a "preventative social medicine, venting the interpersonal tensions caused by the strictures of a highly stratified society."[31]

Hermes' jokes amuse the gods and even settle their arguments, but his jokes are unsettling to them too, as when he steals Apollo's cattle or catches gods in lovemaking. Thus Hermes as messenger-hermeneut (interpreter) reflects play in the chance element of interpretation; he tells fortunes but is no oracle, no Apollo. Because words both express and disguise the meanings they create, Hermes does not guarantee that his messages are fully stated; he promises "never to tell lies, but not necessarily the whole truth." Like revelations, "hermetic messages confirm or disconfirm themselves only in retrospect." Hermes "provides a language for transitions or discoveries (the 'Eureka!' experience of the inventor, poet, initiate), but he does not guarantee their value, or their universality. The hermetic find may bring riches *or* failure." Indeed, concludes Doty, "If Hermes models a hermeneutic, it is an open-ended finding of new meanings that may change interpretive force from one context to another; the values of a way-god must necessarily be flexible and adaptive."[32] Doty could certainly have used Hurston as an illustration of hermetic truth.

Lewis Hyde, author of *Trickster Makes This World*, also dwells upon Hermes but connects him with "ethnic" tricksters more closely and identifies him as an artistic phenomenon. He helpfully confronts many of the dilemmas trickster poses for the literary critic, as in his essay in the present volume on gender. Beginning such traditional figures as Hermes and Coyote and the Monkey King, Hyde also turns to present-day creators of tricksters such as Maxine Hong Kingston and Allen Ginsberg and includes a section on Frederick Douglass. For Hyde the line between the artist and trickster is a thin one: the words "artifice," "artifact," "articulation," and "art" all come from the same ancient root, he points out, a word meaning "to join," "to fit," and "to make." Such linguistic parallels and ambiguities point toward trickster's artistic function as a boundary crosser who confuses clear distinctions—"right and wrong, sacred and profane, clean and dirty, male and female, young and old, living and dead"—and acts as "creative idiot, therefore, the wise fool, the gray-haired baby, the cross-dresser, the speaker of sacred profanities." Trickster creates a boundary by bringing to the surface a distinction previously hidden from sight. In several mythologies gods lived on earth until something trickster did drove them to heaven. "Trickster is thus the author of the great distance between heaven and earth; when he becomes the messenger of the gods it's as if he has been enlisted to solve a problem he himself created. In a case like that, boundary creation and boundary crossing are related to one another, and the best way to describe trickster is to say simply that the boundary is where he will be found—sometimes drawing the line, sometimes crossing it, sometimes erasing or moving it, but always there, the god of the threshold in all its forms." He is a "creator of culture."[33]

Do tricksters appear in the modern world? Not really, according to Hyde, or not as they once did, since they need a traditional, sacred context. But as his own examples from Douglass, Kingston, Ginsberg, and others testify, "if by 'America' we mean the land of rootless wanderers and the free market, the land not of natives but of immigrants, the shameless land where anyone can say anything at any time, the land of opportunity and therefore of opportunists, the land where individuals are allowed and even encouraged to act without regard to community, then trickster has not disappeared. 'America' is his apotheosis; he's pandemic." America is "the fabled land of immigrants, of betrayal of the last generation, of opportunity, blues at the crossroads, and confidence games; the land whose government appeared 'in the course of human events' and whose flag has changed its design a dozen times."[34] It is thus fertile ground for trickster and his (cross-cultural) whims.

Hyde offers a survey of trickster tale types, beginning with the "bait-thief" stories that show trickster evolving a nonoppositional strategy to outwit the predator and fill his belly; these are often creation myths, such as that of Raven, who creates the world when he leaves heaven so that he will have things to eat. Raven forms a contrast to Hermes, who doesn't eat the meat he gets from Apollo's cows, offering it instead as a sacrifice to the twelve gods including himself so that he will garner a better prize: not having to face death. The "prohibition on theft is an attempt to constrain meaning, to stop its muliplication, to preserve an 'essence,' the 'natural,' the 'real.'" Another important trickster tale is the "Bungling Host," in which trickster attempts to imitate other animals because he does not have a "way" of his own, or instinct. Stripped of instinct he is humanized; as Coyote in particular demonstrates, his behavior is plastic and based on adaptation: "Having no way, trickster can have many ways." "Polytropic" skin-changing trickster learns "creative lying," the "construction of fictive worlds." As trickster is "unconstrained by instinct, he is the author of endlessly creative and novel deceptions, from hidden hooks to tracks that are impossible to read," a true traveler. Whether Norse or African, mythology teaches us that "There is no way to suppress change . . . not even in heaven; there is only a choice between a way of living that allows constant, if gradual, alterations and a way of living that combines great control and cataclysmic upheavals. Those who panic and bind the trickster choose the latter path. It would be better to learn to play with him, better especially to develop styles (cultural, spiritual, artistic) that allow some commerce with accident, and some acceptance of the changes contingency will always engender."[35]

Tricksters make us aware of the connections *between* things, Hyde concludes; the single Latin word *articulus* refers both to a joint in the body and a turning point in the solar year, and it is the root of "art." *Artisan* (a "joiner" or maker of things), *artifice* (a made thing), *articulate, arthritis*: "In human speech the tongue and the lips are the organs of articulation. They do the joint-work in a stream of sound. In written language there is joint-work to be done as well," as with *articles* that join parts of a sentence together. Trickster artists are "*artus*-workers, joint-workers." They attack hidden weaknesses, they keep joints moveable and flexible; they disjoint and rejoin the world out of the strict control of fate. As in sacrifice when an animal is dismembered by its joints, tricksters do the work of rearticulation in society. "Prometheus is said to be the first carver; the ancient term for carver, *artamos,* refers to 'the one who cuts along the joints.' When Prometheus divided that aboriginal ox, he articulated (jointed) an animal and a cosmos simultaneously, as did Hermes when he carved his butchered cows." As a ritual of sacrifice, "The stories symbolically knit the animal's articulated body to larger social and spiritual articulation." A body in which all the organs remained discrete could not function; they must communicate with each other and thus give up to some degree their own articulation to forces of transgression. In trickster stories the gods are often quarreling and cannot communicate with each other until trickster enters the picture. "He is the cosmic linguist. . . . Both translation and sacrifice . . . are situated, or come into being, at exactly the points of articulation, and keep those points open; they are the creations of a trickster *artus*-worker, the hunger-artist who inhabits the cracks between languages or between heaven and earth." Thus: "when the shape of culture itself becomes a trap, the spirit of the trickster will lead us into deep shape-shifting." [36]

A now-classic study of trickster as a dimension of multiculturalism is Elizabeth Ammons's introduction to the collection *Tricksterism in Turn-of-the-Century American Literature: A Multicultural Perspective.* Trickster disrupts the traditional academic model of American literature, for he does not privilege Eurocentric notions of "the real, natural, or modern." Unlike "realism," "naturalism," and "modernism," with trickster at the center, the binary opposition of the individual against society, a "master plot" of turn-of-the-century American writings, is replaced by one in which rebellion, transgression, and disruption are seen as necessary parts of the community's life. "Individual desire and group authority cohabit within a framework or web of relations; the dynamic is one of interaction rather than dominance and submission." Ammons points out that "Finding a style in which to write and get published required accommodating the monolithic, racist views of White America. For writers committed to their own people, it also required breaking through them. Such a transaction could only be handled covertly, or by finding strategies to negotiate with a dual audience. . . . From these circumstances . . . 'tricksterism' emerged." In trickster's plot "the disruly—the transgressive—is accepted as part of the community's life. Individual desire and group authority cohabit within a network or web of relations; the dynamic is one of interaction rather than dominance and submission." [37] The disruptive but fundamentally necessary trickster is thus also of special attractiveness to writers like Melville, Twain, and Nathanael West who wish, as Warwick Wadlington puts it, to resist "termination" of meaning in their works and instead evoke the rhetoric of "potential" to convey the "radically unshaped but protean force" they see in trickster's endless creativity and elusiveness.[38]

Inspired by Ammons, Jeanne Rosier Smith emphasizes even more so the multicultural role of trickster in *Writing Tricksters: Mythic Gambols in American Ethnic Literature*. In answer to the question, "Why are tricksters—from the Signifying Monkey to Nanabozho to Br'er Rabbit to Coyote to the Monkey King—such a ubiquitous phenomenon?" she responds that trickster's pervasiveness parallels the growth of ethnic literature in America, for "the borders and boundaries of 'American' literature continually fluctuate and blur." Tricksters are a way of "mediating change," for they

> revel in the hazardous complexity of life in modern America. . . . All sorts of interesting parallels appear when we consider trickster works cross-culturally: the dynamic function of myth in contemporary ethnic literature, the importance of oral traditions to cultural and individual survival, the multivocal challenge to a unified perspective, and the unusual demands made on the reader. . . . Interpreter, storyteller, and transformer, the trickster is a master of borders and exchange, injecting multiple perspectives to challenge all that is stultifying, stratified, bland, or prescriptive. . . . Trickster is a profoundly cross-cultural and therefore truly American phenomenon.

This is especially true in works by American women of color, which form the subject of Smith's study. "Trickster novels use storytelling to set up dialogue among characters and with the reader, thereby lending a sense of orality to the written text. The novels' lack of closure and their privileging of differing perspectives and voices emphasize dialogue, community, and the social process of storytelling." Open-endedness or contradictory endings cause readers to take a more active role in the construction of meaning; this is especially important given the multicultural nature of the novels: "By becoming involved in the interpretive work, the reader becomes more sensitive to cultural boundaries and better equipped to cross them." The "multiplicity of voices" in the novels effect changes in the readers' own openness to new ideas. "As the undefined borderland between two worlds, which is the specific domain of the trickster, the gap represents both an invitation and a challenge."[39]

Quoting Gloria Anzaldúa's statement that "Living on borders, and in margins, keeping intact one's shifting and multiple identity and integrity, is like trying to swim in a new element. . . . There is an exhilaration in being a participant in the further evolution of humankind,"[40] Smith argues that in comparing the use of trickster by different writers, it is important to create "a discursive space" in which their similarities can be seen to intersect but without obliterating their distinctiveness; androgynous trickster is a survivor, a "culture-builder," and "define[s] our national character."[41] Such is the purpose of *Trickster Lives*. By presenting various manifestations of trickster using a variety of approaches—interdisciplinary, cross-cultural, mainstream/marginalized, philosophical, historical, political, literary, folkloristic—we seek to expand the scope of trickster criticism by allowing trickster free movement and interplay among the various forms he assumes, the connections he will challenge, and those he will make.

The collection begins with an essay by William G. Doty that provides a useful and witty compendium of information on how tricksters operate in cultures. Doty gives a strong sense of the contemporary relevance of trickster stories, using primarily Native American Indian examples. As will Hyde, Doty emphasizes the sexual roles of trickster and the connection of his sexuality to creativity: tricksters are "figural marks of the transcendental search for ultimate significance in human experience and its expression in symbols and myths." Trickster's broad function is to "*ennarrate* the grossly human/base/revelatory body" in order to promote community formation, what Doty calls the "holistic *communitas*."

Nancy Alpert Mower and Sandra K. Baringer follow, furnishing specific discussions of tricksters that point to foundational features of all trickster tales. They use the specific examples of Kamapua'a, a Hawaiian trickster, and Brer Rabbit, the best-known of all tricksters in the United States. Mower's story of Kamapua'a, the "pig-child" of ancient Hawai'i, is a shape-shifter whose games and tricks are accompanied by his sacrifice for the "*ohana*," or family of humans he lives among. He is transformed from mischievous baby-god to defender of the oppressed and guardian of the people. One of his many forms is the elusive fish with the tricky name *humuhumunukunukuapua'a,* now the state fish of Hawai'i. Baringer's comparison of Brer Rabbit and the Cherokee trickster Rabbit reveals telling similarities and differences between African American and Native American Indian tricksters. As most animal tales offer satiric comment on human society, so these Naughty Bunnies, despite all their pranks, are in the end "defenders of truth." In the course of her analysis, Baringer relates a number of lively and fascinating tales of unbridled Rabbitry.

A powerful pair of essays on Mark Twain, arguably America's greatest (and trickiest) writer, offer new insights on Twain as trickster in *Adventures of Huckleberry Finn* and *Roughing It*. Sacvan Bercovitch's "Deadpan Trickster: The American Humor of Huckleberry Finn" identifies the book as "a Trickster paradise" in which Twain's "snappers" reveal crucial problems of interpretation. Bercovitch sees Huck's decision to "light out for the territory" as a model "joke." Twain's deadpan humor makes it hard for some, however, to get the joke. This is key: "We can't get any of its jokes without figuring out motive and plot, and we can't possibly do that without assuming a moral position." Bercovitch opposes the claims that the novel is "a radical gesture against interpretation at large," mocking "the very need to find meaning," and that it is "a radical confirmation of the process itself of interpretation," but through study of Twain's humor finds the two poles "reciprocally enriching": "The Huck we are left with represents our powers both of myth-making and of myth-mocking. . . . *Huckleberry Finn* is a savage obituary to the traps of culture which turns out to be a life-buoy (a coffin-lifebuoy) to the possibilities of an ethical life."

Lawrence I. Berkove's "The Trickster God in *Roughing It*" provocatively argues that Twain "regarded God as the greatest trickster of them all." Retaining a suppressed belief in God throughout his life, Twain's "ineradicable" Calvinism led him to see God as more than "stern, angry, and vengeful," but as actually malevolent. In *Roughing It,* what appears to be only a loosely anecdotal set of travel adventures is in fact organized quite compellingly around "a repeated pattern of hoaxes and deceptions" carried out in imitation of the trickster God who set the human stage. Despite all their travels and efforts at silver mining, homesteading, and even writing, and despite the book's rollicking hilarity, its characters learn nothing and do not change. The book's pessimistic themes "characterize progress, happiness, and freedom as divine hoaxes." Twain thought he was escaping the Civil War for the supposed peace and prosperity of the West, but instead he found mostly violence and ugly, monotonous reality. His traveler should have stayed at home, Berkove observes, since while *Roughing It* "looked at from a distance is an extremely funny book about the illusory attractions of travel," regarded up close it is "a tour of ruined Eden overlooking Hell." The trickster God, Berkove concludes, shapes Mark Twain's art throughout his career.

Another pair of essays identify trickster as he appears in realistic fiction of the late nineteenth century. Employing folklore, history, and cultural politics, R. Bruce Bickley Jr. compares archetypes in Melville and Joel Chandler Harris, arguing that their trickster figures demonstrate the influence of oral cultural history and performance. Specifically, their black characters utilize their "illiteracy" as a potent weapon against the strictures of the "literate" culture around them. Tricksters like Babo in Melville's *Benito Cereno* teach that it is "a matter of life and death . . . to wage the desperate battle for freedom from oppression." Gail Jones turns to "the wandering prankster figure from outside" to help us read Jack London's important distinction between two figures of power in his stories, beginning with his earliest Klondike tales: the shaman or priest versus the trickster. Ever a writer who utilized mythology in his works, London became familiar with the Tlingit Raven story cycle while in the Yukon. Following Mac Linscott Ricketts, Jones is able to demonstrate how London differentiates the shaman or priest who acts inside communities to effect mediation between human and transhuman worlds and the trickster who is a "self-transcending figure in whose realities humans can be self-sufficient." She illuminates such Klondike stories as "The Son of the Wolf" and "The Priestly Prerogative" but also addresses a range of other stories, including the Christian allegory "The Seed of McCoy," the folkloristic "The Master of Mystery," and also the later dystopic social satire "Goliah." London's sociopolitical interrogations "navigate the flux of individual and communal identity" by employing the figure of the destabilizing trickster.

The following pair, by Debbie López and Jay Winston, turn to African American instances of a "signifying" trickster. López sees Toni Morrison's character Sula as an instance of "creation's first female trickster," Lilith, the she-demon of Hebraic mythology. As Adam's other wife, she is the legendary seductress, murderer of children, and snake woman. Like Lilith, Sula finds power in breaking gender taboos of all kinds. López identifies the characters and story of *Sula* as patterned by the disruptive presence of the female trickster; for the people of the Bottom, Sula becomes a scapegoat whose trespasses live on in legend in a community that is itself in exile. Jay Winston's study of contemporary American poet Thylias Moss describes the poet's liberation of signifiers from "colonizing, controlling paradigms" through her own particular "productive 'havoc' in which . . . oppositionality itself is critiqued." Winston examines a number of Moss's poems to identify her "trickster metaphysics." As Winston puts it, her agenda is "to 'un-fuck up' the possibilities of truth in language, in racial categories, and, in the poems I've discussed, in religion."

Claudia Gutwirth describes the central role played by Nanabozho, the Chippewa trickster figure, in characterizing Lipsha Morrissey in Louise Erdrich's *Love Medicine* and *The Bingo Palace*. "Nanabozho illuminates the novels' connection to a tribal context and their interconnections with one another" by creating trickster as a metaphor for language itself. As Lipsha struggles for articulation, the multiple meanings of trickster—including the sense of fun—allow the individual voice to connect with that of the community. Gutwirth raises important points as well about how scholars handle trickster as a rule.

Eroticizing and consuming the figure of the gay male Latino in the work of novelists John Rechy and Walt Curtis is the subject of María DeGuzmán's "Turning Tricks: Trafficking in the Figure of the Latino." According to DeGuzmán, both novelists structure their works around the revelation that the mainstream culture's consumption of the "flavorful figure" of the Latino is actually "the dominant culture's john-like investment in an illusion of authenticity." Rechy's and Curtis's portrayals of the Latino "trick the cosanguinity paradigm of ethnicity," but De-Guzmán advances the hope that the identification of their tricks can lead to "un-official and un-sanctioned, one might say queer, cross-cultural identification" to counter "obscene trafficking in ethnicity."

Essays by Lewis Hyde and Houston A. Baker Jr. offer far-reaching meditations on the full range of trickster's possibilities in the areas of gender and race—for Hyde, whether he is in fact a he, and for Baker, what happens when trickster is introduced into contemporary political arguments. Hyde's discussion of trickster and gender explains why most tricksters are male and suggests what can happen when they are (rarely) female. The mother-daughter relationship, despite its ambiguity and "tensions over connecting and not connecting," has not found "mythic elaboration in trickster tales" like the father-son relationship, he argues, for female tricksters in general are even more upsetting to a given social framework than male tricksters. Interestingly, when a male trickster poses as a woman—a frequent ruse—this variation actually reinforces patriarchy. Hyde's analysis of the sexualized trickster identifies some of trickster's most basic characteristics and purposes. However, in the pages that follow, readers will need to decide just what functions are fulfilled by the trickster women characters under study: Lilith, Sula, and the speakers of Thylias Moss's poems.[42]

Trickster Lives concludes with Houston A. Baker Jr.'s passionate critique of black neoconservatism in the United States, which Baker characterizes, using the example of Stephen Carter's *Reflections of an Affirmative Action Baby,* as "rhetorical, conservative, trickster agency." Baker reveals the "tricky speech" of Carter and his intellectual predecessor Shelby Steele as appropriations of tricksterism to advance distinctly untricksterish goals. Their "sacred textual triumphalism" comes under sharp scrutiny by Baker—himself a master of the "free wordplay" he sees as antidote to the allegorizing of pseudotricksters. The problem Jones raised of distinguishing between shamans and tricksters appears here too, and the "shame" in shaman draws Baker's fire. Baker's essay demonstrates how the trope of trickster can leave literature altogether and work on the plane of social commentary and philosophy.

Slippery as he is, trickster moves about freely in this book from essay to essay making connections for us, provoking, teasing, startling—scaring?—us into new knowledge about writers past and present. The essays here give us the joyful riotousness of trickster, his "destructive" creativity, his endless variety, and his eternal coexistence between heaven and earth. Different as these American authors and the critics who write about them are, they are all under the sway of trickster, and I hope readers of *Trickster Lives* will find themselves falling under his spell too.

Notes

1. Zora Neale Hurston, *Mules and Men* (New York: J. B. Lippincott, 1935; rpt., New York: Harper and Row, 1990), 1–4.

2. William J. Hynes and William G. Doty, introduction to *Mythical Trickster Figures: Contours, Contexts, and Criticisms,* ed. Hynes and Doty (Tuscaloosa: University of Alabama Press, 1993), 2–3, 8–9.

3. Paul Radin, *The Trickster: A Study in American Indian Mythology,* with commentaries by Karl Kerényi and C. G. Jung (New York: Greenwood Press, 1956), ix.

4. Carl Jung, in Radin 195–96.

5. Ibid. 206–7.

6. June Singer, *Boundaries of the Soul: The Practice of Jung's Psychology* (New York: Anchor/Doubleday, 1972), 289–90.

7. Hynes and Doty 9.

8. Ibid. 24.

9. Ibid. 34.

10. Cristiano Grottanelli, "Trickster, Scapegoats, Champions, Savior," *History of Religions* 23 (Nov. 1983): 120–21, 135.

11. Laura Makarius, "The Myth of the Trickster: The Necessary Breaker of Taboos," in Hynes and Doty 67–68.

12. Margaret Atwood, "Masterpiece Theater," review of *Trickster Makes This World: Mischief, Myth and Art* and *The Gift: Imagination and the Erotic Life of Property* by Lewis Hyde, *Los Angeles Times Book Review*, 25 Jan. 1998, 7.

13. Henry Louis Gates Jr., *The Signifying Monkey: A Theory of Afro-American Literary Criticism* (New York: Oxford University Press, 1988), 6–7.

14. Henry Louis Gates Jr., *Figures in Black: Words, Signs, and the "Racial" Self* (New York: Oxford University Press, 1987), 237.

15. Lewis Hyde, *Trickster Makes This World: Mischief, Myth and Art* (New York: Farrar, Straus and Giroux, 1998), 124–26.

16. Gates, *Figures* 236–37, *Monkey* 52.

17. Roger D. Abrahams, *Deep Down in the Jungle: Negro Narrative Folklore from the Streets of Philadelphia* (Chicago: Aldine, 1970), 51–52.

18. Gates, *Monkey* 54–55.

19. Gates, *Figures* 240, 242.

20. John W. Roberts, "The African American Animal Trickster as Hero," *Redefining American Literary History,* ed. A. LaVonne Brown Ruoff and Jerry W. Ward Jr. (New York: Modern Language Association of America, 1990), 111, 97, 100–105.

21. Roberts, *From Trickster to Badman: The Black Folk Hero in Slavery and Freedom* (Philadelphia: University of Pennsylvania Press, 1989), 35–37.

22. Roberts, "Trickster as Hero" 104–6.

23. Andrew Wiget, "His Life in His Tail: The Native American Trickster and the Literature Of Possibility," *Redefining American Literary History,* ed. A. LaVonne Brown Ruoff and Jerry W. Ward Jr. (New York: Modern Language Association of America, 1990), 86.

24. Wiget 87, 92. Wiget does observe that such ambiguity "also creates real problems of interpretation, often exacerbated by the sketchiness with which some of the stories are told." There are many audiences for these tales within the one audience, and hence many older people and younger people tend to laugh at different parts of the trickster story. For example, the elders laugh when he

gets his comeuppance; the youths when he is upsetting the social order during the story.

25. Wiget 91–94.

26. Radin 132–35, 195.

27. Wiget 95.

28. William G. Doty, "A Lifetime of Trouble-Making: Hermes as Trickster," *Mythical Trickster Figures: Contours, Contexts, and Criticisms,* ed. William J. Hynes and William G. Doty (Tuscaloosa: University of Alabama Press, 1997), 48–49.

29. Ibid. 50.

30. Ibid. 51.

31. Ibid. 32, 58–59.

32. Ibid. 60–63.

33. Hyde 6–8.

34. Ibid. 10–11, 311.

35. Ibid. 22, 33, 35, 42–45, 51, 59, 65, 74–75, 107, 176–79, 188–89, 191–98. In trickster stories there is often "dirt," Hyde notes, and that dirt "is a by-product of creating order." "As a rule, trickster takes a god who lives on high and debases him or her with earthly dirt, or appears to debase him, for in fact the usual consequence of this dirtying is the god's eventual renewal." As in Bakhtin's "carnival," this happens "when purity approaches sterility." When change is in order "ritual dirt-work" pushes change into being; when it is not, it "offers the virtue of non-violent stability. . . . Trickster tales . . . usually bring harmless release, but occasionally they authorize moments of radical change." In the postmodern world, since we have few shared rituals, our "dirt-work" has settled on fights about transgressive art, such as that of Robert Mapplethorpe and Andres Serrano. The dirt-work could not take place without the transgressive artist and Senator Jesse Helms; it takes "both sides to enact this drama. . . . The team of Serrano & Helms finds the dying god abandoned in the five 'n' dime, exposes him to gross impurity, then raises him up again, newly clean, newly powerful." For Hyde, attacks such as those of Helms "are far more dangerous than the dirt they seek to purge."

36. Hyde 254–59, 280.

37. Elizabeth Ammons, introduction to *Tricksterism in Turn-of-the-Century American Literature: A Multicultural Perspective,* ed. Elizabeth Ammons and Annette White-Parks (Hanover, N.H.: University Press of New England, 1994), vii–ix.

38. Warwick Wadlington, *The Confidence Game in American Literature* (Princeton, N.J.: Princeton University Press, 1975), 5, 16.

39. Jeanne Rosier Smith, *Writing Tricksters: Mythic Gambols in American Ethnic Literature* (Berkeley and Los Angeles: University of California Press, 1997),

xi–xii, 2–3, 16–17, 23–24. On "trickster discourse," see also Gerald Vizenor, *The People Named the Chippewa* (Minneapolis: University of Minnesota Press, 1984), 196.

40. Gloria Andzaldúa, *Borderlands/La Frontera: The New Mestiza* (San Francisco: Aunt Lute Foundation, 1987), ix.

41. Smith, *Writing Tricksters* 7–9, 11, 156. 156. Elsewhere Smith echoes the perspective on language and the trickster given by other theorists. In her study of Zitkala-Ša's trickster, the Lakota figure Iktomi the spider, Smith remarks, "If learning English is the crucial step in enabling Zitkala-Ša to negotiate the two worlds she lives in, Mikhail Bakhtin's conception of language as world view helps to explain the trickster's relationship to language. Because of their marginal cultural position, tricksters can parody languages, and therefore world views. Their location outside the confines of rigid social structures gives them a perspectival advantage." Thus Zitkala-Ša's description of the alienation she felt from whites as she learned English but also from her own mother, who could not help her because she had never been to school and could not read or write, captures "the painful personal isolation which comes from living within the gap between two cultures" (Smith, "'A Second Tongue': The Trickster Voice in the Works of Zitkala-Ša," *Tricksterism in Turn-of-the-Century American Literature: A Multicultural Perspective*, ed. Elizabeth Ammons and Annette White-Parks [Hanover, N.H.: University Press of New England, 1994], 55.)

42. I have chosen throughout the introduction to refer to trickster as "he," following near-universal usage, and I am in general agreement with Hyde as to trickster's usual manifestation as male. However, I would argue for an androgynous definition of trickster that could both accommodate his feminine appearances in works by writers such as Hurston and Morrison and preserve his supernatural identity as both present and transcendent.

Trickster Lives

Native American Tricksters

Literary Figuras of Community Transformers

WILLIAM G. DOTY

*H*ow do we define trickster? Andrew Wiget, Gerald Vizenor, and Jeanne Rosier Smith see him differently, but the differences lead to a shared vision of the freedom he ultimately represents. Wiget describes him as Appetite:

> Trickster the Overreacher fixes his mind on a single goal, but the means required to achieve this goal will effect a radical transformation of his personal identity or of society's norms. He attempts several times to accomplish his aim but meets with failure, expressed either as revenge by the abused power, as in the Offended Rolling Stone, or by an incongruous physical change that can only be called disfigurement, or even by death. These consequences are only temporary, of course; he lives to strive and fail again.[1]

Yet Vizenor warns us, "Those people who dread the trickster and the mind monkey must dread their own freedom."[2]

For Smith trickster reveals himself as "interpreter, storyteller, and transformer, . . . a master of borders and exchange, injecting multiple perspectives to challenge all that is stultifying, stratified, bland, or prescriptive. . . . In multicultural debates, trickster is a lively, diverse, unpredictable, vital actor, enlivening postmodern discourse and everyday lives. It is no accident that many contemporary writers and critics call upon the trickster in their expression of contemporary life and thought. Trickster is a profoundly cross-cultural and therefore truly American phenomenon."[3]

Figuras—literary instantiations of various existentially marked themes, situations, characters—transcend specific narratives and engage large reaches of communication. They recur rather like the comparative archetypes of Northrop Frye's four-sector mapping of literary plots according to spring, summer, autumn, and winter tropes, derived from the poetic permutations of tragedy and comedy in the *Poetics* of Aristotle.

Trickster figuras are properly *mythic* figures, generic types that elucidate usefully one or another crotchet of human or divine behavior; extend significance to apparently random or ad hoc behaviors; or reveal repetitive situations as promising deep significations only delicately traced upon ordinary narrative surfaces. We do not return repeatedly to review comic strips or movies, but the confidence men of the Connecticut Mark Twain or the German/American Thomas Mann, the midwestern Paul Radin's Winnebago trickster, and the Native American accounts from across the continent compel rereadings.[4]

In addition, Raven and Coyote provide creative figuras extending all the way from poetry by Gary Snyder to fiction by Gerald Vizenor.[5] Many of the literary features in contemporary novels that Jeanne Smith cites can be observed readily in traditional American trickster tales.[6] Likewise Lewis Hyde regards as trickster figures musician John Cage, artist Marcel Duchamp, writer Maxine Hong Kingston, and poet Allen Ginsberg.[7] Zeese Papanikolas moves from Shosonean Coyote stories to explore "the themes of technological innovation and utopianism that might have been embedded in the mythologies of the American West from the Stone Age to the present day."[8] Explaining *why* such deeply-rhizomed figuras operate in so many deeply affective/effective dimensions would require a hefty MLA sourcebook, or three or four.

The fifteen-some years it took William Hynes and me to effect publication of *Mythical Trickster Figures* gestated a real appreciation of the many contributions from all the presently walled-apart academic fields such as comparative literature, psychology, cultural studies, rhetoric and communication studies, and religious studies. American trickster figures are so varied that only an inclusive methodological approach can highlight their comic literary features and psychodynamics.[9] The Erdoes and Ortiz reader now organizes a polyphonic overview that inculcates and imbricates the wide terrain.[10] Strong counters to the canonical 1956 collection of Winnebago materials by Paul Radin that promoted a singular trickster figure are provided by more recent collections charting the manifold rather than the singular—including earthdivers, tar babies, vindictive deities of proscriptions, and boundary transgressors.

I focus here not upon that large arena, upon what Vizenor terms "the trickster holotrope," but upon Native American Indian trickster materials (both ancient/ethnographic and contemporary) as *figural marks of the transcendental search for ultimate significance in human experience and its expression in symbols and myths.*

Quacked and farted too loudly for the approbation of many or most American litterateurs, many trickster narratives do indeed incarnate, enflesh, *ennarrate* the grossly human/base/revelatory *body*. This is not, certainly, any gnostic or spiritualistic flight from materiality but rather a wallowing in the grossest forms of Bakhtinian carnival, rampant eroticism, indeed immorality and obscenity, part human no less than part animal.[11] If our sensitivities toward "tricksters' lewdness and immorality have led to a negative perception," Smith observes that "though often bawdy and even anarchic, trickster tales teach through comic example and define culture by transgressing its boundaries."[12]

And as I emphasize repeatedly, recognizing the sitedness of mythic materials in specific sociohistorical settings ought never be lacking in wide-ranging interpretations.[13] Smith reminds us of the "potential challenge to ethnocentricity" and awareness of "the artificiality of culture as such" that criticism of such (perhaps risqué) stories can contribute.[14] Kenneth Lincoln points to the dangers of "slurring 'other' cultures," "playing ethnic," and ignoring cultural tastes or tribal values: "Pan-Indian slurs may turn tribally specific particulars into tasteless parodies."[15]

In this essay the reader will find no whitewashing amelioration of such materials, nor the negative hermeneutics of Freud or Lévi-Strauss. Hardly the allegorists' ploy, according to which statements such as "that twenty-foot-long penis shot clear across the brook, to Princess Buffie's delighted surprise" *really refer to,* oh, say, a deconstructionist revision of patriarchal monotheism.[16]

Rather, in a few examples, I identify some benchmarks that I find instructive indicators that most American trickster talk/tales, while frequently scatological, represent much more than merely scat-songs; that all the elemental trickster features of talking turds and misplaced body parts reflect a cosmological significance beyond the Revlon-esque artificiality of The American Smile and the formaldehyded corpse; and that transgressive, contraestablishment tricksterisms offer a carnivalesque post-postmodernist creativity whose central sociopsychological drive promotes important community-formation.[17]

Indeed that they structure the sort of holistic *communitas* that Victor Turner identified as the essentially *orectic* (stimulating to action) element of appropriately functioning ritual societies—what I like to name *the affective-effective overdetermination of mythical dynamism,* its motivational and stimulating quality. The trickster parables of Jesus, Kafka, or Borges challenge worldviews even as they hint enigmatically at possible new configurations of meaning; and now Smith finds the novels of Native American Louise Erdrich aspiring to "pure storytelling—that is, creation of community through writing her multiply-tricksterish stories.[18] Hence Kimberly Blaeser highlights the "instructive function of [trickster] stories" as transforming "the learning process into a *communal,* joyful, active process," and Vizenor refers to "trickster discourse" as a whole as leading to "engagement in a *communal* sense of ideas, and meaning, and touch, and imagination."[19]

The indefatigable anthologist and critic John Bierhorst devotes one of his reconstructive attempts to retrieving long-ignored Lenape/Delaware trickster materials, remarking initially how earlier accounts simply ignored trickster materials *because* they were humorous or scatological. Some 220 of those texts have already surfaced, of which twelve are first edited and published by Bierhorst.[20]

Likewise Sandra Zagarell reveals how postfeminist (third-generation feminist) methods bring out several literary incarnations *not only* of the long privileged, independent, individualist, often antisocial Western hero, but of the life of *communities* in their local and *everyday,* rather than heroic-transcendental, aspects.[21] Vizenor observes how American criticism has long been dominated by a view of the Native as "the tragic hero who has lost his culture, lost his race, and stands against a withered landscape as evidence of a vanishing race" (a perspective classically graphed in the photographs of Edward Curtis).[22]

Precisely in such a climate of isolated individualism, figures such as tricksters will be infantilized or trashed. But if we recover a deeper sense of *the communal,* pressed inescapably by Zagarell, we will recognize that *comic* situations are those that presuppose communal reflection upon mores and values. Vizenor refers to the Anishinaabeg (Chippewa) woodland trickster as "an existential shaman in the comic mode, not an isolated and sentimental tragic hero in conflict with nature."[23] Vizenor resents the manner in which an American "academic shroud of social evolution" practiced by earlier ethnographers such as Paul Radin imposed the perspective of "the *hypotragic* rather than the comic mode in the language games of tribal literatures."[24] Almost any Vizenor story exhibits his own comic revisionism—one of my own favorites is "Reservation Café."[25]

Already in the second chapter of *Mythical Trickster Figures*, William Hynes and I portrayed some of the manifold resistance to *humorous*, not to mention *explicitly erotic* aspects of tricksters, a reaction based largely in traditional conservative Christian teaching. But perhaps today, as long stable Victorian and modern cultures are criticized for their psychosocial rigidity as well as for all too seldom fostering a healthy sexuality and aesthetics, many postmodernists are ripe for rehearing America's rich heritage of trickster stories. After all, as Erdoes and Ortiz write, "of all the characters in myths and legends told around the world through the centuries . . . it's the Trickster who provides the *real* spark in the action" (Erdoes and Ortiz, *Trickster Tales* xiii). A figure such as the Sioux Iktomi represents sheer potentiality: "I can do most everything. I'm all-powerful" (Erdoes and Ortiz, *Trickster Tales* 94).

Such stories include one entitled "What's This? My Balls for Your Dinner?"[26] Another is about healing one's mother-in-law (who is often taboo, in Native American societies) by fooling her into sitting upon his trickster dick (Swann 150). Others are about transportable vulvas (Swann 384) that satisfy insatiable sexual appetites (Swann 140); or autofellating (Bright 70) or daughter-incesting (Bright 146), or otherwise indiscriminate lecherousness (Bright 65). These are figures labeled by Bright as "grossly erotic" (Bright 21, 72), by Smith, as lewd and immoral, and by Vizenor as "lascivious, an erotic shimmer."[27]

In her *In Favor of Deceit*, Ellen Basso concludes that "in fact, heightened eroticism seems related to a 'trickster' form of sexuality, characteristic of [the] Kalapalo [an Amazonian people], in which things are never what they seem."[28] Such references remind us of already ancient sexual epiphanies of *Dasein* (the fundamental reality-experience in European existentialism) that have long been familiar in sects and cultic practices of the world's various cultures. These epiphanies express divine or at least *surcharged* sexualities, with figuras so intensely, fructively productive because they are "always the most lustful and energetic of the First People" (Bright 49).

But then I am describing cultures that seek not to discourage Johnny or Mary from masturbating but to teach them how to enjoy their bodies most fully, celebrating the brightness of desire—*epi-phanein*: shining upon—as well as recognizing fully the corresponding *dark* side, which is never far away.[29] The classic Raven figura displays fearful magic, evil trickery (Swann 94–105); his wishes are powerful as magic spells (Swann 98, 100). Killing his seal companion ("my best friend," Swann 103), he threads Seal's guts out of his anus (Swann 102); in turn other birds kill him by shitting on him, but "How could I die?"—so he self-resurrects into the body of a young boy (Swann 104).

On the one hand, he is so powerful a creator that he can invent the canoe merely by sketching it in the sand (Swann 97); on the other, the trickster is quite frequently blamed across Native North America for making a wrong choice, the result of which is that *death* enters for the first time into the existential arena of human life.[30] In a Yakima story, Coyote reverses the normal order of things so that the spirits of the dead remain in the land of the dead and no longer come back to life each spring as do the grass, flowers, and trees (Erdoes and Ortiz, *Trickster Tales* 15–18).

Creation/transformation/culture-hero motifs at one extreme, death/ surcease at the other: the American trickster appears as the liminal go-between, the messenger no less than the thanatotic companion, as souls are accompanied between this and that darker plane.[31] Henry Louis Gates Jr. speaks of the African trickster Esu-Elegba's "sexuality [as] a sign of liminality, but [it is also a sign] of the penetration of thresholds, the exchange between discursive universes"—typically tricksterish, he's a living copula/tor, and Native American trickster figuras are right in tune.[32] They often violate taboos (Bright 25, where the violation leads to creative acts) or ritual proscriptions (Bright 452), becoming figures of inversion (Bright 269, 299). *Alive* in the land of the *dead*, trickster becomes what Dell Hymes calls "a principle of inversion. . . . almost inversion itself."[33]

The Cree and Métis story, "Whiskey Jack Wants to Fly" (Erdoes and Ortiz, *Trickster Tales* 195–99), is typical in showing how the trickster (Wesakaychak) can never respect careful proscriptions: dying to gain the power of flight, he persuades geese to lend him an extra-large pair of wings but hasn't the patience to wait the stipulated four days and nights. Of course the wings haven't quite fastened on properly yet, and so Wesakaychak tumbles headfirst into the lake. He bumbles four more times before accepting his place in the scheme of things: "From now on I *walk*," a formulaic response that portrays the trickster figure as learning proper limits to one's aspirations and powers.

Likewise the Blackfoot Old Man gets excluded from civil society because he is too proud, rejecting the chief woman when she appeared before him in her slaughtering outfit (Erdoes and Ortiz, *Trickster Tales* 205–9). "The trickster tricked" is a frequent motif in these stories, although in one Micmac story Glooskap tricks an evil shaman into a contest in which, by means of "the mightiest pipe in the world" that could only be lit by the flames of a forest fire, he puffs the nasty sorcerer right out of the world into nothingness, thereby befriending humankind (Erdoes and Ortiz, *Trickster Tales* 229–30).

But while the trickster draws together in copulation, he also dismembers; his disruptively separative body parts fight one another, the left hand maiming the right before it is over. Or he farts excessively (Swann 455–57; Bright 128). In one tale, a giant skunk trickster kills people by farting at them (Bright 216), and another possesses talking turds that advise him (Bright 40). He is the excremental dude who can indeed fix the toothed vaginas of miserably unsatiated females (Bright 37); replace his gambled-away eyes with berries (Swann 146); or survive by eating his own feces or scabs (Swann 287), an autocoprophagous theme (Swann 301) that is simultaneously hilarious and repulsive.

No wonder such a scatological, obscene, immoral, gluttonous (Swann 102) figure can be regarded (Bright 21) as *the exponent of all possibilities* (compare the often-quoted line from the Navajo: *he makes all things possible*).[34] In southwestern America, the hunchback Kokopelli's hump is full of fertile seeds, a motif that draws him not only into the sphere of reproduction but also into that of the shaman—and indeed contemporary representations in jewelry and ceramics now crown his bent, flute-playing figure with radiating lines, graphing spirit emanations thought to splay outward from his head.

Another sort of emanation—the physical (and perhaps simultaneously the psychological) Shadow—gets integrated into the Omaha Rabbit trickster's persona ("The Long Black Stranger," Erdoes and Ortiz, *Trickster Tales* 175–77). Terrified of his constant companion, one night Rabbit makes a snare to trap it. The next morning he is faced by a furious Sun, caught in his trap, and when he meekly cuts the cords to release Sun, he is burned between his shoulder blades. The story concludes with the etiology that has (as frequently in Native American tales) been part of the occasion for the narration: "Ever since then he has a dark reddish spot there."

In the Tlingit "Raven Lights the World" (Erdoes and Ortiz, *Trickster Tales* 259–65), Raven not only manages, by means of trickster magic, to create the celestial bodies, the oceans, and great rivers, he also tricks an old woman into making the tides ebb and flow. In a Passamaquoddy story, Glooskap transforms rowdy, lecherous, and disrespectful people—they thought about nothing but copulating and gorging themselves with food—into nasty rattlesnakes (Erdoes and Ortiz, *Trickster Tales* 218–19). Elsewhere (Northern Cheyenne, Erdoes and Ortiz, *Trickster Tales* 142–45), the trickster Veeho, through his power of transforming himself, is responsible for the abundance of North American bison.

Coyote makes the first baby, with assistance of Lizard (Karuk, Erdoes and Ortiz, *Trickster Tales* 72–74), and creates people and animals, yet is always ravenous and philandering, even sleeping with his own daughter (Erdoes and Ortiz, *Trickster Tales* 58). His in-between-ness is emphasized in several accounts (Nez Percé, Erdoes and Ortiz, *Trickster Tales* 63–65; Gros Ventre, Erdoes and Ortiz, *Trickster Tales* 162–63) where he wears women's clothes as part of his trickery.

Any primarily fructive *figura* situated in the spaces between and betwixt cultural stasis and generativity is likely to be branded as *gender-ambiguous*.[35] Transcending smartness (in Greek, *mêtis*) is apparently an Odyssean cleverness attained primarily by means not of Newton's simple vision but of everlasting *contradiction*[36] and variation.

The liminal-extraordinary trickster *figura* "represents a site of intersection, dialogue, and connection even while eluding fixed definitions," especially by mocking the fixed dualistic oppositions of Western culture.[37] Hence it can challenge sexism; can appear to be feminine or masculine indiscriminately (Erdoes and Ortiz, *Myths and Legends* 27, 358); or, in Basso's Amazonian materials, alternatively—the principal Kalapalo "male and female tricksters have been clearly developed to complement each other, forming a pair of opposed yet necessarily related images."[38] Hence they shoot well beyond currently politically correct "multiculturalism" into the mixed-blood aggregations of political-hermeneutical significations so richly explored by Gerald Vizenor, Leslie Marmon Silko, Louise Erdrich, and many other contemporary Native American writers, for whom the liminal wanderer Odysseus/Coyote magisterially models motility.

Hyde challenges the "indiscriminate" gendering, refining his statement with respect to gendering: "the standard tricksters are male, some of whom on rare occasions become briefly female," usually for deceitful purposes.[39] Several African American and Native American female tricksters are named by Hyde: Aunt Nancy (derived from Ananse, the Ashanti spider trickster), Entangling Woman from Chiapas, Mexico, and a female Coyote among the Hopi and Tewa. Elsewhere Hyde finds only some clever tricks performed by female characters, but no elaborated trickster career. I am more convinced than he by treatments of several Hebrew accounts of trickery by females, by Susan Niditch, and Cheryl Exum and Johanna Bos.[40]

From the science fiction end of the American literary spectrum, one may turn to Kim Stanley Robinson's Hugo Award–winning Mars Trilogy, with its brilliantly realized epic Coyote figura whose heuristic-educative romps on the surface of the (future, to-be-terraformed) planet of Mars repeat stories familiar from the traditional trickster figuras emphasized here. Robinson's "radical change agent" reflects any number of Native American trickster creators, one of whom creates a habitable world out of mere shifting sands (Swann 106) and who states "[I] only like it when I keep moving" (Swann 105).

This trickster is a peripatetic figure, obviously, as Blaeser paints Native American literary critic–novelist Gerald Vizenor himself, but already treated classically by Barbara Babcock-Abraham's "Tolerated Margin of Mess" with her sixteen-point summary of trickster traits.[41] Likewise, Gates portrays the African American trickster figure as an *ironic* traveler, who has had to survive by his wits in lands outside his own (I return to irony shortly).[42] Vizenor charts the practice of "a hermeneutics of survivance" by which "postindians" have survived the deluded pressures of the American ingressors (see his *Manifest Manners*). Hyde refers to the trickster as "the consummate survivor"; others refer to his role as cultural mediator or border-connector.[43]

The Hopi Masau'u models such a function, which I also establish for the Greek Hermes.[44] And like Hermes, Masau'u is described fully only by a heap of epithets: "a god, a creator, a boundary-maker. He is also a thief, a liar, and a lecher who plays tricks upon men, animals, and inanimate things. He plays jokes even upon his fellow gods. He makes trees grow crooked and makes the faces of humans look ugly or ridiculous so that he can laugh at them" (Erdoes and Ortiz, *Trickster Tales* 233–34). Many Hopi fear this tricky god and are especially wary of flashes of light at night that may indicate his presence. Nonetheless, he teaches them how to plant corn—so there is always a counterrepresentation, an ironic aspect.

But this irony is a mode of the Greek *poiein*/creating. And ironic revisionings ever since the time of the Hellenistic Cynics have functioned to re-vision, to query and challenge the status quo (as recently demonstrated within academic biblical research by members of California's Jesus Seminar, who find many parallels between the Cynic *chreiai* and the aphoristic style of the earliest level of sayings of Jesus).[45] Poiesis itself can be insighted in such a context as *a sort of tricksterish reinterpretation or transformation*, just as much as a *creatio ab ovo* (creation from scratch).

Native American tricksters are exuberantly at home in this trailer park. Raven can self-transform into another figure at will (Swann 97–106); he is a figure *of chaos* (Swann 139–40) precisely because he is intimately associated *with the creation of the world out of chaos* (as in the Ancient Near East—phenomenologically, the Native American trickster is a Gilgamesh-Adamah figure, in terms of effects). For instance Raven tricks Winter into being milder (Swann 215, Erdoes and Ortiz, *Myths and Legends* 140); is transformed into a maggot (Swann 218); or into a shape-changing chameleon (Swann 286).

Creating features of *this* world, his narratives typically end with "the world restored to order" (Swann 719), so that trickster myths are frequently parts of quintessential creation narratives (Swann 750), according to which the cosmos is made available to human occupation (Erdoes and Ortiz, *Myths and Legends* 171). Trickster organizes the stars; creates rivers; and is a healer. Fully enstoried "tricksters are the kind of thought that raises hope, that heals, that cures, that cannot be traced."[46]

Recently psychotherapist Allan Chinen has found such story materials in accounts of mid- and late-life figures not just from Native America.[47] He proposes that developmentally there is an initial period in adolescence where trickster exploits are extremely appealing. But he suggests that in late midlife, tricksterish elements return as men begin to take on roles of nurturing and mentoring the young. Now again there is a love of acting out and frolicking it up, of double-pointed tales that are not always socially acceptable, yet convey some of the wisdom needed to participate gracefully in cultural life.

Erdoes and Ortiz reflect that Raven stories contain "some of the most abstract and bizarrely plotted of all Native American legends. They seem to unfold in a realm of fantasy, totally divorced from the so-called real world" (Erdoes and Ortiz, *Trickster Tales* xix). Why do we attend to crazy trickster stories, full of sublimation and inversion? Probably because "their narratives can be road maps for fundamental change. . . . a new technology for the human race."[48] Like social ceremonies, "trickster stories [are] always restoring some sort of tolerance or balance."[49] Referring to Innu (Naskapi-Montagnais) Wolverine stories as being close to dirty jokes, Lawrence Millman notes that usually before telling traditional lore,

> the teller has to make sure there aren't any evil spirits lurking nearby, or else his story will attract them in much the same way the scent of blood attracts a predator. Wolverine stories, on the other hand, are told anywhere and at any time, since they tend to be anecdotal rather than ritualized. Also, *they invite the one response that makes life in an unhappy, government-sanctioned community livable: laughter.*[50]

Trickster stories are important in terms of creation, and in terms of creative community nurturing. They motivate (often by negative example) change, development, growth, and careful regard for behavioral mores of the community that enjoys them. As Jeanne Smith notes in a citation at the beginning of this essay, "it is no accident that many contemporary writers and critics call upon the trickster in their expression of contemporary life and thought."

Not dusty figures teaching by preaching, these figuras trick hearers and readers into drawing their own morals, even when the stories are lustfully erotic or full of gender ambiguity. By so doing, they affirm ironically the importance of moral standards and set out the task of modeling appropriate change and development as ultimately serious and simultaneously hilarious.

Notes

1. "His Life in His Tail: The Native American Trickster and the Literature of Possibility," *Redefining American Literary History*, ed. A. LaVonne Brown Ruoff and Jerry W. Ward Jr. (New York: Modern Language Association of America, 1990), 83–96, at 88.

2. *The Trickster of Liberty. Tribal Heirs to a Wild Baronage* (Minneapolis: University of Minnesota Press, 1988), 42.

3. *Writing Tricksters: Mythic Gambols in American Ethnic Literature* (Berkeley and Los Angeles: University of California Press, 1997), xiii.

4. Paul Radin, with Karl Kerényi and C. G. Jung, *The Trickster: A Study in American Indian Mythology* (New York: Schocken, 1956).

5. See the range of materials in William Bright, *A Coyote Reader* (Berkeley and Los Angeles: University of California Press, 1993); in addition to Snyder's poetry, such as "A Berry Feast" (13–18), see his essay, "The Incredible Survival of Coyote" (154–76). The prologue to Vizenor, *Trickster of Liberty* (ix–xviii), is his most explicit statement, while the following are instructive *on* Vizenor (if not always adulatory): Kimberly M. Blaeser, *Gerald Vizenor: Writing in the Oral Tradition* (Norman: University of Oklahoma Press, 1996); Kenneth Lincoln, *Indi'n Humor: Bicultural Play in Native America* (New York: Oxford University Press, 1993); and Wiget 1990. Further references to Bright cited in text.

6. Smith 23.

7. Lewis Hyde, *Trickster Makes This World: Mischief, Myth, and Art* (New York: Farrar, Straus and Giroux, 1998).

8. Zeese Papanikolas, *Trickster in the Land of Dreams* (Lincoln: University of Nebraska Press, 1995), ix.

9. Blaeser, *Gerald Vizenor* 138.

10. Richard Erdoes and Alfonso Ortiz, eds., *American Indian Trickster Tales* (New York: Viking, 1998). Further references cited in text.

11. Wiget 86.

12. Smith 8.

13. See "Silent Myths Singing in the Blood: The Sites of Production and Consumption of Myths in a 'Mythless' Society," *Picturing Cultural Values in Postmodern America*, ed. William G. Doty (Tuscaloosa: University of Alabama Press, 1995b), 173–200; and "Exploring Politico-Historical Communications of Mythologies." *Bulletin of the Council of Societies for the Study of Religion* 28, no. 1 (1999): 9–16.

14. Smith 12, 14.

15. Lincoln 153, 154.

16. See Wiget 91, recalling Radin 18–20.

17. See Hyde 185–89.

18. Smith 91.

19. Kimberly M. Blaeser, "Trickster: A Compendium," *Buried Roots and Indestructible Seeds: The Survival of American Indian Life in Story, History, and Spirit*, ed. Mark A. Lindquist and Martin Zanger (Madison: University of Wisconsin Press, 1994), 47–66, at 56; Gerald Vizenor, "Trickster Discourse," *Wicazo Sa Review* 5, no. 1 (1989): 2–7; *Narrative Chance: Postmodern Discourse on Native American Indian Literatures* (Albuquerque: University of New Mexico Press, 1989).

20. John Bierhorst, "Tales of the Delaware Trickster," *Coming to Light: Contemporary Translations of the Native Literatures of North America*, ed. Brian Swann

(New York: Random House, 1994), 489–502. Further references to Swann's collection cited in text. See also his *Mythology of the Lenape: Guide and Texts* (Tucson: University of Arizona Press, 1995), at 493n5; and his *The White Deer and Other Stories Told by the Lenape* (New York: Morrow, 1995).

21. Sandra A. Zagarell, "Narrative of Community: The Identification of a Genre," *Signs: Journal of Women in Culture and Society* 13, no. 3 (1988): 498–527, at 503, 518.

22. Gerald Vizenor, *Manifest Manners: Postindian Warriors in Survivance* (Hanover, N.H.: Wesleyan University Press, 1994), 72–75; see also his *Hotline Healers: An Almost Browne Novel* (Hanover, N.H.: Wesleyan University Press, 1997).

23. *The People Named the Chippewa: Narrative Histories* (Minneapolis: University of Minnesota Press, 1984), 4.

24. Vizenor, "Trickster Discourse" 3.

25. "Reservation Café: The Origins of American Indian Instant Coffee," *Earth Power Coming: Short Fiction in Native American Literature*, ed. Simon J. Ortiz (Tsaile, Ariz.: Navajo Community College Press, 1983), 31–36.

26. Swann 339.

27. Smith 8; Vizenor, *Trickster of Liberty* 88.

28. *In Favor of Deceit: A Study of Tricksters in an Amazonian Society* (Tucson: University of Arizona Press, 1987), 295.

29. See Doty, "Everything You Never Wanted to Know about the Dark, Lunar Side of the Trickster," *Spring: A Journal of Archetype and Culture* 57 (1995): 19–38, and Deldon Anne McNeely, *Mercury Rising: Women, Evil, and the Trickster Gods* (Woodstock Conn.: Spring Publishers, 1996).

30. Richard Erdoes and Alfonso Ortiz, eds. *American Indian Myths and Legends* (New York: Pantheon, 1984), 470.

31. See, with respect to trickster Hermes, Doty, "A Lifetime of Trouble-Making: Hermes as Trickster," *Mythical Trickster Figures: Contours, Contexts, and Criticisms*, ed. William J. Hynes and William G. Doty (Tuscaloosa: University of Alabama Press, 1993), 33–45.

32. Henry Louis Gates Jr., *The Signifying Monkey: A Theory of Afro-American Literary Criticism* (New York: Oxford University Press, 1988), 27.

33. "Coyote, Master of Death, True to Life," Swann 286–306, at 288–89.

34. Wiget 94; see the sample in Bright 92–100.

35. Bright 44; androgynous, Swann 21, 63; Pelton quoted in Lincoln 154: "the double lens of patterned [narrated] ambiguity." See also Hyde's essay in this volume.

36. Blaeser, *Gerald Vizenor* 147; see esp. Marcel Detienne and Jean-Pierre Vernant, *Cunning Intelligence in Greek Culture and Society,* trans. Janet Lloyd (Atlantic Highlands, N.J.: Humanities, 1978).

37. Smith 8, 92.

38. Basso 225.

39. Hyde 336.

40. Susan Niditch, *Underdogs and Tricksters: A Prelude to Biblical Folklore* (San Francisco: HarperCollins, 1987); J. Cheryl Exum and Johanna W. H. Bos, eds., *Reckoning with the Foxes: Female Wit in a World of Male Power. Semeia: An Experimental Journal for Biblical Criticism,* Special Issue, 1988.

41. Blaeser 136. Barbara Babcock-Abrahams, "'A Tolerated Margin of Mess': The Trickster and His Tales Reconsidered," *Journal of the Folklore Institute* 11, no. 3 (1975): 147–86, at 159–60: to a greater or lesser degree, tricksters exhibit "an independence from and an ignoring of temporal and spatial boundaries"; a tendency to dwell at the crossroads or in open public places such as the "marketplace, doorways, and thresholds, . . . situated between the social cosmos and the other world or chaos"; "involvement in scatological and coprophagous episodes which may be creative, destructive, or simply amusing"; the playing of the part of the "Trickster-Transformer-Culture Hero"; possession of "some mental and/or physical abnormality, especially exaggerated sexual characteristics"; an enormous libido without procreative outcome"; the "ability to disperse and to disguise themselves and a tendency to be multiform and ambiguous, single or multiple," especially with regard to sexual status; "a two-fold physical nature and/or a 'double'"; the wearing of motley dress; indeterminant physical stature and age; "a human/animal dualism . . . as a human with animal characteristics or vice versa; a tendency toward the amoral, asocial, aggressive, vindictive, vain, and defiant; a strong relationship with the feminine "in a mother or grandmother bond"; an ambiguous position "between life and death, and good and evil, as is summed up in the combined black and white symbolism frequently associated with them"; freedom from the usual codes of society; the expression of "a concomitant breakdown of the distinction between reality and reflection."

42. Gates 4.

43. Hyde 357n. Bright 152; Gates 6, 37.

44. Doty, "Lifetime of Trouble-Making."

45. See Burton Mack, *Who Wrote the New Testament? The Making of the Christian Myth* (San Francisco: HarperCollins, 1995), or Robert W. Funk, *Honest to Jesus* (San Francisco: HarperCollins, 1996).

46. Vizenor, *Manifest Manners* 70.

47. Allan B. Chinen, *Beyond the Hero: Classic Stories of Men in Search of Soul* (New York: Putnam's-Tarcher, 1993); "Fairy Tales and the Psychology of Men and Women at Mid-Life," in *Sacred Stories: A Celebration of the Power of Stories to Transform and Heal,* ed. Charles Simpkinson and Anne Simpkinson (San Francisco: HarperCollins, 1993), 123–34.

48. Hyde 189.

49. Gerald Vizenor, "Gerald Vizenor," interview by Helmbrecht Breinig and Klaus Lösch, in *American Contradictions: Interviews with Nine American Writers,* ed. Wolfgang Binder and Helmbrecht Breinig (Hanover, N.H.: Wesleyan University Press, 1995), 143–65, at 149.

50. Lawrence Millman, "Wolverine: An Innu Trickster," *Coming to Light: Contemporary Translations of the Native Literatures of North America,* ed. Brian Swann (New York: Random House, 1994), 208–21, at 210, my emphasis.

Kamapua'a

A Hawaiian Trickster

NANCY ALPERT MOWER

*O*h, he was tricky, that pig-god. When being pursued by hunters, he could become the smallest piglet in a sow's litter and convince the hunters that this certainly was not the pig they had been chasing. At other times he could make himself so huge that by leaning up against the mountain, he could gouge out a deep ravine or valley, and stories are told of his creating a furrow in a cliff by eating it out.[1] When he wanted to travel to another island, he turned himself into a fish and swam across the ocean. On occasion he would transform himself into a kukui tree or a clump of *'uhaloa* grass and silently hide from his enemies in the forest. He could also manifest many bodily forms; for instance, he could appear as eight hogs at the same time.

Some refer to him as the hog form of Lono, the Hawaiian god of rain, agriculture, and peace. There is evidence that in some parts of Hawai'i he himself was worshiped as a god, and scholars frequently refer to him as a demigod. Often, however, he was a virile and handsome man, who wooed and won many women, including Pele, the fiery goddess of the volcano. He was Kamapua'a, a mighty Hawaiian trickster.

Kama is the Hawaiian word for "child," and *pua'a* in Hawaiian means "pig." The epic of Kamapua'a, the pig-child, has been called "a wonderful example of the grand tradition of Hawaiian orature,"[2] which flourished in Hawai'i for thousands of years before the introduction of the written word. Many are the tales of this amazing trickster, tales that vary from island to island and from narrator to narrator. There are, however, certain commonalities in all the Kamapua'a legends.

Kamapua'a is the third child of Hina and Kahiki'ula. Hina, who comes to Hawai'i from *Kahiki* (Tahiti), is to marry Olopana, chief of the Island of O'ahu. Because Olopana is in the process of building a *heiau* (temple), he is under a *kapu* (taboo) regarding women. One version of the epic claims that Olopana, therefore, gives Hina to his younger brother, Ka-hiki'ula. Another states that Kahiki'ula makes love to her against his older brother's wishes. All versions of the legend agree that the third child of Hina and Kahiki'ula is born a pig and initially rejected by its parents. (Their fourth child, Kamapua'a's sister, is born a rain cloud, and as we will later see, this sister proves very beneficial to Kamapua'a in his battles with the volcano goddess, Pele.)

When Hina and Kahiki'ula reject their pig-child, the infant's grand-mother takes him in and creates a name chant for him. From the power of this chant emerge the pig's many body forms.

Kamapua'a's mother eventually decides to take her child back. She then gives him as a gift to her eldest son, who thinks at first that he has been given a pet pig. Gradually the boy becomes aware that this little creature is actually his brother. When the two older sons of Kahiki'ula and Hina go to the upland to plant taro, a staple of the Hawaiian diet, Kamapua'a helps his elder brother. Taro planting is very hard work. With the help of the pig, however, this brother's planting is quickly accomplished. When the brothers return home, they tell their parents what happened on the upland—how fast the elder brother's planting went with the aid of his young pig-brother and how much slower was the planting of the second brother. This seems to be when the family first realizes that their pig-child has special powers.

As Kamapua'a grows, he develops a hunger for chickens (not surprising for a pig), which he begins to steal and eat. The pig takes chickens from chief Olopana, who you will remember should have been his father (had it not been for the *kapu*), and who is indeed his father's brother. When Olopana realizes that someone is stealing his chickens, he calls for men to come and capture the thief. Kamapua'a eludes these hunters for quite a while and continues to steal and eat Olopana's chickens. The chief keeps calling for more and more men, until finally there are hundreds searching for the thieving pig. The men finally catch Kamapua'a and bind him with ropes, but as they carry him to the *heiau* to be sacrificed, he makes himself huge, bursts out of his ropes, and kills and eats all his captors.

This happens several times. On each occasion hundreds more men come to capture the pig, and each time Kamapua'a escapes and kills them all, finally killing Chief Olopana himself.

The chicken-stealing portion of the story has been retold for today's children in at least two published versions. In ancient Hawai'i there was no concept of separate literature for children. Children just listened to tales along with their parents. It is interesting, however, to examine the ways in which this story has been retold in recent years.

Vivian L. Thompson, in her *Hawaiian Legends of Tricksters and Riddlers,* has Kamapua'a assume his "man form" after breaking his bonds. Thompson says that as a man he "snatched the dagger, and slew his captor."[3] In an illustrated picture book, *Adventures of Kama Pua'a* by Guy and Pam Buffet, we see the pig bound in ropes and being carried to the altar to be sacrificed. In this book, after breaking his bonds, he becomes "an eight-eyed, eight-legged monster with long shining teeth."[4] Olopana and his men try to flee but they cannot. Overwhelmed with fear, they turn to stone.

Only the chicken-stealing episodes have been written about as stories for children. In the Kamapua'a epics, however, these adventures are just the beginning. There are many more incidents; a few will be briefly mentioned here.

After he slays Olopana, Kamapua'a swims about three thousand miles across the ocean. He does this in his fish form—the *humuhumunukunukuapua'a* (which incidentally is now the Hawai'i state fish). When he reaches Tahiti, he assumes his human body, falls in love with the younger daughter of the chief, and settles down with her. He then goes to the upland to fight the husband of the chief's elder daughter. The husband is a powerful giant with two foreheads, one that cuts mountains, another that cuts forests.

As one narrator puts it, "The people of the land . . . are terrified on account of . . . [this powerful giant] because his strength exceeds that of all others" (Kame'eleihiwa 47). Kamapua'a, still in his human form, easily kills the giant with a spear. He is rewarded with the giant's wife, and for a while he settles down in domestic bliss with the two sisters. (Marrying and living with several sisters, all of whom are daughters of a chief, is a rather common motif in Hawaiian folklore.)

Kamapua'a, however, does not stay with the two Tahitian sisters, for "one night the fires of Pele [come] from Hawai'i to fetch him, to entice Kamapua'a to rise and return to his beloved native sands of Hawai'i" (Kame'eleihiwa 55). Kamapua'a can't resist the call of the volcano goddess, so leaving his two wives in Tahiti, he again becomes a *humuhumu-*

nukunukuapua'a, swims back to the Hawaiian Islands, and goes to Pele's home in a volcano on the Island of Hawai'i.

Now begins a royal battle of words. Kamapua'a assumes his human form, but Pele recognizes him for a pig. The two taunt and insult each other. Pele nearly destroys Kamapua'a with her raging volcanic fires. This is when he calls on his younger sister, the one who happens to have been born as a rain cloud, and she sends a deluge to put out the fires of Pele. In the end (several chapters and many chants later) Pele and Kamapua'a can't resist each other. Pele too can assume many forms. She becomes a beautiful young woman, and she and Kamapua'a mate lustily. They make love continually for four days and nights. According to at least one scholar, this affair produces a child who becomes "an ancestor of chiefs and commoners."[5]

Pele, however, is almost exhausted. Her younger sisters fear for her life and are heard to say,

> This is not the correct way for bodies to be used. This behavior of the pig is very disturbing. If perhaps it were the behavior of a human, then we could not forgive him when his part was finished. (Kame'eleihiwa 115)

These words apparently shame both Pele and Kamapua'a. They stop. They share a meal. Then as a truce they divide up the Island of Hawai'i. The districts of Puna, Ka'u, and Kona will belong to Pele, and these are indeed the areas where one still finds volcanic activity, while the districts of Hilo, Hamakua, and Kohala will belong to Kamapua'a. These are the lush green lands, located on the northern half of the island, where "the rain forests were most suitable for his pig nature" (Kame'eleihiwa 116), that is, verdant and fertile. The volcanoes never erupt in the lands that were given to Kamapua'a.

In the course of this epic tale, Kamapua'a fights many other battles and has love affairs with many other women. As the translator of one version says, "What else can we expect from a pig?" (Kame'eleihiwa 151).

Lilikala K. Kame'eleihiwa, associate professor of Hawaiian studies at the University of Hawai'i at Manoa, tells us that even before the written versions of this epic tale were available,

> Hawaiians . . . would have whiled away their evening hours recounting epics such as this, which is replete with [a] fantastic hero, a complicated plot, and beautiful renditions of chant and hula, interspersed with clever proverbs. (viii)

She goes on to explain,

In orature, the artistic telling of the epic was as important as the story itself. . . . The raconteur would take many hours and certainly many successive nights to present such an epic. . . . In traditional Hawai'i, everyone enjoyed and participated in the arts, ensuring a greater knowledge of the finer aspects of life by the general population than is commonly found in modern American society. . . . Hawaiian poetry and narrative were critically judged by their audience as sophisticated or simple, depending on the levels of *kaona* or hidden meanings presented. (viii–ix)

Kaona is an extremely important aspect of Hawaiian storytelling. The first level is simply the tale at its face value. The second level consists of allusions to ancient events, myths, Gods, and chiefs that have become metaphors in their own right. This can include place names and the symbolism attached to the names of winds, rains, plants, and rocks.

Chants and proverbs add a third level of *kaona,* and there may even be a fourth level, conveyed by the manner in which the story is told, known only to the raconteur and one or two special members of the audience, . . . while everyone else remains oblivious to the message. (Kame'eleihiwa ix)

The *kaona* often include sexual allusions; this is certainly true of the tales of Kamapua'a.

With the introduction of writing to Hawai'i in the nineteenth century, people began to record the Kamapua'a stories. In his book *The Kamapua'a Literature,* John Charlot, who has lectured extensively on the Kamapua'a literature in classes in Hawaiian and Polynesian religion at the University of Hawai'i and at Hawai'i Pacific University, says,

The Kamapua'a literature is extensively represented in published, manuscript, and oral sources, embraces a great number of individual works and genres, and is still being enriched by retellings and performances of received materials and by the creation of new ones.[6]

Although there are a number of English retellings of this legend, or of particular portions of the legend, only three complete versions written in Hawaiian are well known today. One of these was collected by the nineteenth-century scholar Abraham Fornander and published in both English and Hawaiian, along with his three-volume work, *Collections of Hawaiian Antiquities and Folklore* (1917–19). The other two versions were printed serially in Hawaiian language newspapers. Kame'eleihiwa notes that

> between 1834 and 1948, there were dozens of Hawaiian language newspapers, which unlike their English counterparts, consistently published epics and poetry, because their Hawaiian audience preferred reading works of literature to the latest news of the world. Epics were almost always front-page copy, while news and business items were tucked inside. (xiv)

He Moolelo no Kamapuaa (The Story of Kamapuaa), written by G. W. Kahiolo of Kalihi, Oahu, appeared in the weekly *Ka Hae Hawaii,* which ran from 1856 to 1861.[7] The story began in the June 26, 1861, issue and continued through the next thirteen consecutive weeks with each issue starting a new *Helu* (chapter) in the exploits of this pig-child.[8] This version was translated into English in 1978 by Esther Mookini and Erin C. Neizmen, with the assistance of David Tom. The translation was a class assignment for a course in Polynesian religion and directed reading under the guidance of John Charlot. In their introduction to their translation, Mookini and Neizmen cite numerous instances of retellings (in English) of specific aspects of the Kamapua'a legend.[9] *He Mo'olelo Ka'ao o Kamapua'a* (A Legendary Tradition of Kamapua'a) was published in *Ka Leo o ka Lahui* (The Voice of the Nation), a popular Hawaiian-language daily newspaper. This epic was sixty-seven chapters long and ran from June 22 through September 28, 1891. The first twenty-two chapters, representing one-third of the story, were translated into English and published in 1996 by Lilikala K. Kame'eleihiwa, who is currently working on further translation of this publication.

The three versions discussed above differ greatly from one another. Abraham Fornander gives much attention to the warlike nature of Kamapua'a and his superhuman strength. G. W. Kahiolo paints Kamapua'a as a lost soul, constantly in search of his family. The *Ka Leo o ka Lahui* publication has a completely different tenor and is more extensive than the other two; in this version there are more than one hundred chants and proverbial sayings, many of which have sexual connotations and remain unrecorded in other traditional sources. The prose sections are elegant. As the translator, Kame'eleihiwa, says, "this is a tale meant to be read" (xv).

John Charlot points out that the Kamapua'a body of literature is based on traditional Hawaiian perceptions and practices related to pigs. In Hawai'i, before contact with Westerners, the pig was the largest land mammal after humans.

It was both wild and domesticated, a source of wealth, raised in large numbers . . . to satisfy a high demand. As food, it was connected to the chiefs . . . and was often used in religious sacrifices.[10]

In ancient Hawai'i, men and women never sat down to a meal together. The men ate in one *mua* (eating house); the women, girls, and young boys ate in another. Many foods were *kapu* (forbidden) to the women and children; among these was the pig. The fact that this animal could be eaten only by men served to increase its stature.

The pig was considered large and powerful and was thought of as gluttonous because of the quantity and variety of food it consumed.[11] Because it ate a lot, it, of course, also excreted huge quantities. Charlot speculates that "the Kamapua'a literature must have originally included a great deal of 'bathroom humor.'"[12]

Charlot also points out that "pigs, especially males, are loners, having only temporary or loose ties with mates and contemporaries"[13] Kamapua'a's wanderings become one of the main motifs in this literature. In some of the epics, however, he attempts to settle down and become a good family man.

Since the pig played such a major role in the lives of early Hawaiians, it is not surprising that this animal assumed mythic proportions, becoming both a trickster and a hero, a creature to be both feared and admired. He was apparently incorporated into the *Kumulipo,* the Hawaiian creation chant. According to Martha Beckwith, the following lines of the fifth *wa* (section) of the *Kumulipo* refer to Kamapua'a's birth:

His snout was of great size and with it dug the earth
He dug until he raised a great mound
He raised a hill for his gods
A hill, a precipice in front
For the offspring of a pig that was born.[14]

Charlot tells us that over a period of many generations, Kamapua'a gradually came to the attention of the chiefly classes, who applied to this important folk figure their own literary motifs and genres, emphasizing his human characteristics and celebrating in battle stories and name chants his territorial and amorous conquests, gallantry, and qualities as a noble warrior and guardian of his people.[15]

The legendary figure gradually changed from a loner to an affectionate family man, from the rebel who tricked Olopana and other chiefs to a chief himself who cared about his people, "from a boisterous, mischievous god, into a powerful defender of the oppressed and an upholder of the forces of fertility."[16]

The nineteenth-century Hawaiian king, Kalakaua, retold many of his country's myths and legends. Kalakaua had a completely different explanation for the origins of this famous folk figure. The king was convinced that Kamapua'a was an actual historic person, around whom legends were later woven:

the child certainly bore the name through life giving the bards who chanted the story of his acts the cue and pretext for shaping him into the monster depicted by tradition.[17]

Mookini and Neizmen explain that Kalakaua may have felt the "need to rationalize Hawaiian mythological traditions in the face of new western scientific theories of a rational universe."[18] Although some Hawaiian families today trace their lineage back to Pele, who they believe was at one time a living woman, there seems to be no current evidence to support Kalakaua's theory that Kamapua'a was a living man.

As a pig, however, Kamapua'a has been sighted even in our own century. In 1935, an article in the *Honolulu Star-Bulletin* was headlined "Kamapuaa Returns to the Garden Island."[19] And Kame'eleihiwa speaks in her introduction of a sighting that was reported to her in confidence by some pig hunters from Hau'ula on the Island of Oahu. She says,

They were certain it had been Kamapua'a because the pig had been enormous, and even though they had shot him in the head and in the buttocks, he did not even pause, but ran quickly past them. Nor did the pig's wounds bleed at all.

The pig ran at a terrific pace . . . and the hunters . . . followed his tracks to a barbed-wire fence, at which point his hoofprints disappeared completely. The hunters searched the surrounding area and found nothing, not a hoofprint, not a trampled or broken plant, nor a trace of blood. It was this sudden and rather disconcerting disappearance of what had seemed a very real pig that convinced my friends that they had encountered Kamapua'a.[20]

Whether Kamapua'a began as a human and then took on legendary manifestations of a pig, or began as a pig and over time took on legendary traits of a human, one cannot deny that for thousands of years this trickster-hero has played a large role in Hawaiian folklore. He remains a significant folk hero today, and as more of the epic stories of this man-pig-child-demigod are translated from Hawaiian into English, such as the ongoing significant contribution of Lilikala Kame'eleihiwa, Kamapua'a will continue to be a most important trickster-hero in Hawai'i's future.

Notes

1. John Charlot, *The Kamapua'a Literature: The Classical Traditions of the Hawaiian Pig God as a Body of Literature* (La'ie, Hawai'i: Institute for Polynesian Studies, Brigham Young University–Hawai'i Campus, 1987), 14.

2. Lilikala K. Kame'eleihiwa, *A Legendary Tradition of Kamapua'a The Hawaiian Pig-God* (Honolulu: Bishop Museum, 1996), vii. All subsequent references are cited in text.

3. Vivian L. Thompson, *Hawaiian Legends of Tricksters and Riddlers* (New York: Holiday House, 1969), 53.

4. Guy Buffet and Pam Buffet, *Adventures of Kama Pua'a* (Honolulu: Island Heritage Press), 1972.

5. Martha W. Beckwith, *Hawaiian Mythology* (Honolulu: University Hawaii Press, 1970), 201.

6. Charlot 1.

7. G. W. Kahiolo, *He Moolelo No Kamapuaa* (The Story of Kamapuaa), trans. Esther T. Mookini and Erin C. Neizmen with the assistance of David Tom (Honolulu: Hawaiian Studies Program, University of Hawaii, Manoa, 1978), 9.

8. Esther T. Mookini and Eric C. Neizmen, "introduction" to Kahiolo vii.

9. Mookini and Neizmen xiii–xiv.

10. Charlot 13.

11. Ibid. 14.

12. Ibid. 16.

13. Ibid. 17.

14. Beckwith 201.

15. Charlot 3.

16. Ibid. 4.

17. Kalakaua, "His Hawaiian Majesty King David," *The Legends and Myths of Hawaii: The Fables and Folk-Lore of a Strange People,* ed. Hon. R. M. Dagget (Rutland, Vt.: Charles E. Tuttle, 1972).

18. Mookini and Neizmen xiii.

19. Mary Salisbury, "Kamapuaa Returns to Garden Island Haunts!" *Honolulu Star-Bulletin,* 23 Dec. 1935, 7.

20. Kame'eleihiwa xix.

See also Abraham Fornander, *Collections of Hawaiian Antiquities and Folk-lore,* ed. Thomas G. Thrum (Honolulu: Bernice P. Bishop Museum, 1917, 1918, 1919).

Brer Rabbit and His Cherokee Cousin

Moving Beyond Appropriation

SANDRA K. BARINGER

On the issue of cultural appropriation in the context of ethnic and multicultural studies, Gayatri Spivak, bell hooks, and others defend the "strategic essentialism" of ethnic minorities as a defense against "excessive commodification" of their cultural production by whites. Informing this discussion is the concept of "signifyin'," described by Henry Louis Gates Jr. in his seminal text *The Signifying Monkey*. Coco Fusco exemplifies the discussion of these signifying strategies—the practice of "taking elements of an established or imposed culture and throwing them back with a different set of meanings"—in her recently published collection of essays *English Is Broken Here*. Acknowledging that such syncretism has "enabled disempowered groups to maintain their outlawed or marginalized traditions," Fusco criticizes the celebration of multicultural interchange when a dominant culture is borrowing from an oppressed culture. She argues that cultural interchange under such a rubric amounts to "postmodern fetishizing of the exchange of cultural property" that "seems less like emancipation and more like intensified alienation."[1] In other words, she seems to say, what is a culturally positive signifying practice when practiced by marginalized or disempowered groups amounts to appropriation or fetishization when practiced by a dominant group.

The stances of these critics has tended to shift attention in the multicultural arena away from the dynamics of cross-cultural exchange and other "strategically essentialist" practices of signification and transformation to the more limited subtopic of the power dynamics of cultural appropriation. One can generally agree with these critics that rampant cultural borrowing by whites of minority cultural property—as Fusco puts it, "rampant commodification of one's cultural heroes"[2]—has historically offered little in exchange to the minority communities from which such property has been borrowed. For example, blacks and American Indians alike have gained little recognition or other recompense for the commodified evolution from the Brer Rabbit stories to Joel Chandler Harris's Uncle Remus stories, Disney's *Song of the South,* and even Bugs Bunny. But issues of cross-ethnic cultural exchange warrant examination beyond the issue of appropriation.[3] Cultural syncretism that has occurred historically demands analysis, for example, of how dominant histories have distorted or erased Indian, African, and Black Indian syncretic practices and their cultural products, and to what end. Once revealed, these practices and products have interesting things to say about the dynamics of cross-cultural contact and about the cultures themselves. They show how such contact can stimulate creative and historically salient retellings of old stories. They demonstrate, in this instance, the profound connections between African American and Indian concepts about the world and about the spirit world. An appreciation of the value of cultural syncretism is increasingly important because in the contemporary, postmodern arena, signifying practices are rarely just two-way but rather increasingly complex.

Historically the rabbit stories of the southeastern United States are interesting in regard to these questions because even the seemingly simple question of which culture dominated becomes complex. African slaves were unequivocally an oppressed culture, or collection of cultures, in the South, but the Cherokees and the other four Civilized Tribes were both oppressor and oppressed. Their own course of syncretism and assimilation with white settlers in the South reached its zenith in the late eighteenth century, to the point where the affluence of slave-owning Cherokee plantation owners in the early nineteenth century precipitated the forced removal of the Cherokees in 1838. At the same time, many Indians became slaves during the seventeenth and eighteenth centuries and blended into the African American population. Though subsequent generations may have been African in appearance to white slaveowners, cultural retentions from parents and other caregivers, disrupted as slave communities may have been by white slaveowning practices, did not disappear. There were yet other Indians who managed to avoid both slavery and forced removal and whose descendants remain in the Southeast, some of them intermingled with descendants of escaped slaves. In the 1920s it was estimated that one-third of African Americans had some Indian ancestry. More recently it has been asserted that "today just about every African American family tree has an Indian branch."[4] Oral tradition maintained by African American elders in the South prior to the northward migration "kept alive the memories of bonds and ties with Native American cultures."[5]

Given all this contact, interaction, and intermarriage, it makes sense that the rabbit, among several African trickster figures, would have become the dominant trickster figure among the slaves. There would have been both egalitarian cross-cultural exchange among storytelling African and Indian slaves, and also signifying practices—"taking elements of an established or imposed culture and throwing them back with a different set of meanings"—by slaves upon dominant Cherokee and/or white folklore. The significance of dancing and drumming to both cultures as a means of communicating with the spirit world underlies the fact that dancing has continued to be associated with the rabbit trickster in both Cherokee and African American stories. Though the Cherokee rabbit stories do not involve agriculture so much as the Brer Rabbit stories do, the position of the rabbit trickster as a bothersome creature in Cherokee folklore is consistent with a gardening culture. Brer Rabbit stories, on the other hand, carry garden thievery to plantation proportions. The eating of greens may well have been a matter of survival to underfed slaves. It would have been easy, if not inevitable, to identify with the nervous, fast-nibbling and fleet-footed animal who pilfered the master's fields under cover of darkness. And from there, the transition to swashbuckling swindler of wolves is but a short step.

Even before Joel Chandler Harris first published his Uncle Remus stories in 1883, ethnologists had noted the similarities between Brer Rabbit stories and Rabbit stories among the Creek and Cherokee—in particular, two almost identical tales: the well-known tar baby tale,[6] and Rabbit's race with the turtle or terrapin, wherein the turtle prevails, not because Rabbit is overconfident and easily distracted as in Aesop's fable, but because Turtle invokes the aid of all his relatives to pop up and impersonate Turtle at every turning point in the race. Late-nineteenth-century scholars asserted that the African slaves had gotten Brer Rabbit stories from Native American sources, or that they had gotten them from European sources. The issue was most comprehensively addressed in Aurelio M. Espinosa's 1930 article on the tar baby in the *Journal of American Folklore* in which he accounts for 158 versions of the tale worldwide, of which twenty-nine are Native American.[7] He concludes that the story is of Hindu origin, spreading to Europe, and reaching Africa and the Americas through Hispanic and Portuguese mariners. Espinosa's hypothesis is plausible but overlooks the possibility of prior independent contact and migrations.

The 1972 edition of the *Funk & Wagnalls Standard Dictionary of Folklore, Mythology and Legend* comments that "both character and category" of rabbit folklore "has tended to be exaggerated" because of the popularity of the Uncle Remus version, a somewhat odd assertion that not only is dismissive of Cherokee and Creek folklore but can only be interpreted as an inability to recognize African American folklore as significant in its own right. This standard reference tool also offhandedly asserts that the tar baby story was borrowed by Native Americans from European sources. Though its ensuing remark that such tales "have been completely recast in setting, characters, cultural background, style, and thematic emphasis to suit the native pattern" gives a rather global overview of every way in which a minimal plot can be adapted to serve the social, political, and aesthetic needs of a particular culture, this standard reference ignores the issue of African–Native American contact and interchange, as have most scholars.[8]

A 1965 article by Alan Dundes, in defending African origin, implies that all Rabbit tales in Native American folklore come from Africa. Dundes provides a good bibliographic history of the dispute over origins, though he curiously omits Espinosa's work, mentioning it only by way of contesting a remark from Franz Boas in which Boas aligns himself with Espinosa. But Dundes's general conclusion is overbroad:

> In West Africa, the most common trickster figure is the tortoise. But it is a known fact that Negro slaves came from East Africa as well and in East Africa it is the hare which is the principal trickster figure. Therefore since the rabbit is not a trickster figure outside the southeast in American Indian folklore and since there can be no question that African narrative elements were introduced into American Indian tales, one can plausibly argue that the rabbit trickster figure so popular in American Negro tradition is African, not American Indian. In any case, the burden of proof should be on those espousing an American Indian origin theory.[9]

One problem with Dundes's argument is that in setting out to prove that Native Americans have borrowed tales from Africans, he focuses primarily on a strategy of disproving European origins for African tales. Another problem is that he sometimes simultaneously relies on the Arne-Thompson tale type index for much of his evidence and dismisses the implications that don't suit him.[10] Furthermore, it is often far from clear to which index he is referring.

Finally, Dundes's argument is based on a misstatement of fact: rabbit stories were *not* limited to the Southeast—Paul Radin has established that hare stories were widespread among tribes of the north-central area of the continent. Distinguishing between rabbits and hares may be important for rabbit breeders, but it seems an insignificant distinction among shape-shifting tricksters, and Dundes himself conflates the two in discussing African origins. When Dundes argues that rabbit trickster tales occur only among southeastern Native American tribes, he fails to take into account Radin's 1956 book on the Winnebago, which in addition to relating a full cycle of Hare stories, refers also to Hare stories among the Menominee, Ponca, Iowa, and Ojibwa, all tribes of the north-central area of the continent. It is true that Radin is preoccupied with making a distinction between a trickster and a culture hero and thus argues that some of Hare's trickster characteristics, at least among the Winnebago and Iowa, "have been purged in order to make him conform more perfectly to the picture of a true culture hero."[11] But Radin's distinction between trickster and culture hero is somewhat insignificant in an argument of origins. One could likewise argue that Brer Rabbit is more of a culture hero than a trickster. Clearly, indigenous rabbit folklore in North America predated the Middle Passage from Africa.

It is important to start with this observation that the American Indian elements in the Brer Rabbit stories have been largely overlooked or dismissed, though the origin question seems less interesting overall than the process of intermingling elements, divergent paths and surviving themes. The African American Brer Rabbit is a uniquely American creation, having been influenced not by European-based rabbit stories as some have claimed (at least, not much) but by the transmission of stories from a variety of African cultures, by contact with Native American communities, and by the subsequent evolution of the tales to reflect unique aspects of the slave experience in the American South. Gross oversimplifications such as Dundes's assertion that the rabbit trickster is African and not American Indian trivialize the complexities of cultural exchange. That sort of argument of origins is a form of essentialism, but not the sort of "strategic essentialism" that furthers subaltern interests. Rather, it effaces opportunities for the study of cultural exchange that is more complex than one oppressor versus one oppressed. Players in cultural trade may have different sorts of assets and liabilities, as the Cherokees did during slavery, and study of literary motifs as artifacts of that cultural trade may serve to enhance understanding of cultural survival. Like Turtle's cousins popping up at every turn in Rabbit's race, common motifs such as dance and music, and particular trajectories of resistance as in the case of the slave stories, demonstrate both the operation of particular strategies of cultural continuity and the different needs of tribal and of slave cultures.

One interesting cross-cultural motif illustrated in the rabbit tales appears in a group of tales that can be described as the "raining fire" stories. In one African American folktale about Brer Rabbit and Alligator, Alligator asks Brer Rabbit what trouble is. Brer Rabbit replies, "I'll show you trouble," and sets the marsh grass on fire, burning Alligator's hide and thus giving it the rough and scaly appearance it has today. This tale seems to be a variation on an African version from the Ibo of Nigeria, in which the "dupe is persuaded to get into grass in order to learn new dance." But there is no alligator and no rabbit named in the Ibo reference, nor a reference to "trouble."[12]

More than to the Ibo, the tale of Brer Rabbit and Alligator bears similarities to Creek and Cherokee stories. In the Cherokee story of how Otter lost his coat, Rabbit takes Otter camping to a sacred place, the "Fire Falling from the Sky Spot." He persuades Otter to take his coat off for the night so it won't get damaged by the falling fire and then, after Otter goes to sleep, sends him into a panic by throwing hot embers from the fire up into the air with a shovel. Otter, like Alligator, escapes into the water.[13] In the Creek version, it is Panther (Maneater) rather than Alligator who gets rained on. This raining-fire technique also appears in a tale of Simon Brown, the ex-slave storyteller whose turn-of-the-century stories are recounted in William J. Faulkner's *The Days When the Animals Talked: Black-American Folktales and How They Came to Be*. In one of Simon Brown's Brer Rabbit stories, "yellow balls of fire" (Brer Rabbit's friends the hornets) rain down on Brer Fox and Brer Wolf. Brown also tells of how he himself, as a boy, drove the patrollers away from a slave prayer meeting by throwing open the door and tossing a shovelful of hot embers in their faces.[14]

In all these stories, an underdog turns on a predator by wielding a powerful cosmic force, fire. In the Creek tale, Rabbit follows up this feat by causing an ocean to spring up between himself and the angry panther.

In this abrupt shift to global proportions from what had up to that point seemed a quaint, though somewhat brutal, fable of one-upmanship, one gets a glimpse of the supernatural powers and themes that underlie trickster stories. The original meaning of the raining-fire motif in the Cherokee and Creek stories is old and most assuredly has inaccessible sacred connotations. The giant horned snake Uk'ten is the original cosmic monster of Cherokee monster slayer stories; similar horned serpents appear in indigenous folklore all over North America from Canada to Mexico. Cherokee folklorists Jack and Anna Kilpatrick compare Uk'ten to the European fire-breathing dragon, speculating as to a common Mesozoic origin. When Uk'ten was finally slain, "he caused it to rain hot fire. The fire rained until he was completely dead." But fire was also used by the Cherokee warrior who fought Uk'ten. The ritual slaying of Uk'ten involved running from one to the next of seven consecutive "protective, purifying fires."[15]

So when Simon Brown rains fire on the patrollers from the church door, he is invoking sacred power, just as the black preacher inside may be raining metaphorical fire on his parishioners. This mode of articulation is a natural outgrowth of a slave culture in which some combination of variations on these stories were heard from earliest childhood. The storyteller might or might not know the Uk'ten stories, but in a way of knowing the world in which animals are understood to connote spiritual power, the signification of raining fire is likewise understood if not articulated. The fire constitutes not just deadly force but supernatural force—sometimes the only force available to a totally subjugated people.

The most powerful thing a trickster can do is to kill a monster or a witch, and in fact, that is what happens in the story in which Brer Rabbit kills Old Mammy Witch Wise, "the last witch what ever live." It is conventional wisdom in African American folklore that witches often take off their skins at night before they go flying around in other forms.[16] At the behest of the other oppressed animals, Brer Rabbit comes up with a plan: he sneaks up to the witch's house one night, finds her skin on the porch, and rubs the inside all over with hot pepper. When she comes back and tries to put it on, the pain causes her to "fall over in a fit," and the other animals burn her.[17] But the motifs are the same as in the Cherokee story about Rabbit and Otter: burning and removable skin.

Stories get told and retold, almost never twice the same, and it is the interactive and evolving part of storytelling that is effaced from these stories in the anthropologically oriented ventures in recording them over the past one hundred years. This interactive dynamic is the reason that it would be impossible to attempt to show that all Brer Rabbit stories come from Africa, or that all Brer Rabbit stories come from the Cherokees, and so forth. Any such argument of origins misunderstands the way oral storytelling works. A further analysis of the interaction will be facilitated by a brief account of historical contact.

Much of the ethnographic documentation of slave folklore has come from the Gullah people of the Carolina and Georgia coastal areas, many of whom were relative latecomers from Africa in the nineteenth century and thus the focus of studies seeking to trace specific African origins and retentions. As a result of this focus, it has been easy to lose sight of the long history of Africans in the Western Hemisphere. There is considerable basis for speculation, though no hard evidence, of transatlantic contact between Africa and the Americas in pre-Columbian times: the nature of Atlantic currents; the presence of bananas, the yellow type that was indigenous to South America, in West Africa; controversies over the diffusion history of cotton and yams; similarities of Olmec sculpture to African styles.[18] At any rate, systematic introduction of African slaves into Virginia and the Carolinas was well under way in the early seventeenth century. Thus the span of widespread African slavery in this area can be said to encompass two and a half centuries, longer than the history of the United States, and ample time for extensive intermingling of new influences into an African-based culture.

The major tribes in Georgia and the Carolinas were the Cherokee and the Creek. Some of the smaller coastal tribes such as the Catawba along the Carolina coast were diminished almost to the point of extinction (at least, in comparison to the "Five Civilized Tribes": Cherokee, Creek, Choctaw, Chickasaw, and Seminole) by way of a combination of epidemics, enslavement, and assimilation; it could be argued that such "disappearing" tribes were assimilated into African slave culture as much as into white or Cherokee communities.[19] As the Atlantic coastland was converted into a plantation economy, some Cherokees and Creeks acquired African slaves. Slavery existed among these tribes prior to contact with whites but was of an essentially different character. Slaves were captives, usually women and children, taken in battle; they were not generally viewed as a commodity for economic trade and profit. But by the end of the seventeenth century the Cherokee became dependent on European trade goods to the extent that they engaged in warfare with the coastal tribes—the Catawba, the Guales, and others—to obtain slaves for trade.[20] At the same time, there was an active trade in Indian slaves, including Cherokee, throughout the eighteenth century. James Mooney explains, "as the coast tribes dwindled they were compelled to associate and intermarry with the negroes until they finally lost their identity and were classed with that race, so that a considerable proportion of the blood of the southern negroes is unquestionably Indian."[21] Mooney's characterization is an outsider's view, that is, a definition of identity based on physical appearance (to a white eye) rather than sensitivity to evidence of cultural syncretism: social structures both within a slave community and with relation to the dominant culture, spiritual beliefs and attitudes, and the blended body of orally transmitted folklore that both expresses and influences ways of knowing and relating to the world.

European intermarriage with Creek and Cherokee women contributed to a more Europeanized model of agriculture and slave ownership among the Cherokees who escaped slavery. They continued to have a significant presence in the region until Andrew Jackson's defeat of the Cherokees and of the United States Supreme Court culminated in the 1838 Trail of Tears, the forced march of the Cherokees to the Indian Territory, which was to become Oklahoma. Thus it is fair to say that considerable contact occurred among Cherokees and Africans for over two hundred years prior to the forced removal of the remaining "civilized tribes" to Oklahoma. One can even speculate that some of James Mooney's information is traceable to one of these African slaves: Mooney discusses a Cherokee prophet, Yonagusksa, "the most prominent chief in the history of the eastern Cherokee," who died in 1839, noting that Yonagusksa was survived by "an old negro slave named Cudjo, who was devotedly attached to him."[22]

There are many cultural affinities between Africans and Native Americans that neither group shared with European settlers. According to Theda Perdue, "both emphasized living harmoniously with nature and maintaining ritual purity; both attached great importance to kinship in their social organization; and both were accustomed to an economy based on subsistence agriculture."[23] Prior to Christian influence, both had similar concepts of an afterlife in which the soul of the dead person made a journey to another world, though concepts of it differed. A soul could become lost and condemned to perpetual wandering for various reasons: despicable behavior, as in the African American tale of the King Buzzard recorded by Edward C. L. Adams in *Tales of the Congaree*;[24] through a curse; or by some omission on the part of the relatives in dealing with the body. Dancing and drumming were central to the spirituality of both cultures and were (and are) means of communicating with spirits. Spirits were (and are) distinguishable from the souls of the dead; people communicate with spirits through dancing and drumming.

Spirits are often, but not always, associated with particular animals. Camara Laye in his autobiography, *The Dark Child,* commented on the affinity of his mother with her "totem," the crocodile, which enabled her to draw water from the Niger without being attacked by crocodiles.[25] Frequent mention is made in *Drums and Shadows,* a compilation of interviews with former slaves and their Gullah descendants, of inherited food taboos related to particular animals. Such affinities with particular animal spirits among Native Americans are usually inherited matrilineally as clan associations.

Though the rabbit is not a particularly important animal in terms of Cherokee dance and ritual,[26] it is significant in terms of the number of stories that are told about it. It is the primary trickster figure in Cherokee and Creek folklore; it could fairly be said that the rabbit is the main trickster figure among southeastern tribes in general, but the largest story collections available were obtained from the Cherokee and Creek. James Mooney recorded twelve rabbit tales, including versions of the tar baby story and the race between the rabbit and the terrapin. My overview of Cherokee rabbit stories is based primarily on Mooney's ethnological treatise published in 1898 and on Gayle Ross's 1994 book *How Rabbit Tricked Otter and Other Cherokee Trickster Stories* (compiled from Mooney, Jack and Anna Kilpatrick, Jack Gregory, Rennard Strickland, and other Cherokee storytellers). In the Cherokee rabbit tales, Rabbit is a talented singer and dancer who occupies the position of the messenger for the council who goes around to notify everyone of meetings and dances. Since the published Cherokee stories are far fewer than the published Brer Rabbit stories, it is not an insurmountable task to summarize them herein: following is a fairly comprehensive summary of the stories contained in these two sources.

On two of these missions, he steals Otter's coat and conspires to denude Possum's tail, both in order to feed his own vanity before the other animals at the gatherings. On another occasion—in a sequence of events that could be read as a satirical political commentary—Rabbit abuses his position by involving Possum in a scheme to deliver a phony message from the council that "everyone must take a mate at once, and then we'll be sure to get our wives." Possum couldn't keep up and arrived late at the first town, where Rabbit had already gotten himself a wife. So they go on to a second town, purportedly to get a wife for Possum, but Rabbit dupes him by announcing that "as there had been peace so long that everybody was getting lazy the council had ordered that there must be war at once and they must begin right in the townhouse." Consequently Possum walks into the middle of a fracas and survives only by playing dead; Rabbit escapes.[27] This is the most overtly "political" of the Cherokee stories, and will be discussed further in due course.

Rabbit helps Wildcat capture a turkey with his talents as a leader in song and dance.[28] This story echoes that of the Cherokee culture hero Stone Coat who provided hunting songs to lure turkeys from their hiding places; turkey hunters wear simulated wildcat ears when following the turkey hunting ritual described among the eastern Cherokee at Big Cove.[29] Rabbit also escapes from the wolves through his singing and dancing talent; he gets the wolves so involved in stamping their feet that he eventually makes his getaway.[30] Parody and mimicry are key to Cherokee mask dancing; such stories in which Rabbit tricks an opponent by mimicking his adversary—or, better yet, putting words in the adversary's mouth—inform contemporary black signifying practice:

"Why do you say that?" said the (suspicious) old Turkey.

"O, that's all right," said the Rabbit, "that's just the way he [Wildcat] does, and we sing about it."[31]

The dialogue brings to mind rap singer Ice-T's defense of his song "Cop Killer," a first-person narration from the killer's point of view.

Rabbit is made to appear foolish when he has dinner at Bear's house; Bear splits open his side to get some grease to put in the stew, and when Rabbit tries to do the same, he practically kills himself.[32] Deer also prevails over Rabbit: Rabbit loses the race with Deer for the antler prize by getting caught cheating, but he gets back at Deer by convincing him to let him file his teeth down to blunt nubs. But then Deer tricks Rabbit into a jumping contest that ends with Deer conjuring the stream Rabbit has jumped across into an ocean with Rabbit stranded on the other side. In Mooney's version, "the Rabbit was never able to get back again and is still on the other side. The rabbit that we know is only a little thing that came afterwards."[33]

The one truly heroic thing that Rabbit appears to have done is kill Flint, a giant who lived in the mountains, whom the animals hated "because he had helped to kill so many of them." He invites Flint to dinner, waits for him to fall asleep, and drives a stake into his middle, exploding him into the pieces of flint that we now find in many places.[34]

Thus among Mooney's twelve stories, Rabbit is the butt of the joke in six, counting the tar baby and terrapin race stories with which we are already familiar (the other four are being discovered in Otter's coat, injuring himself at Bear's house, losing the race to Deer, and being tricked into banishment by Deer). Among the six stories in which Rabbit prevails in some fashion, he tricks Possum twice, ruins Deer's teeth, escapes from the wolves, helps Wildcat catch a turkey, and kills Flint. Though two of the stories involve Rabbit's skills in song and dance, only the last, when Rabbit kills Flint, involves action of epic and clearly supernatural scope.

Though it is difficult to argue with Mooney's judgment that Rabbit is "first and most prominent in the animal myths," the rabbit stories must be kept in perspective; there is a large body of stories about other animals that is beyond the scope of this discussion, as well as creation stories, historical legends, and stories about supernatural people. For instance, Deer and Bear prevail over Rabbit in the Cherokee stories because they are more significant figures in Cherokee cosmology. Deer was the primary target for hunting, and the deer spirit, described by Mooney as "powerful chief of the deer tribe . . . [,] 'Little Deer'" protects the deer from all but knowledgeable hunters and wreaks revenge on those hunters who kill without offering the appropriate prayer. Bears occupy an even higher position, understood to be transformed Cherokee who, as essentially human, can talk if they want to.[35]

Rabbit's place in Cherokee literature could be described as a cuddly buffoon. This characterization marks the major parting of the ways between the Cherokee Rabbit and Brer Rabbit: the former becomes a nostalgic ne'er-do-well used to convey moral principles to children, whereas Brer Rabbit evolves into a swashbuckling antihero.[36] This distinction is most clearly seen in Cherokee storyteller Gayle Ross's collection, a children's book with illustrations (by a Cherokee artist) of Rabbit as a cute, wide-eyed creature. The collection includes four additional stories not related by Mooney. In one, Rabbit tries to throw a noose around a duck, gets carried up into the air, falls into a hollow tree stump, and gets some children to let him out by singing to them. In another, "Rabbit Steals from Fox," Rabbit gets Fox's fish by playing dead in the road in three different places. Versions of this story appear in both Iroquois and African American folklore.[37] "Rabbit Sends Wolf to the Sunset" ends with the same joke as William J. Faulkner's "How the Cow Went under the Ground"; it is also the only one of the Cherokee rabbit tales to involve an animal not indigenous to North America (the cow). The fourth Ross story not in Mooney's collection, "Rabbit Dances with the People," tells of how Rabbit stole the dance mask of a boy who was very popular with the girls.

Before I attempt any more generalizations it may be useful to compare the Rabbit stories documented among the Creeks around the turn of the century, that is, roughly contemporaneous with Mooney's collection from the Cherokees. The Creeks, though long-standing enemies of the Cherokee, occupied the territory contiguous to the Cherokee on the south, in Georgia and Alabama prior to removal. Frank G. Speck compiled six rabbit stories, among them the turtle race and the tar baby.[38] A third story is actually an elaborate sequel to the tar baby story, in which Rabbit has to escape first from a bag and then a hollow tree. "Rabbit Outwits Tie-Snake," in which Rabbit tricks two snakes into pulling on opposite ends of a grapevine, each thinking Rabbit was pulling the other end,[39] is actually a contest over water rights, like most versions of the tar baby story. Only one story, where Opossum gets Rabbit killed by telling him how to get some persimmons by butting his head against a persimmon tree, seems unrelated to other stories elsewhere.

The sixth story, in which Rabbit rains fire on Panther and then causes an ocean to spring up between them, conflates the Cherokee Rabbit vs. Otter story (raining fire) and Deer vs. Rabbit (making the ocean). In the Creek version Rabbit, not Deer, creates the ocean and Panther, not Rabbit, ends up on the other side. It should be noted that "panther" in these stories, often translated as "Maneater" or "Wildcat," refers to the southeastern American mountain lion—not an African animal.[40] Nevertheless, the motif of the wide ocean compels an acknowledgment of awareness of land on the other side. The theme of insurmountable separation was a resonant one for African slaves who experienced the Middle Passage.

The appearance of tobacco spitting in the African American rabbit stories would appear to be an instance of Native American influence. Rabbit spits at the wolves in the Cherokee story—a way, as Ross points out, "to put a powerful curse on them."[41] In one of the Creek stories, Rabbit spits tobacco juice in Heron's eye when Heron sticks his head in the tree.[42] One might recall that this is what happens to Brer Wolf when he's at the door of Brer Rabbit's house, having killed his wife and children; Brer Rabbit spits tobacco at him to make his final escape.[43] Tobacco is an indigenous American plant, grown by the southeastern tribes and used for religious and ceremonial purposes.

The best known collection of African American Brer Rabbit stories, the Uncle Remus stories of Joel Chandler Harris, has been criticized and vilified for Harris's creation of the character of Uncle Remus, for Harris's exaggerated and inaccurate rendering of dialect, and, according to Bernard Wolfe, Harris's whitewashing of the "malevolent" character of Brer Rabbit himself.[44] A better comprehensive source is Richard M. Dorson's 1956 collection, *American Negro Folktales*, which includes seventeen rabbit tales. But more useful in considering Indian influence is Edward C. L. Adams's folklore collection from South Carolina, *Tales of the Congaree*. First published in 1928, it reflects a picture of Brer Rabbit that has particular affinity with the Cherokee concept of Rabbit as messenger, singer, and dancer. An excellent recent collection is William J. Faulkner's posthumously published *The Days When the Animals Talked*, a group of stories told to Faulkner as a boy starting in 1900 by former Virginia slave Simon Brown. The first part of the book is stories of slave life and the second part consists of twenty-two Brer Rabbit stories. The stories, told to Faulkner in Gullah dialect, are retold by Faulkner in standard English.

Lawrence W. Levine's discussion of Brer Rabbit as trickster in slave folklore ascribes to him a tripartite didactic function: role model for the slave, warning about the duplicity of others, and explication of a fatalist vision of the cosmos—in other words, Brer Rabbit functions "as black slave, as white master, as irrational force." According to Levine, the Hare or Rabbit was the primary trickster figure in East Africa and Angola; he says the trickster of the Yoruba, Ibo, and Edo was the Tortoise, and the Anansi spider trickster was prevalent in "much of West Africa including Ghana, Liberia, and Sierra Leone."[45] Though Melville J. Herskovits's comment that "many elements of the Uncle Remus stories are encountered in the sacred myths" of Africa has apparently gone unchallenged, Levine and Bernard Wolfe have focused their readings of Brer Rabbit as satire on human behavior and thus have paid scant attention to super-natural aspects of the stories.[46]

Many tales obliquely refer to Brer Rabbit's avocation as a doctor. This aspect of Brer Rabbit's character is not present in Faulkner's collection and appears only once in Dorson's, where it is incorporated into the tar baby story.[47] But it appears frequently in miscellaneous tales printed in the late nineteenth century. One such tale is Christenson's version of who stole the butter, wherein Brer Rabbit keeps going off ostensibly to deliver babies.[48] In another tale, also involving a joint farming venture with Brer Wolf, Brer Rabbit "practices medicine" by disappearing while Wolf works, though his profession is a scam.[49] Though Brer Rabbit may not actually heal anybody in those tales, he appears to be a bona fide doctor in the story where Brer Fox doesn't fool Brer Rabbit.[50] Further-more, he actually kills Mammy Witch Wise in the aforementioned tale—the ultimate feat of a root doctor.[51]

The depiction of the supernatural in two of these miscellaneous tales is more understandable when considered in this context. In one, all the animals get together to store food for the winter in a house; rabbit moves in and scares them all away by making a noise so "outlandish . . . de beasties all conclude . . . dat de Sperit, him bin tek persession er de house."[52] In another tale, "Why Mr. Dog runs Brer Rabbit," Mr. Dog's children, after Mr. Dog has frozen his tail, bark "glory, glory" and "hal-lelujah, hallelujah" while chasing Brer Rabbit.[53] Viewed in isolation, the supernatural motif in these two tales could be dismissed as insignificant or satirical. But when juxtaposed with some of the Adams tales, they raise interesting questions about transmission of African concepts of communication with spirits.

In the Red Hill Churchyard tale Brer Rabbit is playing his fiddle in a graveyard, the moon shining bright on the snow. All the animals, at his sign, form a circle around the grave, and Bur Mockin'Bird starts to sing along with the fiddle:

Dat mockin'bird an' dat rabbit—Lord, dey had chunes floatin' all 'round on de night air. Dey could stand a chune on end, grab it up an' throw it away an' ketch it an' bring it back an' hold it; an' make dem chunes sound like dey was strugglin' to git away one minute, an' de next dey sound like sump'n gittin' up close an' whisperin'.

When the music stops, Simon rises from the grave and holds a long con-versation with the animals (especially the owls—"de ole folks always is say dey is dead folks"); when they are finished talking, Bur Rabbit starts playing again; he steps back on the grave and Simon is gone.[54] Sterling Stuckey, in *Slave Culture,* has commented at length on this story and its relation to the significance of the one-string violin in the Mali Empire and today among the Songhai of Upper Volta in the summoning of ancestral spirits; Stuckey also estimates that one out of ten slaves could play the fiddle, based on a study of the Hopeton plantation in Georgia.[55]

Adams tells a similar story, "The Dance of the Little Animals," in which Bur Rabbit ("He ain' no Christian") is playing his fiddle on Christmas in the moonlight, and leads Bur Fox on a chase cross country: "he jes tech (the fiddle) enough to wake dem hound up . . . When Bur Fox pass 'long runnin' Bur Rabbit, den dem hound started to singin' an' cryin'. Dey sound like a choir." Bur Rabbit sits on a stump playing his fiddle and laughing as "dem hound had Bur Fox stretched like a string runnin' a race wid death."[56] This story echoes both the "glory hallelujah" baying of the dogs and two Faulkner stories in which Brer Rabbit sets the hounds on Brer Fox.[57]

Bur Rabbit's musical powers are central to all four of the rabbit stories published by Adams. In "Bur Jonah's Goat," Bur Rabbit uses his fiddle to get Bur Wolf to sing a false confession that he stole the goat that Bur Rabbit stole.[58] As in the Cherokee tale of Rabbit and the turkeys and numerous other Brer Rabbit tales, the temptation to sing along is irresistible. What is clear in the Adams version is that this power is tied to the fiddle.

The fourth and final rabbit story in Adams tells how Bur Rabbit gets back at Bur Spider for cutting his web loose and dropping Bur Rabbit in the river. When they get to the dance they are going to, Bur Rabbit sings a song all about what Bur Spider did: "he make all de gals 'shame' (for makin' great miration over Bur Spider) an' dey turn dey back on Bur Spider an' wouldn't have nothin' to do wid him."[59] This story is significant in two ways. First, the spider was one of the primary tricksters of West Africa: Anansi, rendered as "An Nancy" in some American transcriptions.[60] Clearly, in African American folklore,[61] the rabbit has prevailed over the spider as the primary trickster, even though far more slaves came from western Africa than from eastern Africa where the rabbit trickster is more prevalent. Second, the rabbit prevails over the spider in this story because he possesses the power of song and dance. The contest between rabbit and spider here invites comparison to the Creek contest between Rabbit and Panther and the Cherokee contest between

Rabbit and Deer—all seemingly allegories of power struggles among the supernatural.

The story of the rabbit and the spider, less than one page long, is a historical narrative of the transmission of spiritual power. Several trickster figures crossed over from Africa in the Middle Passage, but through the fragmentation and reassemblage of multiple voices that one would expect in intercultural oral transmissions, it is the rabbit who prevailed among the significant African animal spirits in the southeastern United States—he holds the power of music and dance that is the key to communicating with the spirit world both among Africans and among Native Americans.[62] And it is the Adams stories in which the consistent similarity with the Cherokee Rabbit appears: the rabbit trickster as musician and dancer.

Herskovits says that the African American animal tales

> indicate that the body of African mythology and folk tales has been carried over in even less disturbed fashion than has hitherto been considered the case. The changes that have occurred understandably reflect the flora, fauna, and other elements in the everyday experience of the Negroes in their new habitat. The stories also are changed, in that the supernatural figures among the characters are no longer vested with the power and forms of gods, as they are in African mythologies.[63]

Though the power of African supernatural figures may have been impaired or have changed form, as shape-shifting tricksters are wont to do, the Adams rabbit stories would seem to contest Herskovits's latter assertion and its restatement in Levine's assertion that "divine tricksters such as the Dahomean Legba or the Yoruban Eshu and Orunmila did not survive the transplantation of Africans to the United States and the slave's adaptation to Christian religious forms." On the contrary, these tricksters *evolved* to construct the Brer Rabbit described by Bernard Wolfe and Richard Levine as an antihero of resistance to the slaves' masters, personified as the dupes Wolf, Fox, Alligator, Bear, and so forth. This Brer Rabbit is not as "weak [and] relatively powerless" as Levine sees the African and African American animal tricksters.[64] But insofar as the stories reflect new "flora, fauna, and other elements," this can be seen as true in the Brer Rabbit stories in general. Most of them involve tricks on Brer Fox, Brer Bear, or Brer Wolf—clearly more American than African predators. Brer Possum also figures in a number of the stories. Many of them involve farming such as the slaves were engaged in. Faulkner's (and the Cherokee) story of how the cow went underground is only one example. Of Faulkner's twenty-two stories, four involve cultivation: two of peanuts (pinders), one of corn, and one of things rabbits like—collards, turnips, and carrots.[65] There are many versions, in Dorson and elsewhere, of Brer Rabbit getting some other animal to do all the farm work for him. Though the Cherokees cultivated crops, their Rabbit stories, except for the cow that went underground, do not include any of these tales of farming one-upmanship that are so prevalent in the African American stories. The story in which Brer Rabbit uses another animal as his riding horse is also more African American both in the sense that it doesn't appear in Cherokee or Creek folklore and in the sense that it is a story of dominance and submission.[66] Whatever the sources may have been in African folklore, or even in Mr. McGregor's garden, these are stories that are concerned with the politics of oppression on the plantation and during Reconstruction. Brer Rabbit seems to become more human in the stories in which he is dealing with oppression through guile, subterfuge, and revenge. One could argue that a divine trickster plays tricks more often for entertainment than for survival. Brer Rabbit in this role reflects Ojibwa critic and novelist Gerald Vizenor's conception, more than the Cherokee rabbit does, of the divine trickster as the destabilizer of political tyranny.[67]

By the time Simon Brown was telling Brer Rabbit stories to William J. Faulkner, the politics of Reconstruction were there to be told as well. "Brer Rabbit's Protest Meeting" is an allegory about voting rights in the Reconstruction era: Brer Rabbit calls a meeting to discuss the oppression of the short-tailed animals, but Brer Lion takes over and kicks the short-tailed animals out of the meetinghouse. Brer Rabbit calls on the Lord for deliverance: "one day, by and by, He will answer our prayer, and that's for sure." Simon Brown's Brer Rabbit was an evolution of Wolfe's "malevolent rabbit" into what Radin would term a culture hero. Faulkner says "Brer Rabbit was virtuous, on the side of God." Simon Brown's Brer Rabbit not only ties the tiger to a tree and distributes food and water to all the animals—he rescues all the captives from the dragon's lair, slays the dragon *and* the lion, goes back for the dragon's treasure, and assigns Judge Hooting Owl to divide the treasure "among all the little creatures who deserved it."[68]

Gates has demonstrated in *The Signifying Monkey* the transformation—into the African American signifying monkey—of the divine humanoid West African trickster Esu,

> sole messenger of the gods . . . , he who interprets the will of the gods to man; he who carries the desires of man to the gods . . . guardian of the crossroads, master of style and of stylus, the phallic god of generation and fecundity, master of that elusive, mystical barrier that separates the divine world from the profane.[69]

It seems clear from the Adams stories and supporting evidence from other stories cited above that similar divine powers were transmuted into Brer Rabbit. This process was most likely influenced by contact in the southeastern United States with the Native American Rabbit, messenger and singing, dancing entertainer to the people.

Certainly it would have been easier, in light of religious and political oppression, for slaves to attribute the power of calling the dead from their graves to a fiddle-playing rabbit than to a fiddle-playing Yoruba trickster with a large phallus. And in turn, the rabbit's similarity to the black preacher was perhaps best masked. Just as, in Faulkner's story, young Simon Brown steps from behind the rabbit persona to rain fire on the patrollers, the black preacher in African American folklore sometimes acted like Brer Rabbit. One verse in an old African American folksong, dating back to at least 1836, goes:

> Some folks say that a preacher won't steal,
> I caught two in my cornfield,
> Preachin' and prayin' all the time,
> And pullin' my melons off the vine.[70]

Like Brer Rabbit, black preachers might do what they had to do to survive.

Mooney's speculation that many of the Cherokee animal stories are "worn down fragments of ancient sacred traditions" could be applied as well to the African stories.[71] But whereas the African stories probably have involved more breaking down, reassembling, and assimilating of new cultural material, some of the Cherokee stories may well be more like "worn down fragments" owing to the lesser degree of dislocation and rupture of oral tradition. Certainly the Cherokees have suffered severe depredations from the white invaders, but even in the forced removal to

Oklahoma they have been able to maintain a cultural unity that African tribal units have not. Thus the ancient attributions of specific roles and characteristics to specific animal identities has probably been maintained in Cherokee lore. As Ross says:

> Each animal had its place. Buzzard was known as a great doctor, while Turtle knew the secrets of conjuring. Frog was the marshall at the council house. Rabbit's job was to be the messenger. He was to spread important news. He was also a good singer and often led in the dance. But Rabbit was the leader of them all in mischief, and his bold ways were always getting him into trouble.[72]

Just as Raven is the primary trickster in the Pacific Northwest and Coyote in the Southwest, these roles seem fairly stable among eastern tribes. If the Cherokee rabbit seems more childlike than the African American Brer Rabbit, this aspect is consistent with the relative status of the Cherokee rabbit in comparison to the African American trickster rabbit bearing all that transatlantic baggage on his shoulders. The mixing that has occurred in the African diaspora has lent a certain dynamism to the African American trickster stories that is not, overall, inconsistent with the destablizing and yet timeless role of the rabbit trickster in the Cherokee stories.

Interesting as these interpretations are, it is risky to make too many generalizations on the basis of the work of a few storytellers and transcribers. Mooney's talent was as an ethnographer, not a storyteller. As in Richard Dorson's work, a lot seems to have gotten lost in the sometimes cryptic retelling. Stories vary, and though the African American rabbit may seem to be more dynamic than the Cherokee rabbit, neither can it be said that the Cherokee stories are frozen in time, or in an "ethnographic present." One of the tales in particular, "The Rabbit and the Possum After a Wife" depicts a hare-brained scheme that is profoundly expressive of Native American distrust of authority. When Rabbit abuses his position as messenger, a position of great fiduciary responsibility, to seduce a woman and create general mayhem if not war, the storyteller implicitly makes fun of the people for listening to such a fool—he comes to town and says everyone should get married and they do it; he says it's time to start fighting and everybody starts fighting. Obviously not a children's story, this one is not included in Ross's book. There is no way to estimate its age, but it was being told at the turn of the century when repercussions were still being felt from the violent internal political conflict engendered by the events leading up to removal in 1839.

At the turn of the century, the Cherokees may have been disaffected with messengers, but southern African Americans, according to W. E. B. Du Bois, still had faith in their preachers, despite their human shortcomings: "It was a terrific social revolution, and yet some traces were retained of the former group life, and the chief remaining institution was the Priest or Medicine-Man."[73] The preachers were central to the only sort of community organization available to former slaves; they did not have the same degree of retained infrastructure of tribal council meetings and traditional dances that, despite efforts at suppression, have continued to be central to many Native American tribal cultures (not to say that black churches, especially in the South, have not provided a similar, though tribally syncretic, infrastructure). We see the community dances and council meetings in many of the Cherokee Rabbit stories. Community meetings are rare in Brer Rabbit stories, aside from those of Simon Brown. But Brown's stories, told to Faulkner during the same era in which Mooney was transcribing the tale of Rabbit and Possum after a wife, express a faith in leadership and justice that is the butt of the joke in the Cherokee story.

Certainly Faulkner's Brer Rabbit, reflecting Faulkner's background as a pastor and theologian, is a more righteous character than the "malevolent rabbit" of Bernard Wolfe's analysis. In stories other than Faulkner's, Brer Rabbit's actions are often nothing less than despicable. He serves as a cultural antihero, first for slaves, then for southern blacks of the Jim Crow era, and finally for the urban black migration, much as the myths constructed around the James/Younger gang and other outlaws who "lit out for the Territory" created antiheroes of the rural westward migration. Though postremoval Cherokees were forcibly removed from their homeland, the Cherokee nation remains the largest tribe in the United States, still maintaining two geographical cultural centers—in the Carolinas and in Oklahoma—and the need for the ongoing articulation of resistance against a dominant culture represented by a cultural antihero has been less compelling. The Cherokee rabbit is in a sense outside of time, a creature of the past gone across time's ocean: both a nostalgic reminder of tradition and a warning against vanity, double-dealing, and gratuitous rabble-rousing.

Animal tales in all cultures are probably often at some level satirical commentary about human events and the human condition. Like all literature, some animal stories are timeless and some reflect particular historical conditions and events. Often, they do both. The same figure can appear at times to be a human in animal fur and a waistcoat, and at other times a giant who creates an ocean at the wave of a paw. The supernatural elements in the Rabbit stories constitute a common thread that runs through the Cherokee singer, dancer, and messenger, the African fiddler raising the dead, the wily and thieving agricultural Brer Rabbit, and the defender of truth and justice for all the short-tailed animals. The rabbit may be malevolent and vengeful at times, but in the churchyard or in the dance circle, he can call up the power of the ancestors.

Notes

1. Coco Fusco, *English Is Broken Here: Notes on Cultural Fusion in the Americas* (New York: New Press, 1995), 27, 71. cf. bell hooks's essay "Eating the Other" in *Black Looks: Race and Representation* (Boston: South End Press, 1992), 21–40; see esp. 30–33, 34, 22. Henry Louis Gates Jr., *The Signifying Monkey: A Theory of African-American Literary Criticism* (New York: Oxford University Press, 1988).

2. Fusco 30.

3. Contemporary folklorists, of course, acknowledge the pervasiveness of borrowings of cultural motifs, but my focus herein is on the ramifications of such borrowings for multicultural studies, not for the study of folklore per se.

4. William Katz, *Black Indians* (New York: MacMillan Children's Book Group, 1986). Cited in bell hooks, "Revolutionary Renegades: Native Americans, African Americans, and Black Indians," in *Black Looks* 194. For a more conservative estimate see F. James Davis, *Who Is Black? One Nation's Definition* (University Park: Pennsylvania State University Press, 1991). Davis estimates that as of the 1980 census one quarter of African Americans had some Indian ancestry, 21.

5. Hooks 189–90.

6. There are many versions of the tar baby story, but the only significant difference between Indian and African American versions would seem to be the characterization of the tar baby as a seductive female in some of the latter. Cherokee versions describe a "tar wolf." James Mooney, *Myths of the Cherokee,* Annual Report of the Bureau of American Ethnology 19 (1897–98): 3–548. The seductress version is consistent with the overall development of Rabbit from a being who was not consistently gendered in early Cherokee stories (see Mooney's second version of "The Rabbit and the Tar Wolf," *Myths of the Cherokee*

272–73, for a female rabbit) to something of a ladies' man, at least in his own mind.

7. Aurelio M. Espinosa, "Notes on the Origin and History of the Tar-Baby Story," *Journal of American Folklore* 43 (1930): 129–224.

8. Maria Leach, ed., *Funk & Wagnalls Standard Dictionary of Folklore, Mythology and Legend* (New York: Funk & Wagnalls, 1972), 918, 799.

9. Alan Dundes, "African Tales Among the North American Indians." *Journal of American Folklore* 29, no. 3 (1965): 207–19; 210, 218–19.

10. See, for example, the paragraph on p. 213–14 on duping two animals into a tug-of-war where Dundes seems to be referring to Aarne saying the motif index clearly proves African origin but then says the tale-type index is misleading in implying European origin.

11. Paul Radin, *The Trickster: A Study in American Indian Mythology* (New York: Philosophical Library, 1956), 131.

12. Richard M. Dorson, *American Negro Folktales* (1956; rpt., Greenwich, Conn.: Fawcett, 1967), 79, for reference to the motif index; alligator story in Abigail Christenson, *Afro-American Folk Lore* (Boston: J. G. Cupples Co., 1982; rpt. New York: Negro Universities Press, 1969) 54–57, where the feud with alligator starts at a dance. Dorson's story is rabbit and bear.

13. Gayle Ross, *How Rabbit Tricked Otter and Other Cherokee Trickster Stories* (New York: HarperCollins, 1994), 13–17.

14. William J. Faulkner, *The Days When the Animals Talked: Black-American Folktales and How They Came to Be* (Trenton, N.J.: Africa World Press, 1993), 167, 32.

15. Jack F. Kilpatrick and Anna G. Kilpatrick, *Friends of Thunder: Folktales of the Oklahoma Cherokees* (Norman: University of Oklahoma Press, 1964, 1995), 42–43, 46.

16. Georgia Writers Project, Work Project Administration, *Drums and Shadows: Survival Studies Among the Georgia Coastal Negroes* (1940; rpt., Athens: University of Georgia Press, 1986), 157. See also Faulkner's story "The Ways of a Witch," 46–51.

17. Emma M. Backus, "Tales of the Rabbit from Georgia Negroes," *Journal of American Folk-Lore* 12, no. 45 (Apr.–June 1899): 108–15; "Why the People Tote Brer Rabbit Foot in Their Pocket," 109–11.

18. Jack D. Forbes, *Africans and Native Americans: The Language of Race and the Evolution of Red-Black Peoples*, 2nd ed. (Urbana: University of Illinois Press, 1993), ch. 1; see esp. pp. 17–18 on bananas.

19. According to Mooney, who got his information from an estimate by the North Carolina governor at the time, in 1755 Cherokee "warriors" numbered 2,590, and the number of Catawba men had "dwindled" to 240, *Myths of the*

Cherokee p. 39. In their adherence to their sacred traditions and stories, the Cherokee were described by Adair in 1775 as "a nest of apostate hornets."

In 1840 about 100 Catawba, "nearly all that were left," moved in with the eastern Cherokee, i.e., the ones who had escaped removal, but conflicts developed and most of them "began to drift back to their own homes, until, in 1852, there were only about a dozen remaining among the Cherokee," 165.

20. Theda Perdue, *Slavery and the Evolution of Cherokee Society, 1540–1866* (Knoxville: University of Tennessee Press, 1979), 19–25.

21. Mooney, *Myths of the Cherokee* 233.

22. Ibid. 163.

23. Perdue 42.

24. Edward C. L. Adams, *Tales of the Congaree,* ed. Robert G. O'Meally (Chapel Hill: University of North Carolina Press, 1987), 120–21.

25. Camara Laye, *The Dark Child: The Autobiography of an African Boy* (New York: Farrar, Straus & Giroux, 1954), 74.

26. See generally Frank G. Speck and Leonard Broom, with Will West Long, *Cherokee Dance and Drama* (1951; reprint, Norman: University of Oklahoma Press, 1983).

27. Mooney, *Myths of the Cherokee* 273. Unless otherwise noted, all accounts of Cherokee rabbit tales are from this source.

28. Mooney, *Myths of the Cherokee,* "How the Wildcat Caught the Gobbler," 269–70. A version of this story appears in Ponca folklore; Radin 129.

29. Speck and Broom 92.

30. Mooney, *Myths from the Cherokee,* "The Rabbit Escapes from the Wolves," 274.

31. Ibid. 270.

32. According to Mooney, *Myths from the Cherokee,* this story "is found with nearly every tribe from Nova Scotia to the Pacific," 234.

33. Ibid. 277.

34. Ibid. 274. Jack and Anna Kilpatrick agree with James Mooney that the story of Rabbit killing Flint is "a detail leached out of an eroded national cosmology" exemplifying the "fundamentally Iroquoian material of the Cherokee ethos"—a story in which "one senses a dramatic psychological shift from the sun-lit thought-world of the Southeast to that of the gray and granitic North," 61–62. See James Mooney, "Cherokee and Iroquois Parallels," *Journal of American Folklore* 2, no. 4 (1889): 67.

35. Ibid. 262, 263–64.

36. The Kilpatricks discuss Rabbit's relationship to the more human trickster figure Tseg'sin' and Tseg'sin's relationship, in turn, to the Negro Jack, 62, 99.

37. Dorson 91–94; Joseph Bruchac, *Iroquois Stories: Heroes and Heroines,*

Monsters and Magic (Freedom, Calif.: Crossing Press, 1985), 74–78. The Cherokee are linguistically and historically related to the Iroquois. The Iroquois story about Rabbit and Fox is much more elaborate than Ross's version; Rabbit exhibits extraordinary shape-shifting and conjuring skills and ultimately dupes Fox into eating a tree.

38. Speck, "The Creek Indians of Taskigi Town," *A Creek Sourcebook*, ed. William Sturtevant (New York: Garland, 1987), 149–57.

39. This is a story that Dundes claims is African; see note 16 above.

40. Kilpatrick and Kilpatrick 30–33. The Kilpatricks also note that Maneater often had human qualities in Cherokee stories. Maneater replaces the wolf as the dupe in the version here cited of how the cow went underground.

41. Ross 28.

42. Speck, "Creek Indians" 153.

43. Christenson 34.

44. Bernard Wolfe, "Uncle Remus and the Malevolent Rabbit: 'Takes a Limber-Toe Gemmun fer ter Jump Jim Crow.'" *Commentary* 8 (1949): 31–41.

45. Lawrence Levine, *Black Culture and Black Consciousness African American Folk Thought from Slavery to Freedom* (New York: Oxford University Press, 1977), 120–21, 103.

46. Melville J. Herskovits, *The Myth of the Negro Past* (1941; rpt., Boston: Beacon Press, 1958), 75.

47. Dorson 75.

48. Christenson 73–80.

49. Backus, "Tales of the Rabbit from Georgia Negroes" 108.

50. Emma M. Backus, "Folk-Tales from Georgia," *Journal of American Folklore* 13, no. 48 (Jan.–Mar. 1900): 24.

51. Backus, "Tales of the Rabbit from Georgia Negroes" 109.

52. Charles C. Jones Jr., *Negro Myths from the Georgia Coast* (Boston: Houghton, Mifflin and Co., 1888; reprint, Detroit: Singing Tree Press, Book Tower, 1969), 52.

53. Backus, "Tales of the Rabbit from Georgia Negroes" 112.

54. Adams 235, 236.

55. Sterling Stuckey, *Slave Culture: Nationalist Theory and the Foundations of Black America* (New York: Oxford University Press, 1987), 17–22.

56. Adams 240–41.

57. Faulkner, *Days When the Animals Talked,* "Brer Rabbit Keeps His Word," 95; "Brer Fox Meets Mister Trouble," 137.

58. Adams 237–38.

59. Ibid. 242.

60. Georgia Writers' Project 108, 169.

61. Though I use the term "African American folklore" here, it should be

understood that this body of folklore is syncretic in nature. Indeed, the thesis of this essay is that it is pervaded by Indian influences. Nevertheless, it is important to distinguish a general African·American cultural entity in the United States from more specifically black Indian cultural entities such as the Lumbees, and for that reason I have generally avoided use of "Black Indian" or similar terms in this discussion.

62. The spider is, of course, not unknown in American Indian literature; Spider Woman is a major figure in the American Southwest. But Spider Woman is totally unlike the lecherous Anansi. I am aware of one Cherokee spider story and two Muskogee (Creek) spider stories, all appearing in the children's anthology *Spider Spins a Story: Fourteen Legends from Native America,* ed. Jill Max, pseudonym for Kelly Bennett and Ronnie Davidson (Flagstaff, Ariz.: Rising Moon, 1997). The spider is female in all three stories. Water Spider is bringer of fire to the people in the Cherokee story, and of these three stories of southeastern origin, it is the one, because of the water-crossing motif, that is most provocative of speculation about African influence.

63. Herskovits 275.

64. Levine 103.

65. Though corn and peanuts have been important food sources in Africa since the seventeenth century or earlier, they are indigenous to America, having reached Africa most likely by way of Brazil. Forbes 60.

66. The riding horse story appears in folklore of the Maroons, escaped African–Native American slaves in the Caribbean. Robert Perez, "Brer Rabbit and Ba Nansi: Were They Shipmates?," presentation at University of California, Riverside Winter Conference in History, Jan. 10, 1996. This story seems to echo the closing words of Maya Deren in *Divine Horsemen: The Living Gods of Haiti* (New York: Mcpherson and Company, 1953), describing an episode of Voudoun possession: "the journey around is long and hard, alike for the strong horse, alike for the great rider," 262. Elsewhere Deren asserts that "the African culture in Haiti was waved by the Indian culture which, in the Petro cult, provided the Negroes with divinities sufficiently aggressive (as was not true of the divinities of the generally stabilized African kingdoms) to be the moral force behind the revolution. In a sense, the Indians took their revenge on the white man through the Negro," 11.

Perhaps the most singular contemporary retelling of the riding horse story is contained in Toni Morrison's *Tar Baby* (New York: Plume Penguin, 1982), wherein the protagonist Son, a black man from Florida who is also Brer Rabbit, escapes into the swamps of the Caribbean Isle de Chevaliers to run with the blind ghosts who "gallop; they race those horses like angels all over the hills where the rain forest is," 306.

67. Vizenor is a prolific critic and editor, but he has perhaps most fully ex-

plored his concept of the trickster in two of his novels, *Griever, an American Monkey King in China* (Normal: Illinois State University, 1987) and *The Trickster of Liberty: Tribal Heirs to a Wild Baronage* (Minneapolis: University of Minnesota Press, 1988).

68. Faulkner 115–21, 6, 84. The role of the owl in this tale is evidence, perhaps even more so than the dragon, of European American influence: the owl in both African and Native American cosmogony is a bad omen and messenger of death.

69. Gates 6.

70. Alan Lomax, *Folk Songs of North America* (New York: Doubleday, 1960), pt. 4, pp. 445–595, 509.

71. Mooney, *Myths of the Cherokee* 34.

72. Ross 6–7.

73. W. E. B. Du Bois, *The Souls of Black Folk* (New York: Penguin/Signet, 1969), ch. 10, pp. 210–25, 216.

Deadpan Trickster

The American Humor of *Huckleberry Finn*

SACVAN BERCOVITCH

It is a truth universally acknowledged that *The Adventures of Huckleberry Finn* is funny. That seems to be one of the few points of consensus, amidst all controversies over its meaning. But *what's* funny about the book? We may ask (as many critics have) if we *should* laugh at certain jokes, but that's a different, prescriptive order of inquiry. The fact is, we cannot help but laugh at Huck's adventures, and the question is, what and who are we laughing at (or with)? It's a trickster question, appropriate to a tale told by and about tricksters (from innocent Huck to mischievous Tom to the sinister Duke and King), and the answer may be stated accordingly, as a trickster tautology. What's funny about *Huckleberry Finn* is that it's a humorous story. Here is how Twain explains the trick, in a late piece entitled "How to Tell a Story":

> The humorous story is American, the comic story is English, the witty story is French. The humorous story depends for its effect on the *manner* of the telling; the comic story and the witty story upon the *matter*. . . . The humorous story bubbles gently along, the others burst.
>
> The humorous story is strictly a work of art—high and delicate art—and only an artist can tell it; but no art is necessary in telling the comic and the witty story; anybody can do it.
>
> The humorous story is told gravely; the teller does his best to conceal the fact that he even dimly suspects that there is anything funny about it; but the teller of the comic story tells you beforehand that it is one of the funniest things he has ever heard, then tells it with an eager delight, and is the first person to laugh when he gets through.
>
> Very often . . . [the] humorous story finishes with a nub, point, snapper, or whatever you like to call it. Then the listener must be alert, for in many cases the teller will divert attention from the nub by dropping it in a carefully casual and indifferent way, with the pretense that he does not know it is a nub.[1]

This essay is about the nubs or snappers in *Huckleberry Finn,* and by extension about a distinctive and (according to Twain) a uniquely American mode of being funny—a trickster's mode with an American slant. I refer to deadpan, of course, the comic form familiar to Americans through a wide range of folklore, from Yankee Peddler to Riverboat Conman, and particularly to the protagonist of the western tall tale. The joke is told "gravely"; the teller is straight-faced—he recounts in earnest detail how Davy Crockett at six years of age killed the biggest bear in Arkansas or how you can get the Brooklyn Bridge dirt cheap—and what's funny is the listener who believes and marvels at the exploit. In Twain's case, the joke reflects the peculiar historical conditions of the southwestern frontier. These conditions have often been commented on, but their bearing upon trickster behavior is so striking that they are worth rehearsing at some length:

> "Tall humor," Henry B. Wonham observes, "is American not because it is incongruous—all humor is that—but because it articulates incongruities that are embedded in the American experience. A country founded, settled, and closely observed by men and women with extraordinary expectations, both exalted and depraved, could not help but appreciate the distance that separated the ideal from the real, the 'language of culture' from the 'language of sweat,' the democratic dream from the social and economic reality of the early American republic."
>
> The "gap" between culture and sweat found in frontier experiences— which characteristically included Indian wars, slave-dealing, *herrenvolk* white racial solidarity, endemic violence, economic instability, fluidity, humbuggery, and speculative fantasy—cultivated a vernacular humor of extremes, along with pleasure in horror and depravity (an outgrowth of urban contact zones, as well). . . . "Tall" humor was a form of initiation and survival in response to the radical physical and social uncertainties on the edge of settler-colonial expansion. This humor thrived at the borderland of displacement, migration, and violence, finding much of its pleasure in dethroning the condescension of gentility at the thickly settled Eastern core, while at the same time reproducing the radical incongruities and discrepancies at the root of all American experience.[2]

This setting—a new capitalist nation in the violent process of emergence—is a trickster paradise. Its social and psychological uncertainties, its physical turbulence and shifting borders, make for a world that's not

only ripe for but conducive to all manner of trickster wiles: transgressing boundaries, defying taboos, mocking rules and regulations. And its
"radical incongruities" provide ample scope for trickster fun in what (according to the OED) are the three basic meanings of the word: (1) *Funny*
as in "just plain fun," with the innocence of Young Hermes or Baby
Brahma—the childlike humor we designate as "kidding around." (2)
Funny in its antiquated meaning of "befool," as in "playing a hoax on
someone," with the cruel edge of con games associated with Coyote—a
cunning humor that thrives on "humbuggery and speculative fantasy"
and that often issues as satire, since the hoax that thrives upon the hy-
pocrisies of everyday life—the joke that highlights the "distance sepa-
rat[ing] the ideal from the real"—serves to reinforce social norms *as
ideals*. (3) *Funny* as in "odd or curious," the chilling sense of some sinister hidden meaning, as when we say there's "something funny" about
trickster fox; he might be a killer. This last layer of humor tends towards
"horror and depravity." It's the humor we associate with sick jokes and
the absurd.

Usually deadpan artists specialize in one or another way of being
funny—let us call them innocent, satirical, and sinister—but the humor
reaches its highest pitch, the finest turn of its "high and delicate art,"
when the joke reverberates with all three layers of fun, from (cheerfully)
"that's *funny*" to (suspiciously) "*that's* funny."

Mark Twain's deadpan is trickster fun at its best, and *Huckleberry Finn*
is his funniest book, in the all three senses of the term. What makes
it distinctive, however—what separates it from generic deadpan—is
Twain's deliberate and sustained use of the third, sinister, "odd or curious" sense of funny. Without submerging the cheerful and satirical layers
of fun—indeed, while drawing these out to their limit—his humor involves a drastic turnabout in deadpan effect, virtually a *reversal* of conventional techniques. The novel is a great work of childlike wonder *and*
of social satire whose trickster mode *overturns the very tradition of deadpan it builds upon*. Ostensibly that tradition belongs to the narrator-hero.
Huck speaks "gravely" and often plays the trickster; but the funny thing
is he's *not* a humorist, not even when he's putting someone on (as he
does Aunt Sally, when he pretends to be Tom Sawyer). In fact, he rarely
has fun; characteristically he's in a sweat; and on the rare occasion when
he does try to kid around (as when he tells Jim they were not separated
in the fog) the joke turns back on itself to humiliate him. Huck's voice

may be described as stylized deadpan; it *sounds* comic to the comically disposed listener, but actually it's troubled, earnest. The nub or snapper behind that stylization—the humorous intent of *Huckleberry Finn,* the trickster twist to the joke—is directed *against* Huck's apparent deadpan. For of course the "teller" is really Mark Twain, the Comic Writer, and *this* deadpan artist is not straight-faced (as Huck is), but smiling. He wears the Mask of Comedy. Officially, he's telling a very amusing, sometimes hilarious story and having a wonderful time at every point. His "story bubbles gently along," he's laughing through it all; and so are we.

So here's the trickster setup, American-style, of *Huckleberry Finn:* the deadpan artist is Mark Twain, wearing the Comic Mask, doing his best to conceal the fact that he even dimly suspects that there's anything grave, let alone sinister, about his story—and he succeeds famously. Then, as we laugh, or after we've laughed, we may realize, if we're alert, that there's something we've overlooked. We haven't seen what's funny about the fact that we've found it all so funny. This trickster has conned us, somehow diverted our attention away from the real point, and we have to go back over the story in order to recognize its nub.

Re-cognition in this sense begins with two general premises of trickster humor. The first is that what's funny works as a connective. The joke interweaves the different aspects (innocent, satirical, and sinister) of trickster fun—it makes these volatile, interchangeable. What's a harmless prank as far as Huck is concerned (for instance, Tom's coin trick at the start) may be a hoax on Twain's part. And what seems a hoax to Huck (for instance, the tricks played at the end upon Jim) may have something sinister about it for Twain. In all these instances, satire mingles with brutality and brutality flows into "just plain fun."

The second general premise of trickster humor involves the connectives between the joke and its cultural contexts. The linguistic play of deadpan calls up diverse situations, social, personal, and historical, and by joining these the humor points us toward connections within the culture. The joke may be said to bridge various aspects of life: institutions, practices, beliefs, customs. All humor works in this way more or less, but there's something distinctive (here as elsewhere) about tricksters. They tend to direct their jokes *against* the very cultural connections that their humor invokes. In a recent overview of the trickster figure, Lewis Hyde describes this technique in physiological terms, as an assault upon the vulnerable parts of the social body. He points out that tricksters work best in the intersections of culture, the intricate, delicate links between different social practices and institutions. Home, job, school, church—these variant spheres are connected by joints, which are in fact anatomical weak points. Thus the fragility of the knees (where "the shin bone's connected to the thigh bone") becomes an image for Hyde of cultural weak points, where (say) official religion jars with official politics, or where variant conventions and rules of behavior (residual, dominant, emergent) may overlap and clash. At these junctures, traditionally, the trickster comes most vividly to life—unsettling the system, upsetting its rhythms, exposing conflicts and contradictions.[3]

Mark Twain's trickster trademark is the shock of the funny bone. Imagine a culture like the antebellum frontier (or for that matter the Reconstructionist Southwest), which is both racist and egalitarian, and where that contradiction is the sign not just of hypocrisy (ideal versus real) but of separate, deep-rooted traditions, each involving its own disparities between "culture and sweat," its own configuration of realities and ideals. The minstrel show was a genre born out of precisely these conditions. With this tangled tradition in mind, consider *this* trickster's minstrel act: the audience hears a long funny story about a "nigger" and they laugh along. The nub of course is that *they*'re being laughed at; they're being taken in and made the butt of a joke. Once they see that, they understand what's funny about the story, and they're free to laugh at themselves for having laughed in the first place. That freedom, I'm suggesting, comes with the shock of the funny bone. It's a complex sensation, like the odd "tingling vibration" you feel when you're hit on the funny bone. A light touch might mean no more than a bit of healthy fun—say, the cheerful wake-up call of social satire (the N-joke reminds you of your egalitarian principles). A sharp touch might be unnerving—a bitter protest directed against the system at large (you recognize that you are part and parcel of a deeply racist society). A direct and vicious cut would be painful, a sensation of pure violence, as in the sinister sense of "funny" (you realize that egalitarianism itself is a joke, you're a sucker for having believed in it at all).

Twain's deadpan spans all of these forms. The light touch marks his early career. His tales of the Wild West and of Innocents Abroad are sometimes savage in their exposé of pretense, but their manner and tone emphasize the ebullient Pan in the deadpan. Twain's late career shifts the emphasis to the nihilistic undercurrent in *dead*pan: the deadly laughter of *The Mysterious Stranger,* the doomsday humor of *A Connecticut Yankee,* the absurdist stories collected in *The Great Dark. Huckleberry Finn* might be described as early-middle-but-especially-late Twain. It's the apotheosis of American deadpan, a carefully coordinated synthesis of all three layers of the meaning of *funny.* Twain's mode of coordination—the dialectic behind his synthesis—is the drastic reversal of effect I spoke of: the trickster with the Comic Mask. And the nubs or snappers he delivers constitute the most severe set of shocks in the literature to the American funny bone.

The first shock is that the novel is funny at all. The slave hunt serves as both metaphor and metonymy for the world it portrays: *Huckleberry Finn* describes a slave hunt undertaken literally, collectively, by an enslaved society, a culture in bondage to all the Seven Deadly Sins (in addition to the sin of chattel-slavery), and accordingly characterized by violence, mean-spiritedness, ignorance, and deceit. A fair example is Pikesville, a "nondescript" shantytown somewhere along the river:

> All the streets and lanes was just mud; they warn't nothing else *but* mud—mud as black as tar and nigh about a foot deep in some places, and two or three inches deep in *all* the places. The hogs loafed and grunted around everywheres. You'd see a muddy sow and a litter of pigs come lazying along the street and whollop herself right down in the way, where folks had to walk around her, and she'd stretch out and shut her eyes and wave her ears whilst the pigs was milking her, and look as happy as if she was on salary. And pretty soon you'd hear a loafer sing out, "Hi! *so* boy! sick him, Tige!" and away the sow would go, squealing most horrible, with a dog or two swinging to each ear, and three or four dozen more a-coming; and then you would see all the loafers get up and watch the thing out of sight, and laugh at the fun and look grateful for the noise. Then they'd settle back again till there was a dogfight. There couldn't anything wake them up all over, and make them happy all over, like a dogfight—unless it might be putting turpentine on a stray dog and setting fire to him, or tying a tin pan to his tail and see him run himself to death. (183)

Readers of the novel remember Pikeville not for that bit of "fun" (though that's the town's main source of laughter) but for the Shakespearean soliloquy delivered there by the Duke and the King:

To be or not to be; that is the bare bodkin
That makes calamity of so long life . . .
'Tis a consummation devoutly to be wished.
But soft you now, the fair Ophelia,
Ope not thy ponderous and marble jaws. (179)

That's what we laugh at, as we should. Consider, however, the image of
the dog running himself to death. And now think of the nub concealed
within the Shakespearean parody: the Duke and the King are debased
men, the townspeople are debased, and debasement in both cases is a
metonym for the slave code. The stray dog is Jim on the run, Huck
hounded by sivilization. The animal kingdom parades before us as in a
trickster's Eden-utopia: pigs, "tigers," dogs, and people mingling happily
in the "two or three feet deep" mud (the sow "happy as if she was on
salary," the loafers "laugh[ing] at the fun"); and the joke lies in the calamity we humans make of "so long life." Clearly, this is the world of the late
"dark Twain," the author of *The Damned Human Race* who tells us that
his religion is "Calvinism without God," and who, in his Satanic *Letters
from the Earth,* explains why man, the lowest of all animals, "is first and
last and always a sarcasm."[4]

Question: What's funny about *Huckleberry Finn*? Answer: The teller of
this tall tale has persuaded us that he's a Comic Writer. I mean to explore
his method of persuasion through three typical jokes. The first is Twain's
first: his opening "Notice to Readers" (lv):

Persons attempting to find a motive in this narrative will be prosecuted; persons attempting to find a moral in it will be banished; persons attempting to
find a plot in it will be shot.

BY ORDER OF THE AUTHOR,
Per G. G., Chief of Ordnance

This is a crucial point of the story. It introduces the reader to the text
and connects Mark Twain ("THE AUTHOR") with Huck Finn, who has
written "this narrative." The deadpan connective, "G. G.," links all the
above (narrative, reader, author, and protagonist), and the Notice itself
is a directive concerning interpretation. Overtly, to be sure, it's a directive *against* interpretation, but (we must never forget) it's a deadpan directive, which therefore requires interpretation. For obviously the Notice
is a form of kidding around, a prank of sorts; and then, too, there's a

satirical side to it, a subversive laughter in the "order" that ridicules authority. And finally there's the violence alongside and around the subversive tone—think of the penalties for trespassing (prosecution, banishment, death), and the deadly pun that reinforces them: "ordnance" is not (just) a colloquial misspelling; technically it means "cannon or artillery"; a "Chief of Ordnance" is an officer ready to blow you to pieces.[5]

All this makes for an especially funny situation with regard to the act of interpretation. For the narrative itself—the book that's the subject of the directive against interpretation—*demands* interpretation all the time. We can't get any of its jokes without figuring out motive and plot, and we can't possibly do *that* without assuming a moral position. Take even the simplest joke: say, the story that Huck tells Jim about Solomon and the disputed child (94–96). No reader has failed to laugh at the incident and no careful reader can fail to notice that it concerns key structures of the culture—fatherhood, the Bible, schools, and civil authority—which are also key themes of the novel. It's perfectly natural, then, for Huck to "slide" from Solomon to kings in general. He tells Jim about European ex-kings who migrate to America and teach French; he then proceeds to explain why people need to know different languages (humans are different from one another, as dogs are different from pigs, pigs from horses, and so forth); and Jim counters by pointing out that all people are alike (all people, universally, are different from dogs, horses, pigs, and so forth). If he's a man, Jim declares, "*Well*, den! Dad blame it, why doan he *talk* like a man?"

This is a parody of social pretension: Huck, the master of the colloquial style, is celebrating the language of the elite, as French then was. And in turn the parody is a sick joke about southern history: Jim, the victim of chattel-slavery (the example of man-reduced-to-beast-of-burden), is speaking "the language of culture" (Jefferson's language) *in* "the language of sweat" about the self-evident truths of human equality. How can we *not* interpret? And our interpretation is prodded, if we need prodding, by Huck's concluding response: "You can't learn a nigger to argue. So I quit." Huck doesn't see the fun in all this; he's simply frustrated. We do see the fun because we know we're hearing a comic tale (by Mark Twain, humorist); but in order to take that step we have to interpret. In short, we interpret because Huck doesn't.

Now let me recapitulate what's funny about the Notice. There's a joke here that involves us in a contradiction: the official order prohibits interpretation, but the narrative demands interpretation. The nub or snapper is that the Notice is *calling attention* to interpretation. It's reminding us of our tendency to look for plot, moral, and motive, and then the narrative itself does the rest of the work: it virtually forces us to interpret. Having recognized that much, we should feel uneasy. There's something funny about this invitation to interpret—it's a trickster's invitation. What's *his* motive? What's the *plot*?

To begin to explore the issue I turn to my second example, the last joke in the novel. I refer to what is surely Huck's best-known line—his decision to light out for the territory. Our general impression of the scene is that Huck leaves because he seeks freedom: "Aunt Sally she's going to adopt me, and sivilize me, and I can't stand it. I been there before" (362). And no doubt Huck does want his freedom, but there's another layer of meaning in the text:

> then Tom he talked along and talked along, and says, le's all three slide out of here one of these nights and get an outfit, and go for howling adventures amongst the Injuns, over in the territory, for a couple of weeks or two; and I says, all right, that suits me. (361)

So Huck decides to light out "ahead of the rest," and the nub is: *he's just kidding around.* He plans to get an "outfit" and leave for a while ("a couple of weeks or two"), which we interpret as a flight to freedom—and then (if we follow critical tradition) we proceed to allegorize it as the freedom of the spirit. Over the century that allegory has established itself as a staple cultural/countercultural icon: Huck Finn, the representative rebel, hero of potential and self-definition and the open road.

It's a grand flight of interpretation on our part, but there's something odd about it. Our allegory of this child's prank depends upon a series of exclusions. Just think of the deadpan connection in the episode itself between African Americans and Native Americans: Jim "dressed up for howling adventures amongst the Injuns"! It's a joke akin to the Duke and King's, when they parade Jim through town dressed as a "*Sick Arab*—but harmless when not out of his head" (203). Twain's trickster play here should alert us to the intricate narrative joint we're in. Huck is about to light out from the Phelps's for the territory: this liminal moment joins two crucial dimensions of the social body. First, the dimension of space: the "settlements," as defined by the N-word, are being linked to the "territory," as defined by the I-word. Then, there's the dimension of time:

"Injun" is a clue to the cultural connections implicit in the novel's double time frame. The fictional time, on the one hand, the period of Huck's adventures, is the antebellum South, the slavery era. The authorial time, on the other hand, the decade in which Twain wrote the book, was the era of Indian killing. What joins both time frames is nothing less than the most sinister line of continuity in American history: in the pre-Civil War period, the country's economic growth through slavery; after the Civil War, the country's territorial growth through genocide. For between 1876 and 1885—when *Huckleberry Finn* was begun, briefly abandoned, and then resumed, completed, and published—the territories provided the setting for the final wars (under the notorious banner, "the only good Indian is a dead Indian") against the Native Americans.

Huck's "escape to freedom" is a tall tale that suggests how much can be excluded or concealed in the act of interpretation. And it suggests further what this kind of exclusion makes room for. I refer to the cultural icon ("lighting out") that draws its force from a powerful set of commonplaces: the notion that "the territory" in the United States means (and always meant) freedom; the familiar interpretations of "open land" as promise, opportunity, and possibility. The nub that ends *Huckleberry Finn* is that interpretation may be a trap of culture. I mean interpretation now in its institutional sense, as a process developed, nourished, and sanctioned by society—the official hermeneutic, as it were, by which we confirm our beliefs in what our culture has taught us to believe, and through which (according to this snapper) we conceal the unsavory realities of history. In this case, the incongruity between those realities (slavery, genocide) and those beliefs (freedom, innocence) is funny enough, in the sinister sense, to provide the *finale* to the greatest deadpan act in the history of American humor.

Interpretation may be a trap of culture: Twain's snapper is especially striking in context of trickster fun and games. I said before, following Lewis Hyde, that the joints of the social body are cultural weak points. Hyde adds that tricksters instictively fasten on those weak points through strategies of interpretation; their hermeneutic of invention and surprise, of inversion and perversion, is a kind of endless arsenal of cultural resistance. Thus the trickster becomes for him a figure across time and place, from Greek Hermes to Allen Ginsberg, for the Artist as Subversive. And of course that archetype extends by implication to the discerning critic of Art. The impression it conveys of the powers of interpretation is as comforting as it is familiar. Conversely, Twain's joke about Huck's "flight to freedom" is as discomforting—as shocking and deflating—as it is surprising. The misfit it reveals between the text and the meaning we give it calls attention to the snares of interpretation. Among other things it reminds us that tricksters steal their weapons of ludic resistance (puns, parodies, inversions) from social institutions—institutions of interpretation that are first and foremost centers of social control. Tricksters know where the status quo is most vulnerable, but so does the dominant culture. And historically, across time and place, the social body has defended itself *precisely at its joints* by means of interpretation. Society works through civic mechanisms and economic networks; culture works through the circulation of meaningful artifacts and stories—symbols, emblems, icons, myths. These constitute the moral and spiritual lifeblood of the social body, and its heart is the process of interpretation. Chairman Mao was only half-right to say that power comes out of the barrel of a gun. In fact guns are not even the most effective instrument of state power. They merely force us to submit; interpretation gets us to consent. The effect of a sound cultural heart in a healthy social body is that the body's very joints become a source of strength and revitalization, especially the joints that connect our capacities for creative play with our need for meaning—for purpose, identity, and ideals. Interpretation (so conceived, understood historically, in its institutional context) works by directing that deep and abiding need toward socialization. It turns our world, imaginatively, into a system; it organizes our fantasies and visions in ways that make sense of things as they are; it forges the foundational links between subjectivity and society.

This elemental, conservative, cooptive power is what Twain's deadpan compels us to recognize. The joke is aimed not just against ideology, and not just against organized myth. Its target is the adversarial interpreter. Ideology and organized myth are satirized through the figure of Tom Sawyer. That satire has long provided a source of adversarial criticism, but if we focus on Tom we're being diverted from Twain's deadpan point. His joke centers on Huck, and he means by this (by alerting us to our very impulse to focus on Tom) to identify us as adversarial critics— readers for whom interpretation is the road to free and independent thought (the conceptual equivalent for the "open territory")—*within* the institutions from which we *claim* to light out. We end trapped in the very joints of culture through which we had hoped to escape.

It makes for an unnerving shock to the funny bone, but we owe it to ourselves, and to Twain's art, to account for our laughter. His snapper has the authority of history behind it. One need only consider the fantastic conservative-cooptive force of the fourfold method of medievalist exegesis, with its levels of meaning ascending in a Jacob's ladder from earth to heaven, from literal and political to moral and mystical. It is hardly too much to say that for a millennium in the Christian West the doctrine of the divine right of kings—the biblical-political-moral interpretation of the Great Chain of Being—thus fortified every juncture of the social structure (from the anagogical to the domestic sphere). It linked the king's "two bodies" to the relation between men and women, gender dualisms to the metaphysics of mind and body, and that binary in turn to the double visible-spiritual structure of the cosmos. In America of course (Twain's and ours) the case is altogether different. Officially our interpretative modes are secular, anti-elitist, based on the separation of church and state, and insofar as the legacy of Christian hermeneutics persists—as indeed it does (that legacy is a major butt of Twain's humor)—it is a Protestant mode: basically individualist, geared toward subjectivity, centered in personal conscience rather than in church tradition and papal bull. But the results are no less binding and systemic. The success of society in the United States is due in no small part to the fact that the culture developed a distinctive network of moral-spiritual meanings (iconic, mythic, symbolic) together with a complex set of interpretive techniques appropriate to the civic institutions and economic modes of a modern, free-enterprise, self-centered way of life.

Huckleberry Finn is a deadpan exposé of those techniques—an anatomy of the official hermeneutic of nineteenth-century America as this developed from the Jacksonian era through the Gilded Age. As Huck tells the story, the cultural trap of interpretation is most conspicuously marked by conscience. It's conscience that makes him a racist—conscience that leads him astray at every moral juncture—and we interpret his conscience, properly, as an indictment of the values of the antebellum Southwest. But I believe Mark Twain had another culture in mind. There was no need in 1885 to indict slave society. Primarily, Twain's deadpan is directed against his readership, then and later (and perhaps still today). I refer to the conscience-driven forms of American liberal interpretation, and to its particular modes of socialization as these flowered during the last decades of the nineteenth century, the age of "the incorporation of America."[6] No work of art is more revealing of that process. As a tall tale, *Huckleberry Finn* draws upon an earlier period, the "free and open" Jacksonian Southwest where the joints of the nation's emergent social body seemed weakest, most vulnerable to the blatant "gap between the culture and sweat found in frontier experiences . . . Indian wars, slave dealing, *herrenvolk* white racial solidarity, endemic violence, economic instability, fluidity, humbuggery, and speculative fantasy." As a trickster's deadpan, the novel turns the tall tale (at our expense) into a commentary on the process by which that gap was made a self-revitalizing source of cultural incorporation.

In my first two examples I tried to outline the scope of Twain's design in this regard. Now to specify his technique (the dynamics of his mock-interpretive nub or snapper) I turn to my third and main example. The passage comes at the end of Huck's adventures on the river. He lands at the Phelps Plantation, where he meets Sally Phelps, who mistakes him for her nephew Tom Sawyer. Huck instinctively goes along with his new identity but gets confused in accounting for what now turns out to be his late arrival: Tom had been expected by steamboat some time before. Huck at first explains that the boat had been grounded, then can't think of *which* grounding—but

> I struck an idea, and fetched it out: "It warn't the grounding—that didn't keep us back but a little. We blowed out a cylinder head."
>
> "Good gracious! anybody hurt?"
>
> "No'm. Killed a nigger."
>
> "Well, it's lucky; because sometimes people do get hurt. Two years ago last Christmas your uncle Silas was coming up from Newrleans on the old Lally Rook, and she blowed out a cylinder head and crippled a man. And I think he died afterwards. He was a Baptist." (p. 279)

Again, we're at a key joint of the narrative. The arrival at the Phelps Plantation unites all three sections of the novel (Hannibal, where Tom figures prominently; the journey down the river; and Huck's adventures at the Phelps); and it connects all three layers of trickster fun (innocent, satirical, and sinister). It also demonstrates Twain's hermeneutic imperative—we *must* interpret this scene (its humor leaves us no alternative)—while offering a striking example of what's funny about our habits of interpretation. I take the joke to lie in the (in)famous one-liner "No'm. Killed a nigger." We are then diverted from its nub by Aunt Sally's story of the Lally Rook. To recall Twain's instruction: when the joke comes, "the listener must be alert, for . . . the teller will divert attention from the nub by dropping it in a carefully casual or indifferent way, with the pretense that he does not know it is a nub." The Baptist is a decoy; it allows the story to bubble gently along. The nub is encoded in Huck's throwaway line: "No'm. Killed a nigger." In what follows I mean to decode Twain's deadpan by outlining seven points about Huck's response to which we should be alert.

First, his use of "nigger" is profoundly racist. We can't argue (as too many critics have done) that it's just slang—a poor ignorant boy's way of saying African American. What Huck *means* is far worse than what a bigot means by "wop" or "mick." Huck is saying that a "nigger" is a *no one* (That's the "joke" in response to the straight-man query, "anybody hurt?"). If we're alert, the negational form ("No'm") serves to *highlight* the positive charge of "Killed," especially because of the pause indicated by the sentence break.

Second, Huck's response is gratuitous. As again we're reminded by the sentence break ("No'm. Killed . . . "), Huck could just as well have stopped at "No'm." And be it noted that that kind of gratuitous remark, in all its racist implications, is typical of Huck. The *casual* N-word is fundamental to his vocabulary. As critics over the past three decades have pointed out, the word "nigger" occurs on virtually every page of the novel, and it's worth emphasizing that it took three generations of readers *before them* to take offense. *Huckleberry Finn* was always controversial, but the first debates centered on issues of class, not race. The complaints had to do with Huck's delinquency, bad habits, and poor grammar. The N-word went largely unnoticed until the 1960s, and I believe that the not-noticing was basic to Twain's deadpan. Part of the joke is that the word was woven into the very fabric of Twain's democratic culture. The N-word was at once unexamined and ubiquitous—unexamined because ubiquitous, and ubiquitous because unexamined—and never more so than in the era of Reconstruction, when the minstrel show was the most popular American form of humor. Huck's response is entirely appropriate to him and his readership alike.

It's also appropriate to the plot of the novel. That's the third point to make about Huck's remark. His joke concerns a dead person and death is a main narrative thread—death in the deadpan mode, gilded over by humor. A fair example of the gilding process comes in the early passages concerning Tom's gang:

Tom got out a sheet of paper that he had wrote the oath on, and read it. It swore every boy to stick to the band, and never tell any of the secrets; and if anybody done anything to any boy in the band, whichever boy was ordered to kill that person . . . must do it . . . And if anybody that belonged to the band told the secrets, he must have his throat cut, and then have his carcass burnt up and the ashes scattered all around, and his name blotted off the list with blood. . . .

Everybody said it was a real beautiful oath . . .

Some thought it would be good to kill the *families* of boys that told the secrets. Tom said it was a good idea, so he took a pencil and wrote it in. Then Ben Rogers says:

"Here's Huck Finn, he hain't got no family; what you going to do 'bout him?"

"Well, hain't he got a father?" says Tom Sawyer.

"Yes, he's got a father, but you can't never find him these days. He used to lay drunk with the hogs in the tanyard, but he hain't been seen in these parts for a year or more."

They talked it over, and they was going to rule me out, because they said every boy must have a family or somebody to kill, or else it wouldn't be fair and square for the others. Well nobody could think of anything to do—everybody was stumped, and set still. I was most ready to cry; but all at once, I thought of a way, and so I offered them Miss Watson—they could kill her. Everybody said:

"Oh, she'll do. That's all right. Huck can come in." (9–10)

This is funny, although not to Huck (he's "most ready to cry"). It's Tom who's having fun, along with us. But Twain the trickster has a different point in mind. And (as in the case of Huck's response to Aunt Sally) his point is rather obvious once we're on to his method. Indeed, it's a point that's basic to deadpan technique, as Twain describes it: the humor "depends for its effect upon the *manner* of the telling . . . [as distinct from] the *matter*." Once we look as it were through the narrative manner to its matter the snapper to the gang oath is as plain as the ubiquity of the N-word. Death and violence are writ large throughout the novel. The blood bond that Tom invents is a mirror-reflection of the world of *Huckleberry*

Finn. It foreshadows the death hoax that Huck invents when he leaves for the river ("I pulled out some of my hair, and blooded the ax good" and made a track so that they'd look "to find the robbers that killed me") and the horrific scene earlier, when his blind-drunk father chases him around the shack with a "clasp knife," cursing and roaring (and laughing with "*such* a screechy laugh") that Huck is the Angel of Death, "saying he [Pap] would kill me and then I couldn't come for him no more" (41, 36). These fantasies come to life, as it were, in the Boggs murder, in scenes of lynching and tar-and-feathering, in the Grangerford-Shepherdson clan massacre. According to Twain scholars, there are thirty-three corpses in *Huckleberry Finn,* and that does not include the section Twain omitted, surely one of the most vivid and most morbid he ever wrote, describing Pap's dead body.[7] It's not too much to say that dead bodies, real and imagined, are the anatomical links of Huck's story. It's appropriate that G.G.'s "ordnance" (the Notice authorized by a Chief of Cannon and Artillery) should warn that anyone seeking a plot would be shot. Getting killed is a key to the novel's plotline.

The fourth point to make about Huck's "joke" concerns the cause of death. On the river he travels, explosions are a common experience. Aunt Sally confirms this in the case of the poor Baptist, and we can find many other examples in the novel (steamboats grounded, blown up, cutting rafts in two). The point is: this river is dangerous. Critics have tended to sentimentalize the "natural setting" in *Huckleberry Finn* ("the river-god" called the Mississippi), and to be sure the sentiment is invited by its comic author. But Twain the Trickster makes it plain that the river is a constant threat. "Nature," Satan reports in *Letters from the Earth,* "is a killer," and *Huckleberry Finn* might have been his proof-text.[8] The river here is the source of storms and water snakes, it calls up the fog that keeps Huck and Jim from reaching Cairo; its currents and countercurrents, twists and turns, carry the raft ever deeper into slave territory; it is ubiquitously "troublesome" to those who live near it:

> the houses was sticking out over the bank, and they was bowed and bent, and about ready to tumble in. . . . People lived in them yet, but it was dangersome, because sometimes a strip of land as wide as a house caves in at a time. Sometimes a belt of land a quarter of a mile deep will start in and cave along till it all caves into the river in one summer . . . the river's always gnawing at it. (183)

This river affords Huck and Jim some wonderful moments together; and to underscore their "idyll" critics have often quoted Huck's description of life on the raft: "what you want, above all things, on a raft, is for everybody to be satisfied, and feel right and kind towards the others" (165). But they have generally failed to add that that's how Huck *rationalizes* allowing the King and Duke to have their way ("it warn't no use to tell Jim")—and they have generally failed to note that *for much of the river journey* (more than half of it) life on the raft is controlled and directed by those "scoundrels" (268), as Huck charitably calls them. (Huck and Jim spend eleven days together on the raft [chapters 11–16 and 18]; the Duke and King invade the raft in chapter 19 and remain for at least 15 days, until chapter 31, when the raft arrives at the Phelps Plantation.) Huck and Jim may be in flight on the Mississippi, but the Mississippi is the natural habitat of the Duke and King, just as it is naturally the cause of mudslides. In this book the river is emphatically not an emblem of Nature's Nation; it belongs to the world of Hobbes and Darwin, not of Rousseau and Emerson. Nothing is more natural about Huck, nothing more clearly shows how close he is to the river, than does his spontaneous invention of the exploding cylinder that (only) "Killed a nigger."

Not that Huck needs the river to prompt his invention; he always thinks in terms of death and disaster. That's the fifth point to note about Huck's casual response. It alerts us to the fact that he's a morbid, haunted young boy. I'm referring now to the way he thinks and imagines rather than to his experiences. Twain provides two clues to Huck's inner world: the lies that Huck tells and the images that he conjures up when he's alone—in other words, the reality that Huck himself makes up, for others and for himself. In both cases, it's the reality of the grotesque. The stories he invents for strangers are a series of horror tales: families dead, dying, or diseased. And his solitary musings take exactly the same form, except that the dead return as ghosts. One such moment occurs on his arrival at the Phelps Plantation:

> When I got there it was all still and Sunday-like, and hot and sunshiny; the hands was gone to the fields; and there was them kind of faint dronings of bugs and flies in the air that makes it seem so lonesome and like everybody's dead and gone; and if a breeze fans along and quivers the leaves it makes you feel mournful, because you feel like it's spirits whispering—spirits that's been dead ever so many years—and you always think they're talking

about *you*. As a general thing it makes a body wish *he* was dead, too, and done with it all. (276)

What's funny about this description—in both the fun sense of the term and in its "odd or curious" implication—is that actually it's a lovely Sunday morning. There's no reason for Huck to think this way, except that that's the way he thinks.

One more example must suffice. I take this from the first chapter, Huck alone in his room at night, conjuring up the world out there in what may be read as an introduction to his general angle of vision:

> I went up to my room with a piece of candle, and put it on the table. Then I set down in a chair by the window and tried to think of something cheerful, but it warn't no use. I felt so lonesome I most wished I was dead. The stars were shining, and the leaves rustled in the woods ever so mournful; and I heard an owl, away off, who-whooing about somebody that was dead, and a whippo-will and a dog crying about somebody that was going to die; and the wind was trying to whisper something to me, and I couldn't make out what it was, and so it made the cold shivers run over me. (4)

What I termed Huck's casual response—his spontaneous invention of a dead person (or nonperson)—is in fact perfectly characteristic, a typical product of his "mournful" fantasy life.

But of course it's not pure fantasy when he invents the cylinder explosion; this time Huck is not alone; on the contrary, he's trying hard to please someone else. He's being led on by Aunt Sally, who prods him about the grounding. He knows what she'd like to hear, and he knows she'll think a "nigger" is "no one," just as he knows she wants him to be like Tom. And naturally he complies. That's the sixth point to note about his response. Huck *wants* to conform. More precisely, he's a conformist who can't make it. Huck would like to please everyone, even Miss Watson. He would even like to live with Pap, if Pap would let him live; he tries as best he can to "satisfy" the Duke and King; he'd certainly like to join the Grangerfords (at the expense of abandoning Jim) and no doubt the Phelpses as well; and he'd *love* to be Tom Sawyer—but he can't. Huck Finn is Woody Allen's Zelig in reverse: a deadpan artist's Zelig. Zelig may not want to be a Chinese chef or a Nazi, but he can't help becoming just like whoever he's with. Huck's dilemma is just the opposite: he can't help being different. Certainly, we sympathize with his difference, we applaud it, but the nub remains. Huck's desire to fit in is underscored by his inability to do so. And he wants to fit in because he believes in society and its values. He believes in racism, class hierarchy, southern aristocracy, Sunday School religion. Why else would he be so disappointed in Tom's plan to "steal" Jim?

> Well, one thing was dead sure, and that was that Tom Sawyer was in earnest, and was actuly going to help steal that nigger out of slavery. That was the thing that was too many for me. Here was a boy that was respectable and well brung up; and had a character to lose; and folks at home that had characters; and he was bright and not leather-headed; and knowing and not ignorant; and not mean, but kind; and yet here he was, without any more pride, or rightness, or feeling, than to stoop to this business, and make himself a shame, and his family a shame, before everybody. I *couldn't* understand it no way at all. It was outrageous. (292–93)

If this were a children's book called *Tom Sawyer,* we could read this passage as a healthy piece of social satire. The white-trash boy is at once denouncing (when he shouldn't) and looking up to (when he needn't) the respectable head-of-the-gang. But *Huckleberry Finn* is something else altogether. As Huck describes the difference in the opening paragraph, *Tom Sawyer* is marred by "stretchers" invented "by Mr. Mark Twain" ("I never seed anyone but lied one time or another")—and he, Huck, is going to set the record straight. As we come to understand the difference, however, *Huckleberry Finn,* as *opposed* to *Tom Sawyer,* is a complex, sophisticated narrative about a black-white relationship. To recall Twain's phrase, it's a work "of high and delicate art . . . [as] only an artist can tell it"—in which an African American takes on extraordinary human force. Jim, we learn, is the noblest person in Huck's life, the novel's most sympathetic adult figure, the father Huck deserves and never had. Can it be funny that Huck thinks like *this* after their long experience together on the river? After all he has seen of Jim—having actually acknowledged, however reluctantly, Jim's goodness, intelligence (he "was most always right"), and caring (he'd "do everything he could think of for me")—can he believe that it would be "ignorant," "leather-headed," and "mean" for Tom to "stoop to this business" (270)?

In order to explain this nub we need to rehearse its context. The last narrative section (the Phelps adventures, occupying about a third of the novel) has become a familiar critical crux. Twain scholars have debated its merits ever since Hemingway advised readers to skip it altogether. Tom's tricks at the Phelpses amount to a series of minstrel-show send-ups: Jim locked in a wood-shack, following the silly-cruel instructions of a couple of adolescent pranksters, who "smuggle" spiders into the shack, instruct him to write messages in blood, and feed him a corn pone with a candlestick hidden in it ("it most mashed all his teeth out"). "Jim he couldn't make no sense in most of it," Huck comments, "but he allowed we was white folks and knowed better than him; so he was satisfied" (309). Tom's higher knowledge in this case comes from the romances of Alexander Dumas; he names his scheme the Great Evasion; and the joke, it turns out, is that Jim has already been freed. Miss Watson (who earlier had intended to sell him down the river for eight hundred dollars) set him free on her deathbed (after his escape), so that Tom's games are a hoax, as *in effect* were Huck's efforts all along to help Jim escape. If we carry the logic of this hoax to its absurd end, we could say Jim was *lucky* he didn't get to Cairo and the North, since he would then never have known he was a free man.

Evidently Tom's games did amuse the minstrel-show audience of the 1880s and 1890s, but by the 1920s (as Hemingway's remark indicates) they had become troublesome, and over the past half century critics have roundly denounced them and all that they imply. It's now safe to say (T. S. Eliot and Lionel Trilling to the contrary notwithstanding) that the last third section of *Huckleberry Finn* is a grand sarcasm on Twain's part directed against Tom Sawyer. But it's worth repeating that this is a trickster's sarcasm. The satire of the Good Bad Boy (whose mischief-by-the-book we see through and, accordingly, to whom we feel superior) is a Great Evasion to divert us from the nub. What's really funny about the hoax is that the Bad Bad Boy, the rebel hero Huck Finn, *our* Huck, goes along. He has the same respect for Tom at the end that he does at the start. Fundamentally, "Tom Sawyer's Comrade" (as the novel's subtitle funnily puts it) *is* the same Huck at the end that he was before he set out on his adventures. That's what makes it appropriate for him to respond to Aunt Sally as he does, in spite of all he has learned about Jim. Or rather, *because* of all he has *not* learned, for (as his gratuitous "Killed a nigger" should remind us) Huck never develops. He speaks and thinks and feels at the Phelpses' pretty much as he does at Miss Watson's. There's a technical reason for this: *Huckleberry Finn* is Huck's autobiographical retrospective, and if he had realized what we'd like him to have realized—if his Devil's Pact on the river had had any enduring positive value; if it would have signaled a genuine conversion *to* Jim's humanity, rather than just one more confirmation of his own fatalistic low self-esteem (his sense of being damned anyway, in a wonderfully grim-funny display of what Twain meant by "Calvinism without God")—then Huck would have written an entirely different book. He would have felt differently not only about Jim but about Tom and all others, including himself. The boy who might have emerged as critics have told us he did would never have said early in his river-journey that "you can't learn a nigger to argue"; he would have expressed *some* regret, or at least offered some explanation, for having abandoned Jim to live with the Grangerfords; and certainly he would not have expected Jim to join him and Tom in the territory. That is to say, if Huck Finn had really grown morally, Twain the trickster could not gull us into thinking that he does. There would be no point or nub or snapper—no "point"—to the whole story. Humorously speaking, his tall tale would be un-American.

Huck doesn't develop so that we can be conned into believing he does: in this case, there's something funny about the nub itself. The joke suggests it's a good thing that Huck doesn't change. It reminds us that what we believe in ultimately is Huck's integrity. He has the same fantastic innocence from start to finish. He's always the same lovable boy with the "sound heart"; from the outset his innate decency is set in contrast to society's "deformed conscience"; we come to see in Huck a kind of essentialist Romantic-natural opposition to "sivilization." What's *funny* here (in the con-man sense of the term) is that it's Huck's unchanging quality that makes him admirable. And to draw out this con game, it's precisely that admirable aspect of him—the potential we discern *within* Huck's transparent innocence—that invites us to interpret his narrative. As I noted earlier, Twain's hemeneutical imperative turns on the snapper that we interpret because our hero doesn't. Which is to say: Huck doesn't develop, therefore we do it for him. We know him better than he knows himself. Indeed, we know him as he *cannot* know himself, since his na-iveté, his *unfulfilled* potential, *is* what we know about him, and what we cherish. Thus we understand (as he never does) what's *really* happening—with him, to him, and around him.

The deadpan this involves posits two contrary responses on our part:

first, our distance from Huck and our superiority to him; and second, our love of Huck and our identification with him. The link between these responses—the joke's nub—lies in Twain's directive for interpretation. I said earlier that the deadpan Notice invites us to seek moral, motive, and plot; the trickster's point is to guide us into a certain mode of exegesis. We might call it a comic mode in the classic sense of the term. Its purpose is to resolve contradiction and restore order. The snapper this entails is dramatically illustrated in the scene that critics have rendered the locus classicus of Huck's moral progress. It comes at the point when Huck learns that the Duke and the King have disclosed Jim's whereabouts. Dismayed that Jim may be "sold down the river . . . amongst strangers," Huck decides it would be preferable to return him instead to Miss Watson, "his true and proper owner," so that he can "be a slave at home where his family was." Then Huck succumbs to conscience-stricken memories of how he himself has been responsible, directly or indirectly, for helping this "runaway nigger":

I tried the best I could to kinder soften it up somehow for myself by saying I was brung up wicked, and so I warn't much to blame: but something inside of me kept saying, "There was the Sunday school, you could a' gone to it; and if you'd 'a done it they'd a' learn't you there that people that acts as I'd been acting about that nigger goes to everlasting fire."

It made me shiver. And I about made up my mind to pray, and see if I couldn't try to quit being the kind of a boy I was and be better. So I kneeled down. But the words wouldn't come. . . . You can't pray a lie—I found that out. . . . At last I had an idea: and I says, I'll go and write the letter—and then see if I can pray. . . . So I got a piece of paper and a pencil, all glad and excited, and set down, and wrote:

Miss Watson, your runaway nigger Jim is down here two mile below Pikes-ville, and Mr. Phelps has got him and he will give him up for the reward if you send.

HUCK FINN.

I felt good and all washed clean of sin for the first time I had ever felt so in my life, and I knowed I could pray now. But I didn't do it straight off, but laid the paper down and set there thinking . . . [and went on thinking] and then I happened to look around and see that paper.

It was a close place. I took it up, and held it in my hand. I was a-trembling. . . . I studied a minute, . . . and then says to myself:

"All right then, I'll go to hell"—and tore it up.

It was awful thoughts and awful words, but they was said. And I let them stay said and never thought no more about reforming. (269–71).

What's funny about this scene is that it's (1) playful, a mock-conversion that turns into a Devil's Pact; (2) satirical, a sweeping indictment of the ravages of southern evangelical Calvinism; and (3) odd, curious, and sinister, a savage mockery of our relation to the text. For in order to "get the joke" we *have* to interpret and yet we feel sure that our interpretation is voluntary. The meaning we find seems entirely subjective, a meaning "from the heart," and yet it's entirely predictable, a meaning directed step by step by trickster deadpan. To begin with, we're led to interpret in a *consistent* pattern of inversions. Huck says "conscience" meaning the Right Thing to Do, and we think "source of evil"; he says "wicked" and we think "kind"; Huck laments that he was "brung up wrong" and we're glad that he has held fast to his virtues; he tells us he shivered with fear and we think he's brave and independent; he says, trembling, "I'll go to hell" and we think "he's saved!"

This pattern of inversion is an act of protection. That's the second step of interpretation. Whether or not we're aware of it, we're reading between the lines in order to save the "true" Huck from everyone around him, from Tom and Miss Watson and the Grangerfords and the Phelps family. And our act of protection is in turn a claim to ownership. We might call this the triumphant final step of interpretation. It makes Huck *ours*. The opening gang-oath is worth recalling in this regard. The question that Tom raises about family hostages expands into a much larger question: to whom does Huck belong? The narrative plays out a series of options—Pap, Tom's gang, Jim—until it becomes obvious, whether or not we're conscious of the dramatic shift in perspective this entails, that Huck belongs *only to us*. We adopt him, once and for all; we take him into *our* True American family, into our hearts; we interpret him into our likeness. Hermeneutically, we recreate Huck as the child-in-us.

Now, all of this (to repeat) is predictable, an interpretive design forced upon by the humor itself. That is, it's a design carefully elicited from us—with all the trickster's "casual" airs and sly diversions (just "bubbling along")—by Mark Twain, Humorist.

Let me explore the snappers. First, there's the issue of "manner" (Twain's key to the deadpan relation between form and content). Huck

Finn is a great writer; his grammar and spelling are faulty, but that simply accentuates the beauty of his style, which is extraordinarily simple, spontaneous, and direct. And yet we have to protect him all the time from his own text. We have to explain away his words, to redefine the emotions he records, to reverse the convictions he sets out. Huck is a master of the literal statement; he writes with unfailing directness, lucidity, and vivid effect; he's the prime example (as Hemingway noted) of the American plain style. And yet we have to save Huck at every turn from his own plain meanings. We have no choice, as it were, but to recast "shiver" (when Huck says "it made me shiver") into *something* positive, to deny the import *for Huck* (the stated effect) of his decision to choose damnation, to white out not only his numerous N-words but the "no one" by which he glosses the word, at the Phelpses' and elsewhere. Once we've done all that, we can laugh along *with* Huck, *our* Huck, the uncorrupted child in us who (we're certain) does *not* believe, would never *really* think, that "you can't learn a nigger to argue." To paraphrase Jim: we're sophisticated folks, and so we know better, and can smile contentedly and be satisfied. (Imagine reconstruing Hemingway's "plain" meanings in this comic fashion!)

Still, we should be suspicious by this point about the process we're engaged in. Our interpretation has led us step by logical step from protection to adoption to identification; and at the end our laughter expresses the child-in-us—who is *us*? The answer, I've suggested, is the liberal white reader of 1885, and beyond. For the term "liberal white" here refers to a social-symbolic system, an official hermeneutic, an institution of interpretation designed to fortify a certain way of life. "Liberal" so understood is a code word that can stretch to accommodate a wide range of positions, from (say) communitarian to libertarian, from Left Democrat to Right Republican. And "white" in this configuration can stretch accordingly to include a liberal rainbow-gamut of colors (black, brown, red, yellow). *Huckleberry Finn* has always been controversial, and many casebooks have documented the polemical zigzags. Nevertheless, a consistent liberal theme dominates the discourse, a critical main current that runs through virtually all sides of the argument (provided that the critic does not dogmatically, illiberally, and foolishly condemn the book for being merely trashy or utterly racist). I refer to what Jonathan Arac has recently labeled the "hypercanonization" of Huck Finn. To judge from a century of Twain experts, Huck is "the individual in nature," "independent," "self-reliant," "the spirit of youth," "the spirit of adventure and expansion," the soul of "mobility," "enterprise," "unboundedness," and "exploration." More than that: Huck and Jim on the raft have been taken as a kind of communitarian utopia, the emblem of the "ideal society." In contrast to the settlements, they represent the "spiritual values" of "voluntary association," "personal freedom" in a context of "true brotherhood," "responsibility and equality entwined." Critics have applied these abstractions as universals, but clearly they are universals within a distinctive historical frame, a configuration of beliefs and ideals that make up a singular *cultural* vision. As Norman Podhoretz, editor of the conservative journal *Commentary,* has written: "Sooner or later, all discussions of *Huckleberry Finn* turn into discussions of America." Or in the words of the late Irving Howe, writing in his left-wing journal *Dissent,* "Huck is not only the most American boy in our own literature, he is also the character with whom most American readers have most deeply identified." Or once again, in the words of the centrist Americanist scholar Eric Sundquist: *Huckleberry Finn* is "an autobiographical journey into the past" that tells "the story of a nation." [9]

Twain's trickster humor stands out brilliantly *against* the background of this liberal consensus-in-dissent. The nub or snapper of our interpretation of *Huckleberry Finn*—both of the narrative and of its "autobiographical" hero—is that what begins as our subjective assessment, and often our oppositional perspective (against "sivilization"), leads us happily *into* the institutions of culture. Thus it was all but inevitable that in our multicultural era, Huck should be discovered to be (in addition to everything else that's positively American) multicultural. This is not the place to discuss Huck's "blackness," but it's pertinent here as elsewhere to recall Twain's warning that interpretation may be a trap of culture. *Huckleberry Finn* is an inexorable journey into deadpan, toward a devastating nub. The plot is a river story, the style is a flow of humor, and our interpretation is a raft that promises protection (from conscience, from Tom's games, from social enslavement, from racism and ethnocentrism, from all the slings and arrows of outrageous adulthood). But the river keeps returning us again and again to the settlements, the raft proves to be a very insecure haven, and on this "raft of trouble" (77), on this river that betrays and kills, we're left with two mock-symbolic figures. One is Huck Finn, bond-slave to society, mostly scared to death, speaking a language we don't trust, and (as Pap puts it, in a drunken flash of insight) an Angel of Death. The other is Jim, the fugitive Black who need never have run off, who leads Huck into a Devil's Pact, and who, in doing so, ironically enacts his own version of the official hermeneutic: "Dey's two angels hoverin' round 'bout [every person]. One uv 'em is white en shiny, en t'other one is black. De white one gits him to go right a little while, den de black one sail in en bust it all up. A body can't tell yit which one gwyne to fetch him at the las'" (27). So the nub is: the Angel of Death and the Black Angel, on a trickster's raft to freedom, drifting deeper and deeper into slave territory. It makes for a savagely funny obituary to the American dream.

I mean *funny* now in the manner of the late Twain, the comic nihilist who wrote that "only laughter can blow history to rags and tatters at a blast," the "laughing mortician" (as one of his heirs, Nathanael West, put it) who felt "quite sure that (bar one) I have no race prejudices nor color prejudices nor creed prejudices. Indeed I know it. I can stand any society. All that I care to know is that man is a human being—that is enough for me—he can't be any worse." For that deadpan artist, humor was a systematic expose of the abstractions that held history together. He states the rules of the game in "How to Tell a Story," and he shows how they work explicitly (exposes the nub itself) in *The Mysterious Stranger*. Here Satan, the divine trickster, pairs up with a poor-white, innocent, sound-hearted little boy—a boy not unlike Huck—befriends him and conjures up for him a variety of alluring spectacles and promises, only to reveal, at the end, the absurdity of each one of them. "You perceive *now*," Satan declares, that it "is all a dream, a grotesque and foolish dream." And then the boy's epiphany: "He vanished, and left me appalled; for I knew, and realized, that all that he had said was true." That's the humorous point of *Huckleberry Finn,* if we're alert. The novel's underlying moral and motive, its deadpan *plot,* is that this exhilarating flight to freedom—black and white together, the individual regenerated by nature—was all a dream, a grotesque and foolish dream. That's the enlightened reader's appalling post-snapper insight, accompanied by the invitation to laugh at ourselves for having laughed along with Huck. As Melville puts it near the end of his comic-satiric-nihilistic "Piazza Tale": "truth comes in with darkness." [10]

Where does that leave the problem of interpretation? No doubt the ready formalist response is Bakhtin's theory of dialogics, especially as applied to the *skaz,* the traditional Russian comic-colloquial monologue.

And indeed it's tempting to consider Twain's novel in light of Bakhtin's analysis of the three types of *skaz* he defines in *Problems of Dostoevsky's Poetics*. But here the voice of what I called "our Huck" poses a peculiar problem. I refer to the compelling subjectivity we sense within or beyond that voice, once we have recognized—*after* the trickster's last deadpan twist—that we do not own Huck after all. We might imagine this sense of beyondness (to follow Levinas's terms) as the Face of Huck that "*precedes* individuation . . . the anonymous, impersonal state [that] precedes the formation of the material 'I'"—specifically, the "I" whom we have interpreted into heroic existence. So understood, the furthest reach of Twain's "high and delicate art" yields a Huck Finn "for whom suffering is a direct consequence of being imprisoned in the experience of personal identity"—the experience of being "Tom Sawyer's Comrade," the imprisonment of our wish-fulfillment of freedom. Levinas speaks of this recognition on our part as a sense of the other's "enchainment"; and in Huck's case enchainment extends from Pap to Miss Watson to Tom to (most imprisoningly perhaps) the Huck we re-create in the image of our culture-bound dreams.[11]

I would like to think of this suffering-comic Face of Huck as the potentially hopeful juncture not of the parts of the social body but on the contrary as the culture-resistant juncture between interpreter and fictional subject, as between self and Other. Like Twain's opening deadpan connective between reader and text—the joking "authority" ("*Per G.G., Chief of Ordnance*") that prohibits interpretation on pain of death—it entails a set of open-ended connectives that leads, to begin with, into an absurdist impasse. We must interpret (to get the joke), we can't interpret (without making a joke of ourselves). It's a comic position bereft of every traditional sustaining device of comedy—stripped of the social norms embedded in satire, stripped of the moral or philosophical alternatives implicit in irony and parody, stripped even of the immemorial "liberating magic" of the folktale (since the deadpan exposes liberation as a storyteller's magic *trick*).[12] What remains is the sheer volatility of the fun that Twain sets loose. Considered as a trickster's monologue, Huck's story has a certain brilliantly controlled authorial point-to-it-all. As humor, however, its layers of meaning are not only different but contradictory— cheerful, satiric, sinister—and yet they coexist, interpenetrate, modify, and undermine of another. I've called them layers to distinguish the relationship between them from what we traditionally mean by levels of meaning. Levels imply a unifying, bottom-line interpretation, as in the medieval fourfold method, or in our deep interpretation of Huck's innocence (or his radicalism, or his multicultural representativeness). By contrast, layers of meaning are mobile, shift-shape, like a kaleidoscope. It depends which way you turn them; and they are by definition always subject to another turn or series of turns. Thus what's funny about West's image of the laughing mortician (or about my description of *Huckleberry Finn* as a "savagely funny obituary") is that "mortician" (like "obituary") is apocalyptic, the mark of an ending, whereas to laugh at something signals a different perspective on the matter: the possibility of another, different, and/or contradictory layer of interpretation.

That comic perspective does not transcend Twain's deadpan; it does not release us from the implications of his nubs and snappers. But it seems to me the most positive of those implications, since it follows from the *intentionality* of the humor itself as distinct from authorial *intention*. Twain's intention is embedded in the humorous levels of his "stretchers"; but the layered intentionality of his humor turns our laughter against any form of hierarchical, bottom-line interpretation. It reminds us that deadpan itself is quintessentially systemic, the very model of Deep Meaning. We're asked to get *the* snapper, *the* realization that explains (even as it undoes) everything that has come before. In the Levinasian view, however, the monologue flow undoes the deadpan design. Twain's nubs remain the key to the artistry by which he takes us in; with which he then guides us, if we're alert, to perceive the traps of culture; and through which he offers us the opportunity to have a good laugh at ourselves, good enough perhaps to blow history to rags and tatters. Nonetheless, those nubs are *dependent* on the extraordinary creative power of *Huck's* (as distinct from Twain's) storytelling. Huck says at the start that his aims are different from Twain's; and although he's referring here to *The Adventures of Tom Sawyer* ("a true book, mainly," but there "was things which he [Twain] stretched" [1])—although, moreover, this is transparently a joke on Twain's part—nonetheless the story that Huck tells turns Twain's joke *against* the novel's deadpan. For really we do not get beyond the narrative "surface" when we get the nub. The "true" Huck who comes in with trickster "darkness" remains a figure of negotiation. Within his own world (*his* monologue), Huck remains alive and well, buoyant, on the go; and he remains too, from our critical distance, *enhanced* by the satire we see through his straight-faced observations, fortified by the very layers of tricksterisms (Tom's, Huck's, the Duke and King's, and above all Twain's) by which we are ensnared into wonder and belief.

In short, Huck's voice is not contextualized (let alone submerged) by Twain's. The text works (to repeat) in layers, not levels of humor, and the dynamic this entails becomes a continuous, fluctuating, myth-making/myth-mocking interplay between perceptions that tear meaning apart and protective revisions that build up meaning. Finally, that is, the novel's protagonist (hero-butt-conformist-rebel) emerges as someone we can't really know because we can't fix him into categories. The unforgettable human presence, Huckleberry Finn, is neither merely what he says he is (poor white trash), nor merely a version of the American Ideals we project upon him, nor (again) merely the laughing-stock of a Tall Tale. Thus he remains a figure outside of our interpretive control; we respond most fully to his subjectivity when we laugh at our very urge to appropriate him. So understood, what's funny about *Huckleberry Finn* is that this savage deadpan obituary to dreams turns out to be a life-buoy (a Trickster's coffin/life-buoy) to the possibilities of an ethical life.

Notes

1. Mark Twain, "How to Tell a Story" (1897), *How to Tell a Story and Other Essays,* ed. Shelley Fisher Fishkin (New York: Oxford University Press, 1966), 3–4. This essay was first delivered as a talk (without the emphasis on the trickster) at the University of Vermont and subsequently published in the *New England Review.* I want to record my gratitude to the audience then at the University of Vermont, especially to Professors Mary Louise Kete and Stephen Donadio. The present substantially altered essay was inspired by Professor Jeanne Reesman, who organized the memorable Trickster Conference at Reno, Nevada.

2. Hilton Manfred Obenzinger, *American Palestine: Melville, Twain, and the Holy Land Mania* (Princeton: Princeton University Press, 1999).

3. Lewis Hyde, *Trickster Makes This World* (New York: Farrar, Straus and Giroux, 1998), passim.

4. Mark Twain, *The Adventures of Huckleberry Finn,* ed. Walter Blair and Victor Fischer (Berkeley and Los Angeles: University of California Press, 1988), 183, 189 (all subsequent references to the novel are from this edition); Mark Twain, *The Damned Human Race,* ed. Janet Smith (New York: Hill and Wang, 1962), 62, and *Letters from the Earth,* ed. Bernard De Voto (New York: Harper and Row, 1962), 7.

5. I owe this reading of the Notice to Professor Susan L. Mizruchi; more generally I am indebted for her insightful close reading of the entire essay.

6. Alan Trachtenberg, *The Incorporation of America* (New York: Hill and Wang, 1982), passim.

7. Did he omit it because he feared it would blur the Comic Mask he wears and so undermine the deadpan?

8. Twain, *Letters from the Earth* 6.

9. Howe, Podhoretz, and Sundquist, quoted in Jonathan Arac, *Huckleberry Finn as Idol and Target* (Madison: University of Wisconsin Press, 1997), 3. For critical comments on Huck see Arac, passim, and the essays collected in Gerald Graff and James Phelan, eds., *Adventures of Huckleberry Finn: A Case Study in Critical Controversy* (New York: Bedford/St. Martin's Books, 1995), passim.

10. Nathanael West, *Novels and Other Writings,* ed. Sacvan Bercovitch (New York: Library of America, 1997), 770; Mark Twain, "Concerning the Jews," *Mark Twain: Collected Tales, Sketches, and Essays,* ed. Louis J. Budd (New York: Library of America, 1992), 355; *The Mysterious Stranger,* ed. William M. Gibson (Berkeley and Los Angeles: University of California Press, 1969), 405; Herman Melville, "The Piazza," *Herman Melville: Pierre, Israel Poter, The Piazza Tales, The Confidence Man, Uncollected Prose, Billy Budd,* ed. Harrison Hayford (New York: Library of America, 1984), 634. I mean to suggest here a certain American comic line (running through Melville to West) that underlies Twain's concept of the American "humorous story." Indeed, what I called the Levinasian Face of Huck may be discerned as well at the end of Melville's "Piazza": "every night, when the curtain falls [over the dream of 'fairy-land'], truth comes in with darkness. No light shows from the [deceptively 'magical'] mountain. To and fro I walk on the Piazza deck, haunted by Marianna's face," now become the face of the Other.

11. Mikhail Bakhtin, *Problems of Dostoevsky's Poetics,* trans. R. W. Rostel (New York: Ardis, 1973), 153–63; Emmanuel Levinas, *Otherwise Than Being, or Beyond Essence,* trans. Alphonso Lingis (The Hague: Martinez Nijhoff, 1981), 199ff.; Levinas, paraphrased and quoted in Sharon Cameron's enormously suggestive essay, "The Way of Life by Abandonment: Emerson's Impersonal," *Critical Inquiry,* 25 (1998): 28–29; Cameron cites Levinas's *Time and the Other,* trans. Richard A. Cohen (Pittsburgh: Duquesne University Press, 1987), 51, 57.

12. Walter Benjamin, "The Storyteller," *Illuminations: Essays and Reflections,* ed. Hannah Arendt, trans. Harry Zohn (New York: Schocken, 1969), 102; that magic, writes Benjamin, speaking in particular of Nikolai Leskov, leads back to "the earliest arrangements that mankind made to shake off the nightmare of which history had placed upon its chest." What I would suggest here is the prospect of a comparatist study of the American monologue and the Russian *skaz.* The most promising beginning for such a study (from the perspective of Huck's

monologue) is Donald Fanger's brilliant analysis of the *skaz* as a send-up of its readers—a monologue that parodically mirrors the larger text of which it is a part, "so that in laughing at the audience who listens to the story-teller we laugh at our own proxies"—in *The Creation of Nikolai Gogol* (Cambridge, Mass.: Harvard University Press, 1979), 102ff., 178. Another rich source of comparison—along with Gogol and Leskov—are the great monologue figures of Sholem Aleikhem, among them the orphan boy Motl Peisi.

The Trickster God in "Roughing It"

LAWRENCE I. BERKOVE

All of his life, Mark Twain was haunted by a sense that life was a practical joke. Early, middle, and late, his work teems with the ironies, surprises, reversals, unexpected twists, and tricks that are associated with practical jokes. "The Celebrated Jumping Frog of Calaveras County" (1865) is a veritable nest of practical jokes, one inside the other. *Roughing It* (1872) contains the famous but obvious image of the trickster coyote who slyly induces a dog to follow him, draws the dog farther and farther from his home by pretending to be near exhaustion, and then puts on a burst of blinding speed and leaves the dog alone in the wilderness, baffled by the sudden turn of events. In *Huckleberry Finn* (1885), Tom Sawyer's unexpected announcement at the end of the book that Jim was free means not only that Jim and Huck had been put through idiotic and humiliating rituals just to satisfy Tom's appetite for romance but that the reader had also been deceived. In "The Man That Corrupted Hadleyburg" (1899), the mysterious stranger plays a diabolic practical joke on the town in order to avenge some unspecified slight he had received in it. And in *Letters from the Earth* Satan gleefully describes how mankind is doubly deceived, first by "the Law of God"—the dictates of imperfect human nature, which can never avoid running afoul of God's moral law, and then by its own foolish insistence on piously maintaining that God is benevolent in the face of overwhelming evidence that He is not. But whereas those who have read widely in Twain's latter works especially are able to see that he did not regard God as benevolent, it may still not be self-evident that for most of his adult life Twain regarded God as the greatest trickster of them all. It was never a compliment.

Despite his overt claims at various times in his life that he regarded the God of the Bible as a patently ridiculous superstition, that he himself was a Deist (in his early years) or a determinist (in his later years), Twain retained a suppressed belief in God. His works are saturated with religious imagery, religious allusions, religious ideas and attitudes. Even in his later years, when he wrote so bleak a deterministic view of mankind's inherent nature in *What Is Man?* (1906), in other works he reverted to considerations of God, Satan, supernatural messengers or agents, predestination, and notions of Heaven or Hell. Twain's early indoctrination into Calvinism was ineradicable. He could later differ with it, oppose it, and detest it, but he could never quite extirpate it from himself. The main reason for this was that it made sense. Calvinism preached the corruption of human nature, and this lesson was reinforced for Twain almost every day of his life. Calvinism affirmed predestination, and Twain saw freedom as a mirage. Calvinism preached a stern, angry, and vengeful God, and insofar as Twain observed what might be called God's providence at work, it was apparent to him that Calvinism was right again. But in one main matter Twain did break with Calvinism sufficiently to be heretical. Calvinism viewed God as omniscient, omnipotent, and benevolent. Twain would have agreed with the omniscience and omnipotence, but he early came to regard God as malevolent. Twain saw the world and man as the victims of a God who did not mean them well. God played tricks on creation, and the tricks were not funny. In his latter years, after he became established, Twain was fairly direct about describing God as maliciously whimsical in works such as "Letters from the Earth" (1909/1962) that he set aside to be published after his death. But while he was still anxious to ensure that his books sold well, he was more devious or circumspect in his major works about hiding his beliefs beneath dark hints and veiled clues—usually by means of ironic levels of language in his layered style. This may be seen by an examination of *Roughing It,* in which these vestiges of Calvinism not only appear in abundance but also combine to unify the book around a central theme.

On its entertaining but deceptive surface, *Roughing It* appears to be only a loosely anecdotal travel book that recounts Mark Twain's travels to, and humorous adventures in, the Far West and Hawaii. Looked at more closely and deeply, however, the book may be seen to be surprisingly serious and its structure a repeated pattern of hoaxes and deceptions. The travels of *Roughing It* are ironic; distances are traversed, time passes, and variety is experienced, but the changes are illusions. The characters in the book remain the same; they learn nothing, gain nothing, and in the long run have gone nowhere and might as well have stayed at home. They start off as sinners, act as sinners, and wind up as sinners. It is not that there is no difference between home and the scenes of the travels but that they are similar in that both resemble ruined Eden, or are reminiscent of Hell, which, as sinners, the characters are never far from. The pattern of repeated ironic undercutting of all hopes and enthusiasms supports the book's pessimistic themes that characterize progress, happiness, and freedom as divine hoaxes.

On its broadest and most literal level, the book opens with its callow narrator excitedly confessing that "that word 'travel' had a seductive charm" for him (1:1–2)[1] but concludes with the now experienced narrator drawing the discouraging moral that "If you are of any account, stay at home and make your way by faithful diligence; but if you are 'no account,' go away from home, and then you will *have* to work, whether you want to or not." Upon his own return home, the narrator reports, he found it "a dreary place" with few of his acquaintances prosperous and happy: "some of them had wandered to other scenes, some were in jail, and the rest had been hanged." At the end of his travels and adventures he was therefore hardly farther ahead than his fellow townspeople for what started out as a three months' "pleasure trip" to Nevada had turned out for him to be "seven years of vicissitudes" (79:542).

What sort of vicissitudes? It may be noted that although *Roughing It* abounds in episodes that are hilarious to read about, the narrator never joins in the hilarity. For the reader, the contrast of the humorless narrator with the rollicking stories he tells is one of the humorous features of the book, but if we probe his humorlessness we uncover a truly serious and extensive dimension to him and the book that reflects Twain's underlying religious values.

Like *Huckleberry Finn* and *Connecticut Yankee* after it, *Roughing It* is rooted in Twain's deeply internalized Calvinism.[2] Early, middle, and late, Twain saw the human race as doubly damned both by its fatally flawed nature and by divine predestination.[3] He saw postlapsarian life as designedly hellish, marked by mankind's Sisyphean efforts to escape God's curse of Adam: that he would earn his bread by the sweat of his brows. *Roughing It*'s underlying unity—and the book is far more unified than has been generally recognized—is largely accomplished by the thematic operation of Twain's bitter belief not in the justice of this view of existence but in its empirical accuracy.

The book's central and unifying theme appears explicitly in chapter 36, where the narrator, after having worked a week at a quartz mill, observes: "It is a pity that Adam could not have gone straight out of Eden into a quartz mill, in order to understand the full force of his doom to 'earn his bread by the sweat of his brow'" (233). Twain understood when he wrote this line that, granted the truth of the Bible, man can no more escape his destiny than he can change his nature. Nevertheless, the ignorantly futile hope to escape this predestined curse by striking it rich was one of the reasons the narrator went to Nevada in the first place. An earlier and indirect statement of the theme occurs in chapter 30, when the narrator and his partners, having begun the labor of excavating the ledges of their silver mine claim, decide that there has to be an easier way of making money than actually working: "We never touched our tunnel or our shaft again. Why? Because we judged that we had learned the *real* secret of success in silver mining—which was, *not* to mine the silver ourselves by the sweat of our brows and the labor of our hands, but to *sell* the ledges to the dull slaves of toil and let them do the mining!" The theme is here somewhat disguised by irony. Using the simple past tense, the narrator appears to have made a triumphant discovery. At this point, however, he withholds from the reader the later discovery that the "*real* secret" did not amount to anything. But in the quoted passage, the slang meaning of "sell"—to hoax or to swindle—suggests that the ledges were also not worth anything and that the only way the narrator and his partners could profit by their claim was to take advantage of some "dull" party. Here and elsewhere throughout the book, humans, following their nature, are shown to have no hesitation in cheating their fellow men for easy profit. This view of things conforms to the tricky double-bind of the Calvinistic doctrine of double damnation: most men are damned to hell because of original sin, but even if they were not damned by predestination, their sinful natures would inevitably damn them.

The book abounds in such examples. For instance, the narrator is taken advantage of in the "genuine" Mexican plug incident in chapter 24; stockholders in a mine are deceived by a phony assessment in chapter 35; and chapter 44 is largely devoted to hoaxes ranging from salting worthless mines with slugs of silver cut from silver dollars to journalists (including Twain) who, bribed by presents of "feet" in prospective mines, "followed the custom of the country, used strong adjectives and frothed at the mouth as if a very marvel in silver discoveries had transpired" (287). These are fairly obvious examples of human deceit and trickery, and there are many more of them, but perhaps Twain's strongest examples of the divine Trickster's handiwork are the deftly subtle ones that illustrate the corruption of human nature and that function in such as way as to include the readers in the human tendency to misinterpret sins as virtues. One famous episode, chapter 47's delightful narrative of Buck Fanshawe's funeral, may serve as such an example.

The chapter is almost universally regarded as a classic specimen of pure Twainian humor. Indeed, on the face of it it is one of the richest examples of humor in the book. The humor is apparent even in paraphrase. Scotty Briggs, a Comstock miner, asks a clergyman to officiate at the burial of his friend, Buck Fanshawe. Scotty, however, is incapable of speaking in correct conventional English; his first language is mining jargon largely made up of colorful metaphors that are incomprehensible to someone from a different region of the country. The clergyman is that someone, but he also speaks in his own professional ecclesiastical jargon, which is equally incomprehensible to Scotty. After a number of hilarious false starts, the two finally understand each other, the minister accommodates Scotty's request and officiates at the funeral, and Scotty eventually is converted and henceforth teaches the Bible to the local Sunday school children using the lingo they all understand.

The narrative takes on a deeper and ironic level, however, when we shift our perspective from plot to language. Buck Fanshawe is disarmingly categorized as "a representative citizen," but ensuing details undercut this. "He had 'killed his man,'" "kept a sumptuous saloon," "been the proprietor of a dashing helpmeet whom he could have discarded without the formality of a divorce," and been "a very Warwick in politics." Subsequently, under the influence of typhoid fever, he "had taken arsenic, shot himself through the body, cut his throat, and jumped out of a four-story window and broken his neck." Twain then diverts his readers to a new target, the coroner's jury, which "brought in a verdict of death 'by the visitation of God.'" This is a superb example of how the whole can be greater than the sum of its parts, for the general propositions of the case become unstable when they are connected.

The ironies escalate if the language is inspected more closely. Most readers pay scant attention to the minor detail that Buck had a mistress, but the text's description of him as the "proprietor" of his mistress is a clear implication that Buck was a pimp as well. The funeral itself is also not as innocent as might seem at first glance. It is a lavish affair, and the clergyman delivers an impressive eulogy, for which he is well paid. But in the final analysis the minister hired out to praise a brawler, a killer, a saloon keeper, the pimp of a mistress who was a whore, a devious politician, and a suicide. Is this serving his religion, or selling it for his own profit?

The chapter ends with two seemingly warmhearted sentences: "It was my large privilege, a month before he died, to hear him [Scotty] tell the beautiful story of Joseph and his brethren to his [Sunday School] class 'without looking at the book.' I leave it to the reader to fancy what it was like, as it fell, riddled with slang, from the lips of that grave, earnest teacher, and was listened to by his little learners with a consuming interest that showed that they were as unconscious as he was that any violence was being done to the sacred properties." Twain generally used sentiment ironically, and the details of phraseology in these sentences point to the conclusion that this is no exception. Although the narrator appears to approve of Scotty, Twain does not; he is satirizing Scotty. This may be deduced from the textual hints that Scotty is "unconscious" of the "violence" caused by his rendition of the Bible story, and the pregnantly ambiguous phrase that the story "fell, riddled with slang," from Scotty's lips. The "violence" referred to can be understood when it is remembered that the kind of slang Scotty indulges in includes complimenting someone for being "white" or because "he warn't a Catholic," referring disparagingly to people as "Greasers" or "niggers," and using the slogan "no Irish need apply." Such prejudice-loaded slang would of course violently taint the "beautiful" story of Joseph or any other Bible text. Conforming the Bible to local slang brings down (that is, fells) the moral lessons of the Joseph story by riddling it (that is, shooting it full of holes) with the biases of the mining camp. The main point of this episode, however, is not to ridicule what may be fictional characters, or even to suggest that Bible lessons might be undesirably altered by reducing them to vernacular, but to demonstrate that human nature is so thoroughly corrupt that neither the characters in the story nor the readers recognize the fact of corruption let alone the degree of it. Indeed, we are entrapped by the author's consummate skill into believing that we are reading a benevolent tale of the goodness of human nature when what underlies the text is the cynical moral that the innate viciousness of our nature is concealed from us by a depraved conscience and an innate tendency to moral blindness. As Mary Edwards of "The Man that Corrupted Hadleyburg" (1899) would have said, "Lord, how we are made—how strangely we are made!"[4]

In *Roughing It* the hope of escaping the curse of work is always characterized as a delusion, a dream. "Silver fever," the lure of wealth that attracted everyone to Nevada in the first place, is characterized by the narrator as a "disease" (26:175). Infected by it on a prospecting trip, he "fled away as guiltily as a thief" from his comrades, "crawled about the ground," and collected glittering stones, believing in "a delirious revel" that the glitter was precious metals (28:185). When one of his partners subsequently identifies the stones as mere mica, the narrator falls from romantic "ecstasy" into romantic despair: "So vanished my dream. So melted my wealth away. So toppled my airy castle to the earth and left me stricken and forlorn" (28:188). Later, the partners travel to a mining camp where all claims are given "grandiloquent names" and are hyped with the "frenzied cant" of hyperbole. The miners are described as "stark mad with excitement—drunk with happiness," but retrospectively the narrator admits that it was all "a beggar's revel. There was nothing doing in the district—no mining—no milling—no productive effort—no income—and not enough money in the entire camp to buy a corner lot in an eastern village" (29:193). Not only are the narrator and his friends caught up in these dreams, but all prospectors as well. Trying to escape work, they unwittingly condemn themselves to lives of solitary wandering and hard labor.

The pocket miner of chapter 60 is described as one decaying example among multitudes who were "dead to the common interests of men, isolated and outcast from brotherhood with their kind," and who lived in "the most touching and melancholy exile that fancy can imagine." The pocket miner in particular is "one whose dreams were all of the past, whose life was a failure; a tired man, burdened with the present, and indifferent to the future; a man without ties, hopes, interests, waiting for rest and the end" (412–13). Here we may see the hellish enormity of the deception that began with the hope of escaping conventional labor by discovering wealth but ultimately brings the pocket miner to abandon all hope.

The pattern of deception occurs again in chapters 31 to 33, one of the choice scenes in the book, when the narrator and his partners leave an inn to go to Carson City, get lost in a snowstorm, and follow a trail of footprints. Their leader brags that "his instinct was as sensitive as any compass" and that if he were to deviate "a single point out of the true line [it] would assail him like an outraged conscience" [31:207], but he soon discovers that they had been "circusing round and round in a circle" in their own tracks for two hours. Failing to start a fire and believing that their end is near, the partners renounce the error of their ways and throw away into the snow the pleasurable tokens of their sinful lives: a bottle of whisky, a pack of cards, and a pipe, and resign themselves to death and oblivion. Their oblivion is only that of sleep, however, and they awaken in the morning chagrined to discover themselves barely fifteen steps from a station like the one they left and not much closer to Carson City. For two hours the men sulk in the station until one by one they leave the building to hunt in the snow for the discarded objects of their vices so that they can enjoy them once again. So much for conscience, so much for reform, and so much for human nature. They might have stayed where they were and not put their lives in danger for all the progress, geographical or moral, they made. This episode is, in miniature, the pattern of the entire book.

Wherever the narrator goes, there are reminders that his vision of glories is illusory and that all about him are hints of ruined Eden or of Hell. Chapter 56 begins, for example, with the seemingly innocent remark that "all scenery in California requires *distance* to give it its highest charm." Several sentences later, the narrator explains the illusion of this charm.[5] Once he gets close to the scenery, he finds "a sad poverty of variety in species, the trees being chiefly of one monotonous family." He further notes that "at a near view there is a wearisome sameness of attitude" of the trees' branches. "Close at hand, too, there is a reliefless and relentless smell of pitch and turpentine; there is a ceaseless melancholy in their sighing and complaining foliage; one walks over a soundless carpet of beaten yellow bark and dead spines of the foliage till he feels like a wandering spirit bereft of a footfall; he tires of the endless tufts of needles and yearns for substantial, shapely leaves; he looks for moss and grass to loll upon, and finds none, for where there is no bark there is naked clay and dirt, enemies to pensive musing and clean apparel" (385). The narrator's complaints undercut the common notion that Paradise is a place of unchanging peace and beauty by suggesting that part of man's doom is an innate restlessness and, consequently, an inability to enjoy what he has. More than that, the smells of pitch and turpentine strongly suggest Hell, as does the tightly consistent pattern of negative modifiers: the smells are "reliefless" and "relentless"; melancholy is "ceaseless"; foliage is "sighing" and "complaining" and its spines are "dead"; the tufts of needles are "endless"; and the clay and dirt are "naked," devoid of any moss and grass.

Indeed, the narrator himself is the best example of doomed restlessness in the book. He suffers from an internal hell and is never satisfied. An archetypal man, he leaves home because he finds it boring and is attracted by the variety of travel, but after he gets to some place that seems idyllic, he tires of its monotonous perfection. The unpleasant reality of where the narrator is always contrasts to the attractive but illusory aspect that is lent to it by distance. Hence, from a railroad car approaching California from the snows of the Sierras, he looks down "as the birds do, upon the deathless summer of the Sacramento Valley, with its fruitful fields, its feathery foliage, its silver streams, all slumbering in the mellow haze of its enchanted atmosphere, and all infinitely softened and spiritualized by distance—a dreamy, exquisite glimpse of fairy-land, made all the more charming and striking that it was caught through a forbidding gateway of ice and snow and savage crags and precipices" (56: 390). This romantic vision uses such loaded words as "deathless," "enchanted," "spiritualized," "dreamy," "fairy-land," "charming" and "striking" to set up the reader for the ironic contrast which follows. In the next sentences, a close-up view of the Sacramento Valley shows the ravages of gold-mining operations: "its grassy slopes and levels torn and guttered and disfigured by the avaricious spoilers of fifteen and twenty years ago. You may see such disfigurements far and wide over California—and in some such places, where only meadows and forests are visible—not a living creature, not a house, no stick or stone or remnant of a ruin, and not a sound, not even a whisper to disturb the Sabbath stillness" where only shortly before stood a "fiercely flourishing little city." In the first sentence the distant vision *charmed, enchanted,* and *spiritualized* like a *dream,* but close-up one is *struck* by the realization that what was seen was *fairy-land,* an illusion. In the second sentence "fiercely" and "flourishing" are oxymoronic except in an ironically hellish sense. The towns flourished by bustling with activity, noise, and commerce but were fierce by consisting of "gambling hells crammed with tobacco smoke, profanity" and "labor, laughter, music, dancing, swearing, fighting, shooting, stabbing—a bloody inquest and a man for breakfast every morning— *everything* that delights and adorns existence" (57:391). After the Fall from Eden, all succumbs to ruin, and existence is hellish.

The narrator also finds the climate of the San Francisco region hell-ishly monotonous. At first it is described as "as pleasant a climate as could well be contrived . . . and is doubtless the most unvarying in the whole world." He explains that "during eight months of the year . . . the skies are bright and cloudless, and never a drop of rain falls. But when the other four months come along, you will need to go and steal an um-brella. Because you will require it." In other words, change hardly ever comes, and when it does it simply introduces something else that also becomes tiresome. The narrator later puts it more vividly. In the middle of the "dismal monotony" of the quiet rains of the rainy season, "you would give *anything* to hear the old familiar thunder again and see the lightning strike somebody. And along in the summer, when you have suffered about four months of lustrous, pitiless sunshine, you are ready to go down on your knees and plead for rain—hail—snow—thunder and lightning—anything to break the monotony—you will take an earthquake, if you cannot do any better. And the chances are that you'll get it, too" (388). What appears to be the narrator's indulgence in hyper-bole turns out to be prophetic two chapters later when he recounts how he "enjoyed" his first earthquake, which came without warning on a bright October day in San Francisco, when "all was solitude and a Sab-bath stillness" (58:398). The seemingly offhand details that one will "*need* to go and *steal* an umbrella" and that the earthquake comes in a moment of "*Sabbath* stillness" are subtle hints, repeated throughout the book, of Twain's belief that man's nature is inclined to break the com-mandments and that the Sabbath is associated with the punishment of man rather than his refreshment.[6] Twain later links the monotony of weather and the deceptive character of the Sabbath in his 1897 story, "The Enchanted Sea Wilderness," when the ship *Adelaide* enters upon the region of the Everlasting Sunday, a doldrums contrast to the stormy re-gion of the Devil's Race-Track which surrounds it.[7] The narrator there-fore exposes the deception of California when he describes its weather: the "endless winter of Mono," the "eternal spring of San Francisco," and the "eternal summer of Sacramento" (389). It looks like Paradise but it feels like Hell.

The narrator's first, romantic, impression of Hawaii, of "a summer calm as tranquil as dawn in the Garden of Eden" (63:433), typically is followed by a realistic undercutting. "It was tranced luxury to sit in the perfumed air and forget that there was any world but these enchanted islands. It was such ecstasy to dream, and dream—till you got a bite. A scorpion bite." Eden had its snake, and Hawaii has its equivalent, the scorpion. And mosquitoes, tarantulas, and a centipede in bed that had "forty-two legs on a side and every foot hot enough to burn a hole through a raw-hide" (434). As before, romantic words like "tranced," "enchanted," "ecstasy," and "dream" set up the reader for a fall. The first chapter about Hawaii thus continues the pattern found in the rest of the book, and subsequent chapters abound in references to a ruined Eden and to Hell.

Even the volcanic origin of Hawaii is fraught with opposing double meanings of picturesqueness and ominousness. The narrator walks on a layer of "lava and cinders overlying the coral, belched up out of fathomless perdition long ago through the seared and blackened crater that stands dead and harmless in the distance" (63:433). But in chapter 74, a trip to the volcano Kilauea, a close-up view of a crater that is neither dead nor harmless, the narrator sees perdition in action, boiling lava with scattered fountains of fire ejecting "a shower of brilliant white sparks—a quaint and unnatural mingling of gouts of blood and snow-flakes! We had circles and serpents and streaks of lightning all twined and wreathed and tied together" (511). When Twain has the narrator comment at the end of the chapter that "the smell of sulphur is strong, but not unpleasant to a sinner" (512), this is an inadvertent admission of the narrator, who confessed to the sins of envy, covetousness, and seduction in the first chapter of the book, that he is a sinner, for he is not alarmed at recognizing the presence of Hell by its smell.[8]

Indeed, wherever he has traveled the narrator has never been far away from the wreckage of Eden and the reminder of Hell. Although Mark Twain does not admit it in the book, he fled the hell of the Civil War for the supposed peace and prosperity of the Far West. Instead of peace he found a lawless society where vice and violence were rampant; where murder and other crimes were frequent occurrences; where charm, enchantment, or dreaminess also signified an illusion; and where the beauty of distance was always undercut by the ugly or monotonous reality of what was close-up. In other words, despite the traveling, the narrator could have had essentially the same experience by staying at home. He was not meant to escape the common doom of mankind nor did he for more than an occasional moment of illusion. *Roughing It* looked at from a distance is an extremely funny book about the illusory attractions of travel, but regarded close-up it is a tour of ruined Eden overlooking Hell. It is proof that the trickster God derived from the deep and gloomy Calvinism that drove Mark Twain's art in *Huckleberry Finn* and *Connecticut Yankee* is not only at large in this early masterpiece but shapes ironically its conception of existence.

Notes

1. In addition to succumbing to the "seduction" of travel, the narrator also "envies" his brother and "covets" his distinction. With such an unpromisingly sinful start, it is ironic that when his brother invites him to come along, he unwittingly invokes Revelations 6:14 and 21:1 in his enthusiastic response: "it appeared to me that the heavens and earth passed away, and the firmament was rolled together as a scroll" (1:1–2). The passages alluded to refer to Judgment Day, when the final reckoning will be made. One does not expect a sinner to look forward to judgment for sins that he admits so frankly to enjoying. All parenthetical page references to the book follow the text of *Roughing It*, ed. Harriet Elinor Smith and Edgar Marquess Branch (Berkeley and Los Angeles: University of California Press, 1993). Where chapters are not specified in my text, the chapter number precedes the page number in parentheses.

2. The impact of Calvinism on *Huckleberry Finn* is discussed in my article "The Poor *Players* of *Huckleberry Finn*," *Papers of the Michigan Academy of Science, Arts, and Letters* 53 (1968): 291–310. For Twain's extension of his Calvinist vision to *A Connecticut Yankee*, see my articles, "The Reality of the Dream: Structural and Thematic Unity in *A Connecticut Yankee*," *Mark Twain Journal* 22, no. 1 (Spring 1984): 8–14; and "*A Connecticut Yankee*: A Serious Hoax," *Essays in Arts and Sciences* 19 (May 1990): 28–44.

3. A short summary of the main dogmas of the Calvinism that Twain was taught as a child and reluctantly accepted throughout his entire life, not at all because he approved of them but because he thought they were true, are presented in my article, "Mark Twain's Mind and the Illusion of Freedom," *Journal of the Humanities* [Kobe, Japan] Special Issue (1992): 1–23.

4. "The Man that Corrupted Hadleyburg," in Mark Twain, *Collected Tales, Sketches, Speeches, and Essays, 1891–1910,* ed. Louis J. Budd (n.p.: Library of America, 1992), 398.

5. The dispelling of this illusion is strikingly similar to the young pilot's realization, at the end of chapter 9 of *Life on the Mississippi* (1883), that the glorious sunset he experienced on the river and all the picturesque effects he noticed and took pleasure in, at the level of a layman, were instead specific tokens of danger. Then, from the perspective of age, the narrator observes that human

appearances are also deceptive. "Since those days, I have pitied doctors from my heart. What does the lovely flush in a beauty's cheek mean but a 'break' that ripples above some deadly disease? Are not all her visible charms sown thick with what are to him the signs and symbols of hidden decay? Does he ever see her beauty at all, or does n't he simply view her professionally, and comment upon her unwholesome condition all to himself? And does n't he sometimes wonder whether he has gained most or lost most by learning his trade?"

6. See Twain's discussion of temperament as a law of God that runs contrary to the Bible's commandments in Letter 8 of "Letters from the Earth."

7. In his discussion of "Everlasting Sunday," R. Kent Rasmussen observes that Twain "associated Sundays with stillness and inactivity," and that "throughout his writings, he generally uses 'everlasting' in a negative sense" (132). *Mark Twain A to Z* (New York: Facts on File, 1995). Rasmussen might have gone even farther and noted that Sunday almost always has negative connotations in Twain's works.

8. Chapter 74 is strikingly adumbrated by the narrator's experience at Lake Tahoe in chapter 23. At first, he and his friend find the loveliness "fascinating, bewitching, entrancing" (152) where even talking would have "interrupted the Sabbath stillness and marred the dreams the luxurious rest and indolence brought" (153). After their campfire carelessly gets out of control, however, the resulting forest fire devastates the area until "as far as the eye could reach the lofty mountain-fronts were webbed as it were with a tangled net-work of red lava streams. Away across the water the crags and domes were lit with a ruddy flare, and the firmament above was a reflected hell!" The implication of humans turning an Eden into its opposite is almost inescapable in this passage. Maybe "almost" is not needed, for the narrator's admission, "We were homeless wanderers again" (156), recalls the expulsion from Eden, and "again" is ominous in its implication of a pattern.

John, Brer Rabbit, and Babo

The Trickster and Cultural Power in Melville and Joel Chandler Harris

R. BRUCE BICKLEY JR.

*O*ral folklore and orally transmitted cultural history are central influences on Melville's and Joel Chandler Harris's works. Furthermore, in their works oral-language performance, augmented by body language and other visual cues, expresses both cultural identity and cultural expectations. Moreover, language as oral performance becomes an especially powerful rhetorical weapon when it is successfully employed by black trickster folk heroes in Melville and Harris. In fact, under particular circumstances, oral language used skillfully by unlettered African performers proves, ironically, to be more potent than the cumulative effect of several centuries of European and American civilization and literacy. Thus the tongue can be mightier than both the sword and the pen; furthermore, supposedly "primitive" African slaves can control, at least for a time, their presumably more powerful and educated Western masters—and in the process broadcast a compelling call for freedom.

Comparable in several ways to the celebrated *Amistad* mutiny of 1839, most recently interpreted by Steven Spielberg's 1997 film adaptation, one of Herman Melville's two most frequently analyzed short stories for several decades running has been the rhetorically complex, richly multicultural "Benito Cereno." Melville's tale was also based on an actual shipboard slave rebellion, which had taken place in 1804; his fictional reworking of the events was first published in *Putnam's Magazine* in 1855 and has been regularly anthologized in college textbooks from the 1950s to the present. Two handbooks on the story, edited by Seymour L. Gross and John P. Runden, respectively, were published in 1965. In her 1986 bibliographical compendium, *A Reader's Guide to the Short Stories of Herman Melville,* Lea Bertani Vozar Newman devotes her two most extensive essays, of approximately 60 pages each, to scholarship on the critics' perennial favorite, "Bartleby," where she cites 233 studies, and to commentary on "Benito Cereno," which includes 160 citations. In 1992, Robert E. Burkholder edited a major collection of essays on "Benito Cereno" that also included three specially commissioned articles on the narrative.[1]

In 1876, two decades after Melville published "Benito Cereno," Joel Chandler Harris printed his initial Uncle Remus Brer Rabbit stories in the *Atlanta Constitution*. The first of the seven volumes of Uncle Remus tales printed during Harris's lifetime, *Uncle Remus: His Songs and His Sayings,* was published by Appleton's in November 1880. Harris's first collection of Brer Rabbit stories has never been out of print, and it remains the most extensively analyzed of his Uncle Remus books. We have no evidence that Harris was influenced directly by Melville's works. Rather, both writers drew on folk archetypes, some of them centuries old, that had been appearing in orally transmitted tales well before Melville's and Harris's times—first in African stories and later in the southeastern United States, in African American slave folklore.[2]

In the introductions to *Uncle Remus: His Songs and His Sayings* and to his second volume, *Nights with Uncle Remus* (1883), Harris discussed the folkloristic significance of the oral-tradition animal stories he was retelling, through the complex persona of Uncle Remus. In his introductions, Harris cites contemporaneous discussions of folklore origins and transmission, including studies by the Smithsonian's John Wesley Powell and by Herbert H. Smith, Robert F. Hartt, W. H. Bleek, George M. Theal, and other ethnologists. He also explains that, even though Appleton is including his book in their catalog of humorous publications, his intent in gathering these folktales is "perfectly serious." Harris subscribed to the British *Folk-Lore Journal* and also became a charter member of the American Folklore Society, and he carried on extensive correspondence during the middle of his career about folklore and ethnographic theory. Although he was a conservative white author living in the largely unreconstructed South who had many affectionate memories of the old plantation era, Harris, for his day, had progressive political leanings about race. Moreover, Harris appreciated at least some of the allegorical dimensions of the stories he was retelling. As he observes, it needs "no scientific investigation to show why he [the Negro] selects as his hero the weakest and most harmless of all animals, and brings him out victorious in contests with the bear, the wolf, and the fox."[3] Also, Harris's recovering and popularizing the Brer Rabbit cycle of stories helped spur folkloristic studies of trickster traditions, and their complex sociologies, all around the world.

Melville, like Harris, was influenced during his entire career by folklore, the anthropology of the folk, and the oral tradition. From his first novels, *Typee, Omoo,* and *Mardi* (1846–49), through *Redburn, White-Jacket,* and, of course, *Moby-Dick* (1849–51), in his late poetry, *John Marr and Other Sailors* (1888), and in his final work, *Billy Budd* (1891), Melville regularly, and often profoundly, drew upon the oral folklore and physical culture of seafaring. Furthermore, urban folklore and rural New England folktales surface regularly in his domestic short stories and in *Pierre* (1852); and Mississippi River lore is part of the atmosphere and thematic patterning in *The Confidence-Man* (1857). In the 1817 source document for "Benito Cereno," a narrative of voyages written by the original American captain, Amasa Delano, Melville found an absorbing account of rebellion and the overthrow of authority.[4] But he may not have fully realized that, in retelling this dramatic sea narrative, he was helping to transmit fascinating and powerful incarnations of not one but two African and African American trickster folk traditions: the Old Master and John-the-slave tale, and the Brer Rabbit trickster story.

The John-the-slave tales apparently evolved on the cotton, rice, and indigo plantations in the southeastern United States sometime after slaves brought the Brer Rabbit stories over from more identifiable African oral folktale traditions. In a series of essays, John W. Roberts explores the complex, nonlinear, recursive character of African and African American folk traditions across cultural groups on both continents. Roberts analyzes the ways in which game and food shortages and the quest for status and power, as well as economic, social, moral, ethical, and religious values, were woven into both native African and African American slave folktales.[5] In a typical John tale, a trusted black slave, or a black slave driver who enjoys the confidence of his white master and a certain deferential respect from his fellow slaves, finds a dozen reasons not to complete a job for his master; or lies to avoid dire consequences for some malfeasance; or manipulates his master for personal gain or to acquire temporary power for himself or for the slaves who work under his supervision; or plays on his master's gullibility. John also uses various stratagems and rationalizations to evade work or responsibility, or to leverage at least a modicum of freedom for himself—or, again, for other slaves on the farm or plantation.

Although we find occasional parallels with this tradition in his canon, Harris rarely drew on the John tale cycle. Melville, however, helped transmit a dynamic contribution to the John tale trickster tradition in "Benito Cereno." In the original episode on the high seas off the coast of Chile, and in Melville's enriched fictionalized narrative, the slave leaders organize their black companions to play John-the-slave to three gullible owners and masters, Spanish and American. Reconstructing the historical setting and events that underlie Melville's story will help put the John tradition in context.

In February 1805 the original Captain Amasa Delano from Duxbury, Massachusetts (coincidentally, an ancestor of Franklin Delano Roosevelt), had encountered the Spanish slave vessel *Tryal* in some distress, approaching the harbor of Santa Maria island, off the coast of Chile. The well-intentioned American captain boarded the *Tryal* and remained there for several hours, arranging with the Spanish captain, Benito Cereno, to transfer supplies, food, and water aboard the ship. Captain Delano did not realize, however, that the slaves had successfully staged a shipboard rebellion about two months earlier and that, led primarily by Babo and by his son Mure, the slave who played the part of Cereno's attentive and dutiful man-servant, they had totally taken charge of the vessel.

In his illuminating essay, "*Benito Cereno* and New World Slavery," Eric Sundquist explains why Melville moved the encounter back to 1799, renamed the slave ship the *San Dominick,* and added or deleted other facts in his fictional retelling. In particular, the back-dating and renaming of the ship are complex, multilayered puns on the explosive 1790s slave rebellion on French San Domingo, given the native name Haiti in 1804, that culminated in the celebrated black general Toussaint L'Ouverture's triumph over European colonial planters and political leaders. The aftermath of the rebellion proved excessively brutal, too, when L'Ouverture's successor Dessalines butchered white landowners after falsely reassuring them about their safety. Well into the middle 1800s, European planters in the Caribbean and in South America—and American plantation owners also—remained panicky that the Haitian revolutionary fever would spread among other slave populations throughout the Caribbean and even into the southeastern United States, producing insurrections everywhere. In 1793 alone, ten thousand white planters had fled San Domingo for refuge in the United States. Nat Turner's rebellion in 1831, the freeing of the slaves in British Jamaica the same year, and the *Amistad* revolt in 1839 only served to keep anxieties high.[6]

Thus Melville's fictionalization of yet another slave revolt, on the *Tryal*, which he published on what turned out to be the very eve of our own Civil War, could not have been more timely. Note how the John-the-slave trickster tradition works both in Melville's source and in his story, as a reflection and an ironic refraction of racial themes and concerns of the colonial and postcolonial period. When the slave-laden *Tryal* had begun its voyage from Valparaiso, Chile, in December 1804, the slaves' owner, Don Alexandro Aranda, had assured the boat's captain, Don Benito Cereno, and the Spanish crew that Babo, Mure, and the other slaves were entirely "tractable" and would therefore not need to be secured with iron shackles. Well before their rebellion, then, the black slave leaders had already learned to play John-the-slave to their gullible master, Aranda. The shipboard conditions were overtly repressive on the *Amistad,* however, where the slaves were apparently chained to the ship's stanchions. The slave leaders in Melville's source document had continued to wear their masks of dutiful cooperation and uncomplaining accommodation to slavery right before Old Master's unseeing eyes—until a week out of port. Then they had suddenly and decisively unleashed their brutal rebellion, quickly murdering at least twenty-four of the forty or so Spanish crew members, officers, and passengers but saving Don Benito, whom they needed as their navigator to guide them to Senegal, their ultimate destination. Several days later the slaves had also killed their owner, Aranda, to demonstrate their complete freedom from his mastery and probably to send an additional warning to Cereno about their deadly serious commitment to their cause.

Melville added his own historical symbolism and irony to his story when he explained that the slaves had also removed the ship's Christopher Columbus figurehead, discoverer and first-wave explorer/exploiter of the New World, replacing his effigy with the skeleton of their former owner, Aranda, whom Melville portrays as Cereno's good friend. Neither the Columbian figurehead nor the implied cannibalism were part of the original *Tryal* narrative. In Melville's story, the slaves had also chalked the motto "Follow your leader" below Aranda's canvas-shrouded skeleton, as a constant warning to Don Benito that Columbus was no longer his leader but that the slaves most emphatically were—and that Cereno absolutely had to follow their commands and sail them to Senegal, or lose his life. Another part of Melville's symbolic irony plays off the fact that Columbus himself had named the Spanish, eastern half of the island Santo Domingo (now known as the Dominican Republic) in honor of Saint Dominick. So Melville's renaming the ship *San Dominick* reinforces both the revolutionary turning over of French San Domingo to the blacks and the absolute erosion of the legacy of Columbus himself—that revolutionary voyager who had opened up the Caribbean, and ultimately the New World, to European exploitation and who could once name the lands he touched for anyone he chose to. The bottom line is that in both the original Third World rebellion and in Melville's rendering of it, shufflin' John-the-slave is now completely in charge of his ole Spanish marster.

But with the American Captain Delano's arrival on the ship, John has the chance to play his trickster role again, with even more flair. In Melville's story, during the several hours the "good Captain Amasa Delano" is on board the *San Dominick,* Cereno's body servant brilliantly plays a fawningly obsequious, even oleaginous, John-the-slave—both to his titular Spanish master, Captain Benito Cereno, and now to the well-meaning, good-Samaritan, "generous" Captain Delano. In casting Cereno's servant, instead of Mure, Melville selected Babo, who, again, was Mure's father in the original narrative; Melville chose to portray Babo as about thirty years old in his story. As some critics have suggested, perhaps Melville liked the disarming, humorous lilt of Babo's name or perhaps Melville was thinking about its more African animalistic connotation, like "baboon." After spotting the American vessel in the Santa Maria harbor, the rebellion leaders had only an hour or maybe two in which to organize their ranks and train the entire shipload of illiterate slaves to play a chorus role as suffering blacks or in some cases to adopt individual John-the-slave parts. Their purpose, in both the factual and fictional versions, was to play on the American captain's sympathies and persuade him to give them the supplies they needed to make it back to Senegal.

Mure, Babo, and the entire cast succeed beautifully in wearing theatric masks, both in the original 1817 source document and in Melville's own 1855 fictionalized remake. In Melville's more detailed and creative rendering of the original events, the shipload of supporting actors and assistant producers—scores of seemingly distraught slaves, the enchained

Atufal, the hatchet polishers and oakum pickers, Francesco the steward, the nursing Negresses—should be given posthumous Academy Awards for their performances. And the script Babo designed for them deserves the award for Best Picture. But in Melville's highly visual, filmic story Babo plays John-the-slave brilliantly. Robert Lowell effectively captures Babo's unctuous style in his verse-drama rendering of Melville's story included in *The Old Glory* (staged in 1964; published in 1968). Melville's shirtless, shoeless, self-abasing, Spanish-flag-and-razor-flourishing black slave Babo deserves the award for Best Actor.

Perhaps without actually realizing what he was, in fact, transmitting, Melville in his 1855 narrative also enriched the second folklore tradition, featuring Brer Rabbit as trickster. Babo is an authentic analogue to Brer Rabbit; although Delano can only see the black slave as a fawning, devoted, eager-to-please-his-master "shepherd's dog," the animal analogy still works. Like his equally devious and inventive kinsman, Brer Rabbit, who can act "mighty humble" when he needs to, Babo is of "small stature" and in front of Delano pretends to be powerless. As Babo protests to the good American captain, he is not a noble or accomplished servant and says he was, in fact, only "a black man's slave" in his native Africa. But behind his mask of humility and deference, Brer Babo had used brain to compensate for lack of brawn, had used his wits to mind his time and work with his fellow slaves to spring their uprising at the moment of best opportunity. Then they use their wits again—to play the elaborate ship-wide theatric performances that so misled the original Captain Delano that, like Melville's captain, he had walked the Spanish vessel's decks and negotiated details with Cereno and his body servant for several hours, completely unaware that the slaves were in control.

Melville repeatedly describes Babo's physical position, normally standing close by Cereno's side, his arm securely around Don Benito's waist; and on several occasions he pictures Babo literally supporting or even catching his master when Cereno faints from weakness or from sheer fright at the horrifying events he is forced to recall. Babo is like one of the smaller animals in Joel Chandler Harris's woods. No one could possibly assume that a creature of Babo's diminutive stature could be top dog on the Big Road—top fish on the High Seas—and the terror of the more culturally dominant, larger animals. Babo regularly murmurs "Poor, poor master" or "This excitement is bad for master" before circumspectly extracting Cereno from a dialogue with Delano that might reveal the actual situation on board ship, or before taking Don Benito below deck. Here, graphically, we have trickster Brer Rabbit, or trickster Brer Babo, "signifying" at a powerful visual and oral-performance level, except that the signifying is even more complexly ironic than usual. The American captain—and most of us, too, as first-time readers of this powerful story—do not see that Babo is both signifying and countersignifying through what he is saying and obsequiously acting out. Brer Babo *is* literally saying that all the excitement is not good for his master and that his master *is* literally in very poor health. Babo *does*, in fact, literally and figuratively make himself the dutiful servant, the force behind Don Benito, shoring him up, keeping him barely alive just long enough to navigate the vessel to Africa. And Babo shaves Cereno with such pleasurable symbolic intensity that Babo literally *is* "a Nubian sculptor finishing off a white statue-head." And Babo literally *does*, many times, take his master "below," to revisit the horrors of total domination, murder, and even cannibalism.

Just as Brer Rabbit was caught by Brer Fox's tar-baby, Babo and his fellow slaves, before their powerful rebellion, seemed inextricably trapped in the epoxy of slavery itself. In Harris's famous inventory of reverse-psychology appeals, Brer Rabbit urges Brer Fox to "hang me," or "drown me," or "skin me," or "snatch out my eyeballs," or "cut off my legs," just as long as the fox doesn't throw the rabbit into the briar-patch. Horrifyingly, these options are all historically documented punishments for rebellious slaves. If the chattel slaves on the *San Dominick* "skinned" Alexandro Aranda and "snatched out" his eyeballs—reminding Cereno and the other surviving Spaniards that a similar fate awaited them, too, if they did not cooperate—is it not hypocritical to protest about black brutality and revenge-taking on board the *San Dominick*? What about three hundred years of white brutality?

To see another fascinating analogue to Melville's story, read Harris's "The Awful Fate of Mr. Wolf," which, like the tar-baby story, was also published in *Uncle Remus: His Songs and His Sayings*. Brer Wolf has been raiding Brer Rabbit's previous homes for months, carrying off baby rabbits each time. Symbolically, then, the predatory race has been progressively annihilating the subordinate race's offspring—thus threatening to terminate its gene pool. This time, however, Brer Rabbit builds a secure stone house for his family, complete with a basement room too small for the wolf's invasion. Brer Wolf tries, himself, to use Brer-Rabbit-style reverse psychology to get inside and scope out Brer Rabbit's seemingly impregnable stone fortress. One day, Brer Wolf bursts through the accidentally unlocked door, pretending that hunting dogs are chasing him, and asks for temporary shelter. The Little Rabs who had survived the wolf's earlier raids immediately bolt for the cellar, while Brer Rabbit tells Brer Wolf to hide quickly in a stout wooden chest "en make yo'se'f at home."

Amazed at this stroke of good luck, Brer Rabbit promptly locks the chest lid, deliberately walks to his looking glass, knowingly winks at himself, draws his rocking chair in front of the fire, and takes out a big chaw of tobacco. ("Tobacco?" interrupts Uncle Remus's skeptical little white listener. "Rabbit terbaker, honey," responds the tricky old narrator.) Brer Rabbit thoroughly enjoys every minute of his dominance—luxuriates in it, in fact, just as Brer Babo luxuriates in the physical and oral power games that he plays on Cereno and on Captain Delano, too. Like Don Benito, who is quite literally made a prisoner on his own ship, which Melville pointedly describes as a floating wooden hearse or sarcophagus, Brer Wolf is now a prisoner in a wooden box that turns out not to be a temporary sheltering "home" but a more permanent place of rest. Brer Rabbit next puts some water on the stove ("W'at you doin' now, Brer Rabbit?" asks an increasingly nervous Brer Wolf. "I'm fixin' fer to make you a nice cup of tea," Brer Rabbit hospitably reassures his adversary). Then he bores holes in the chest-lid ("I'm a bo'in' little holes so's you kin get bref," he calmly explains to his now panicky adversary). Then he adds more wood to the fire ("so you won't git cole, Brer Wolf," he continues). And next he fetches out all his surviving children from the cellar, to tell them "w'at a nice man you is." Finally, he pours the boiling water through the holes in the chest-lid, meanwhile reassuring Brer Wolf that he's only feeling the fleas "a bitin." And then "de scaldin' water done de bizness." Brer Wolf dies inside the sheltering box that has now become his wooden sarcophagus, and Brer Rabbit later hangs up his hide on the back porch and calls in all the neighbors for a communal celebration.

Harris screens from the Little Rabs' and the reader's eyes Brer Wolf's terrifying death inside the chest, but the progressive intensification of the physical and oral torturing-unto-death of Brer Rabbit's enemy is strongly reminiscent of Babo's rhetorical trickery and physical/mental/oral torturing of Cereno in Melville's famous story of rebellion and incarceration. In both the tar-baby tale and in the wolf-in-the-chest story, the master animal is mastered, the wolf's attempts at mind-game trickery and domination not equal to master trickster Brer Rabbit's countermoves. Furthermore, the graphically displayed skeleton of Cereno's friend Alexandro Aranda in Melville's story is visually and symbolically parallel to the nailed-up hide in Harris's tale. In the latter tale, too, Uncle Remus makes sure to point out that the slave-hero's children are present at the execution of the creature who had murdered their own siblings. Uncle Remus has certainly made this a cautionary tale for both white and black children—and for their parents.

Brer Rabbit not only survives but dominates in "The Awful Fate of Mr. Wolf." In Melville's source and in his intensely rendered fictional story "Benito Cereno," however, the black trickster-hero's rebellion is put down at the last minute by the redoubtable Captain Amasa Delano of Duxbury, Massachusetts. Babo, the master of rhetoric, body language, oral performance, and double-signifying, after his capture takes his power and dignity unto himself and absolutely refuses to speak again. Moreover, in the *Tryal* slave rebellion and in Melville's version of it, no John Quincy Adams effects Mure's or Babo's release. In Melville's source and in his own story, the whites burn the ringleaders' bodies to ashes and put their severed heads on display in the city square. Yet as Melville closes his story, we see Babo's head, "that hive of subtlety," fixed on a pole on the Plaza at Lima, where it met, "unabashed," the gaze of white onlookers and passersby. Across the Plaza, too, Babo's dead eyes look toward the monastery where, three months later, Don Benito Cereno, his wasted body borne on a funeral bier, did indeed follow his leader, Aranda, and now his leader Babo, into death.

Babo's Old-Master-and-John-the-slave play-acting kept the Spanish and American captains under his control only temporarily, and technically his shipboard rebellion failed. Yet even after death, Brer Rabbit's archetypal brother-trickster, Babo, still has the power to arrange the events of the universe. His far-seeing eyes look backward across generations of blood spilled from the brutalized bodies of black slaves, including those thousands thrown overboard during the Middle Passage. And Babo's eyes look ahead prophetically toward the Civil War, the most destructive conflict America would ever know—and his eyes gaze still further ahead toward the violent civil rights struggles of the twentieth century, all around the world. Early in the story, Melville notes of Amasa Delano that his "undistrustful good nature" would never have led him to believe in "the malign evil in man." A racist to the end whose only sympathies are for the plight of his dying friend Cereno, Delano's moral blindness to the horrors of slavery makes him part of slavery's very malignity. It would take a terrible Civil War to get the attention—if even then—of the Delanos of our nation.

A mythic trickster-hero of the black slave's imagination, Brer Rabbit is permitted to survive assault after assault from the stronger creatures who systematically devour his children and who would finally cannibalize him too, if they could have their way. Unlike Cinque who had his champions, the tricksters Babo and Mure lost their particular battle when the slave ship was recaptured by Delano. As in the celebrated escapades of Brer Rabbit and the enduring tales of John the slippery slave, however, Mure's and Babo's resolution, intelligence, and heroism live on in the world mythology of the trickster. Moreover, their powerful rebellion against slavery continues to have implications, in our own times, for the three inextricably interrelated world cultures in their respective stories—African, European, and American—and for the larger world too, north and south, east and west, from Belfast to Bosnia, from Boston to Bagdad, from Auschwitz and Tiananmen Square to Ruwanda and Kosovo. Mure's and Babo's violent attempts to free their fellow slaves and the resultant killing or maiming of persons from all three world cultures on board the *Tryal* renamed *San Dominick* starkly remind us that it is truly a matter of life and death—all around the world—to wage the desperate battle for freedom from oppression, ignorance, racism, and fear.

Notes

1. Seymour L. Gross, ed., A *"Benito Cereno" Handbook* (Belmont, Calif.: Wadsworth, 1965), includes Melville's story, his primary source document, chapter 18 of Amasa Delano's *Voyages and Travels* (1817), and a representative collection of criticism. Similar to Gross's study, John P. Runden, ed., Melville's *"Benito Cereno": A Text for Guided Research* Boston: D. C. Heath, 1965), Runden's volume reprints Melville's story, his primary source document, and several critical essays. Lea Bertani Vozar Newmann, *A Reader's Guide to the Short Stories of Herman Melville* (Boston: G. K. Hall, 1986), 18–78, 95–153. Newman thoroughly summarizes scholarship and criticism on "Benito Cereno" through the mid-1980s and provides a full bibliographical checklist. Robert Burkholder's *Critical Essays on Herman Melville's "Benito Cereno"* (New York: G. K. Hall, 1992) includes a helpful introduction and reprints two contemporaneous reviews and sixteen book chapters and articles, along with the three commissioned essays.

2. Florence E. Baer, *Sources and Analogues of the Uncle Remus Tales* (Helsinki:

Academia Scientiarum Fennica, 1980). Approximately two-thirds of the Uncle Remus stories have origins or strong analogues in African sources. Also see Baer's "Joel Chandler Harris: An 'Accidental' Folklorist," in *Critical Essays on Joel Chandler Harris,* ed. by R. Bruce Bickley Jr. (Boston: G. K. Hall, 1981), 185–95. Here Baer summarizes key folkloristic findings from her 1980 monograph.

3. Joel Chandler Harris, *Uncle Remus: His Songs and His Sayings,* ed. by Robert Hemenway (New York: Penguin Books, 1982), 39, 44. "The Wonderful Tar-Baby Story" and its second half, "How Mr. Rabbit Was Too Sharp For Mr. Fox," are printed on pp. 57–59 and 62–64; "The Awful Fate of Mr. Wolf" on 89–92.

4. Amasa Delano, *A Narrative of Voyages and Travels, in the northern and southern hemispheres: comprising three voyages round the world, together with a voyage of survey and discovery in the Pacific Ocean and Oriental Islands* (Boston: E. G. House, 1817), 76–104. See the collections of criticism edited by Gross and Runden for reprintings of Melville's primary source. Herman Melville, *The Piazza Tales and Other Prose Pieces, 1839–1860,* ed. by Harrison Hayford, Alma G. MacDougall, and G. Thomas Tanselle (Evanston and Chicago: Northwestern University Press and Newberry Library, 1987). "Benito Cereno" is printed on 46–117.

5. John W. Roberts, "Strategy, Morality, and Worldview of the Afro-American Spirituals and Trickster Tales," *Western Journal of Black Studies* 6, no. 2 (1982): 101–7. Spirituals and folktales reveal both overt and covert ways of psychologically and physically resisting slavery. Roberts, "Br'er Rabbit and John: Trickster Heroes in Slavery," *From Trickster to Badman: The Black Folk Hero in Slavery and Freedom* (Philadelphia: University of Pennsylvania Press, 1989), 17–18, 19–64. African and African American folklore reveals a complex, nonlinear sociology, structure, and value system. Roberts, "The African American Animal Trickster as Hero," *Redefining American Literary History,* ed. by A. Lavonne Brown and Jerry W. Ward Jr. (New York: Modern Language Association, 1990), [97]–114. Roberts discusses the African roots that feed African American trickster tales.

6. Eric J. Sundquist, "*Benito Cereno* and New World Slavery," *Reconstructing American Literary History,* ed. by Sacvan Bercovitch (Cambridge, Mass., and London: Harvard University Press, 1986), 93–122. A complex history and racial sociology underlie Melville's source materials and his story.

Bibliographic Note

Joel Chandler Harris (Athens: University of Georgia Press, 1987) is a reprint of R. Bruce Bickley's 1978 Twayne U.S. Authors Series biography and critical study and incorporates an updated annotated secondary bibliography. Bickley and Hugh T. Keenan are the authors of *Joel Chandler Harris: An Annotated Bibliography of Criticism, 1977–1996; With Supplement, 1892–1976* (Westport, Conn.:

Greenwood Press, 1997). The authors compile 448 abstracts of Harris commentaries in books, dissertations, book chapters, essays, and reviews. This volume is a sequel to Bickley's *Joel Chandler Harris: A Reference Guide* (Boston: G. K. Hall, 1978), an annotated secondary bibliography that includes 1,442 abstracts of reviews, articles, book chapters, dissertations, and books on Harris from 1862 to 1976. Bickley's *The Method of Melville's Short Fiction* (Durham, N.C.: Duke University Press, 1975), a critical study, contains chapter 6, "Experiments in Omniscience," which treats "The Bell-Tower" and "Benito Cereno" (95–108). William B. Dillingham's *Melville's Short Fiction, 1853–1856* (Athens: University of Georgia Press, 1977) addresses "Benito Cereno" in chapter 10, "A Dark Similitude: 'Benito Cereno'" (227–270). In *Going Under: Melville's Short Fiction and the American 1850s* (Baton Rouge and London: Louisiana State University Press, 1977), Marvin Fisher discusses "Benito Cereno" in chapter 4, "Truth Comes in with Darkness" (104–17). See also Joel Chandler Harris, *Nights with Uncle Remus: Myths and Legends of the Old Plantation* (Boston: James R. Osgood, 1883); and Eric J. Sundquist, "Uncle Remus, Uncle Julius, and the New Negro" and "'De Ole Times,' Slave Culture, and Africa" from chapter 4, "Charles Chesnutt's Cakewalk," *To Wake the Nations: Race in the Making of American Literature* (Cambridge, Mass., and London: Harvard University Press, 1993), 323–59. Harris and Chesnutt "exploited" black language but developed different rhetorics in their complex folk stories. H. Nigel Thomas in *From Folklore to Fiction: A Study of Folk Heroes and Rituals in the Black American Novel* (New York: Greenwood Press, 1988), 3–81, finds that the Brer Rabbit and John tales teach that being black in America and surviving require the trickster's skills. Although he does not discuss the black trickster figure in "Benito Cerno," Kevin J. Hayes explores Melville's extensive use of other folk traditions in *Melville's Folk Roots* (Kent, Ohio: Kent State University Press, 1999).

Tricksters and Shamans in Jack London's Short Stories

GAIL JONES

*F*or many, trickster is a cultural hero, a wandering prankster whose antics have brought great gifts to humans, including fire, light, and heat, which provide an important and welcome opportunity for change. However, defining trickster as a cultural hero is limiting; for what can be gleaned from the hundreds of trickster tales and cycles profiles a shape-shifting character of contradictions: a figure both profane and sacred, foolish and clever, absurd and profound, marginal and, yet, central. In whatever incarnation, trickster shakes up the status quo, rearranging boundaries and reordering our reality with amusement and laughter. The transforming, transcending trickster operates along boundaries, borders in flux.

Because trickster challenges our boundaries, he has been and remains a popular figure for those negotiating ethnocentric barriers, including linguistic ones. Although some critics, such as William Lenz, have explored earlier literary trickster figures, they primarily focused on the nineteenth-century confidence man as used by Twain, Melville, and Poe and ignored other writers, including Jack London—even though London makes frequent use of trickster and trickster figures.[1] The wandering prankster from outside negotiates many of the cultural boundaries in print that London negotiated in life. Jack London struggled for acceptance for most of his life. His illegitimacy, childhood struggle with poverty, strange spiritualist mother, rejecting father, and later celebrity status separated him as an outsider of conventional society. The frequent moves and erratic economic conditions in his childhood established the journeying pattern of the questioning outsider seeking accommodation from inside that London would continue in adulthood and in his writing.

The transforming trickster is often a rhetorical strategy for many writers, particularly contemporary women of color, and as Jeanne Rosier Smith argues, "the [modern] focus on tricksters . . . suggests kindred impulses toward challenging the possibility of a unified perspective, disrupting perceived histories of oppression, and creating new narrative forms."[2] Trickster surges whenever we seem to be at a crossroads. Yet, new possibilities, even radical revisions, follow in the wake of trickster antics. As Andrew Wiget explains, "Trickster functions not so much to call cultural categories into question as to demonstrate the artificiality of culture itself. Thus he makes available for discussion the very basis of social order, individual and communal identity."[3] This fluidity of trickster appears to have held a special appeal to Jack London.

London, a noted socialist of his time, continually questions the social order in many of his works; for example, his exposé, *The People of the Abyss*, details the horrific, hopeless conditions in London's East End during the height of the British Empire. In addition, much of London's fiction navigates the flux of individual and communal identity; indeed, London's semiautobiographical novel *Martin Eden* suffers at times from the lengthy doctrinal discussions of socialism versus individualism. For some critics, London is, like trickster, a contradictory figure, a writer who professes a deep passion for the socialist cause while some of his works seem to glorify the super-individual.[4] However, many surface contradictions dissolve when the deeper mythic underpinnings framing London's writings are exposed.[5]

The mythic underpinnings in London's earlier writings have been underexamined—overshadowed at times by aspects of London's political and personal life.[6] Yet, mythic images and tales influenced and helped shape London even as a beginning writer. London began writing during the late nineteenth century, a time of unprecedented interest in reexamining the Greek and Roman tradition within a scientific framework. However, this interest explored in exhaustive detail—James G. Frazer's *Golden Bough* ran to twelve volumes, while Wilhelm Schmidt's *The Origin of the Idea of God* ran eleven volumes—was not limited to classical mythology. Men such as Franz Boas and Bronislaw Malinowski, ushering in the new discipline of anthropology, had already been collecting and publishing collections of various Native American myths and stories, even though the work of Boas's student Paul Radin, *The Trickster: A Study in American Indian Mythology*, was not first published until 1937, well after London's death in 1916. Although Boas's first fieldwork and publication centered on the tribes of the Northwest Pacific Coast, it is not certain if London read his writings. However, Boas's work and London's interest were formed within the same milieu, fascinated with exotic and "primitive" cultures.

Most likely, the short time, less than a year, that London spent in the Klondike introduced him to the Tlingit Raven cycle; he seems to have spent most of that time observing the local traditions. During his return home, London traveled for a time with Father Roubeau, a Jesuit priest who by the time London met him had already spent twelve years in the Klondike with various Tlingit clans. Father Roubeau would have been an informed source as he spent much of his time with the Tlingits "'reducing the language to a grammar.'"[7] London was certainly impressed by Father Roubeau, and as Franklin Walker notes, "London's journal plays up [Father Roubeau's] absorbing conversations."[8] Whether from Father Roubeau or from a different, unidentified source, London absorbed tales of Raven, Bear, and Fox, later using them in his Klondike tales while emphasizing his own cultural hero, Wolf.

When we see how pervasive fluid trickster figures are in literature, we are often tempted to flatten cultural and historical distinctions and differences calling every tricky, slippery figure trickster and forgetting the deep, religious significance of trickster and his reordering the universe.[9] Yet, remembering trickster's religious significance is critical. Among hunter-gatherers, tricksters are closely linked with shamans. Because shamans are often unpredictable religious specialists, many hunters viewed shamans as witches and feared them; hunters would tell humorous stories about shamans to lessen their power. However, there are important distinctions between shamans and tricksters. Mac Linscott Ricketts views both trickster and shamans as religious figures "represent[ing] two diametrically opposite poles of spirituality" (87).[10] Ricketts notes that shamans and priests act from *inside* the community as "mediators between the human and transhuman world" whereas tricksters are self-transcending figures in whose realities humans can be self-sufficient (105). Trickster comes from *outside*. For trickster, supernatural powers are to be overcome, even mocked. As Ricketts explains:

> But the two figures relate themselves differently to the realm of unseen powers. The shaman has been accepted into that other world, and consequently he looks upon it as a potential source of help as well as harm for man. But by the contrast the trickster is an outsider whose attitude toward that world of superhuman powers is a negative one. He has no friends in that other world,

and for him it is a realm opposed entirely to the will of human beings. All that humans have gained from the unseen powers beyond—fire, fish, game, fresh water, and so forth—have been obtained by necessity through trickery or theft. . . . What the trickster obtained from the supernaturals was their *goods* only; unlike the shaman he did not also obtain superhuman powers or spiritual friendship. The Trickster apparently sees no need to have powers other than those with which he is naturally endowed: his wits and his wit. (91–92)

Ricketts acknowledges that his argument that trickster can be best understood as a modern humanist is in complete opposition to Joseph Campbell's view of trickster as the mythological counterpart to the shaman. In effect, Campbell's view would cast trickster as divine and shamans as primitive priests. However, as Ricketts argues, if trickster is divine, why does he not have divine or superhuman powers? Why does he win through use of trickery and not through the use of some divine or superpower? Ricketts suggests that "Campbell has been overly impressed by the tricks shamans perform as a part of their 'technique,' and by the seeming titanism of the shamans in their willingness to set themselves in opposition to spirits" (104). However, as Ricketts points out:

The shaman opposes only *certain* spirits, not the whole supernatural, divine realm. We must remember that the shaman has friends as well as foes in that other world. The Trickster has only enemies there. The shaman is not irreligious, but devout: his or her defiance is a function of "faith," not the antithesis of faith. He or she reverences those spirits before whom one stands in awe, and the shaman would undertake nothing dangerous without their companionship. The trickster, on the other hand, looks to no higher power for aid, . . . but by using his one weapon, his devious brain, he attacks and defeats the supernaturals, none of whom are his friends. (104)

Ricketts argues that "the shaman, as mediator between the human and the transhuman world, is the forerunner of the priest, not his antithesis. The Trickster is the true opposite of the shaman *and* the priest" (105). Ricketts's distinctions between trickster and shaman/priest become important as London made the same distinction between trickster and shaman/priest. The often biting irony in some of London's tales is missed by readers who do not decode the differences between trickster and shamans and messiahs and false messiahs as perceived by London.

London blended Tlingit tales of trickster and shamans into his Klondike tales using these figures in a very distinct pattern, a Tlingit pattern, to create inversions. As in the cycles he appropriates, London's shamans and priests are insiders not to be trusted; they are often impotent figures leading their followers astray, as exemplified in two London stories, "The Priestly Prerogative" and "The Son of the Wolf."[11] In both, the shaman or priest is either impotent or incorrect. In "The Priestly Prerogative," Grace Bentham, a sympathetic Medea figure to her husband, Edwin, delivers Edwin's version of the Golden Fleece to him. Edwin, like Jason, ignores and abuses Grace. Soon Grace falls for another man, an appreciative man, and in an attempt to run off with this man, is almost caught by her husband. The priest, Father Roubeau (named for the historical Father Roubeau), lies to and tricks Edwin to save Grace from discovery and effects her return to her husband, thus restoring order, a proper move if the restoration of the given order—in this case, the sanctity of marriage—is of primary concern, and definitely a proper move for a priest prior to 1898. However, if the primary concern is the welfare of Grace, this restoration is devastating for her. Even the priest acknowledges this. In the conclusion, Father Roubeau, still disturbed because he knows what is proper for order is not proper for Grace, confesses his discomfort to his friend Malemute Kid, saying, "Yet, this thing remains. I knew it and I made her go back" (194). Although Father Roubeau uses trickery, he is still clearly within a priestly/shaman role here; he is an insider whose trickery maintains the order rather than upsets it. It should be noted here that this is the only story that features Father Roubeau in a "priestly" mode, and when he appears as a recurring character in other Klondike stories in different modes, he is always portrayed as courageous and adventuresome, suggesting that the assumption of the "priestly" mode causes his human error.

A story written immediately after the "The Priestly Prerogative," "The Son of the Wolf," also questions societal value versus true value of a woman. The Son of the Wolf, Scruff MacKenzie, is seeking a wife, and, in conflict with Raven, Fox, and Bear, challenges the wisdom of Raven's shaman by saying, "The shaman is without power. Thus! I spit upon his face." Although this is noted as sacrilege, there is no uproar, for the Son of Wolf is challenging the shaman, *not* Raven. The shaman has been advising the tribe to kill Wolf, and although there is combat, the conflict is not as deadly as advocated by the shaman. Ignoring the shaman's advice,

Raven, Fox, and Bear reach consensus with Wolf, creating a new, a different order. Even Fox is satisfied as he does receive his promised plug of tobacco. In this story, the ending provides a positive future for the wife because the confining order is not maintained by the shaman. In "The Priestly Prerogative," London suggests that those who follow the advice of either priests or shamans, whose function is maintenance of the social order, suffer; in "The Son of the Wolf," those who use their own wits, rejecting mediation, fare much better.

In "The Master of Mystery," London presents yet another impotent shaman figure, Scundoo, who regains his potency by becoming a trickster figure. As a shaman, Scundoo is impotent, "disgraced; his known magic could not be called upon to seek out the evil-doer" (62). The village has sent for another shaman, Klok No Ton, to dispel the witchcraft responsible for the disappearance of valuable blankets, the jealously guarded treasure of the village. Klok No Ton fails to find the blankets because Scundoo, aided by Raven, tricks Klok No Ton into identifying the wrong man as perpetrator. Scundoo tricks the guilty party—indeed, the entire village—and ends up owner of the blankets, the wealthiest, most comfortable one in the village. This shaman regains his potency by shifting into a trickster mode, successfully acquiring *material* rather than *spiritual* goods. Certainly the focus on material rather than spiritual comfort is a hallmark of the Raven—a realm for successful endeavors by tricksters, *not* shamans.

However, the other negative representations of shamans and priests are not a rejection of the spiritual by London, for when a character moves beyond the shaman/priest category into a messianic realm, the messiah figures are potent. London seems to be rejecting blindly following a shaman or/priest; rather London favors potential self-sufficiency as offered by tricksters and messiahs.

For instance, in "The Seed of McCoy," McCoy, chief magistrate of Pitcairn Island and a descendent of McCoy (one of the *Bounty* mutineers) and his Tahitian wife, pilots a burning ship, *Pyrennes,* which has been on a tangled journey across the Pacific, to a safe harbor. McCoy reluctantly assumes his leadership category, ship's pilot, because he is asked to do so by the captain and crew. However, McCoy continually has to remind the captain and the crew that he is not their navigator, only their pilot; the captain and crew must keep control and guide the ship themselves.

As the captain misses island after island, the crew, frightened by the "hell-fire" under them, is often close to mutiny. Yet, McCoy's tranquillity provides the necessary example for the crew to maintain faith in their journey. Certainly McCoy's physicality does not prevent a mutiny by intimidating the crew; he is described as a simple beachcomber with feminine brown eyes and the voice of a dove who possesses the simplicity of a child and the gentleness of a woman. McCoy is more than an mediator or messenger of the gods; he is an empowered outsider, a messiah piloting the ship to safe harbor. The ship finally reaches a safe harbor because the captain and crew do their work; each time a possibly safe harbor is missed, either the captain or crew failed to do their jobs adequately, relying instead on the hope that McCoy would do it for them.

Clearly self-sufficiency is an attitude that London values; in his stories, those relinquishing their self-sufficiency to a mediator, such as a shaman or a priest, suffer from impotency. Recognizing the distinction London makes between shaman or priest and a trickster or a messiah helps clarify the problematic science-fiction tale, "Goliah." In "Goliah," a shadowy, disguised figure, an empowered outsider, takes political and social control of the world through blackmail, extortion, and trickery. By the end of the story, Goliah transforms into a benign, beloved figure. An editorial note at the end of the text places this narrative as an award-winning essay of a fifteen-year-old high school student in the year 2254, which partially helps to explain the unquestioning, admiring tone of the story. This panegyric to the all-seeing wisdom of Goliah discounts Goliah's killing of all the captains of industry, politicians, military leaders, and scientists who "failed to accept his invitation" (1204). Some do accept Goliah's offer and the world turns upside down—there is no Wall Street, no buying, selling, and speculating, and no private interests. There is no greed, and no need to commit crime. The workday is eventually reduced to five hours, and the standard of living increases to the extent that consumption cannot keep up with production. Removal of Goliah's disguise reveals a "little man" weighing only 118 pounds, with quizzical blue eyes laughing at the "huge joke" he has played upon the world, trapping it, in spite of itself, into happiness and laughter (1220). On a monument to Percival Schultz, Goliah's true identity, Percival's motto is inscribed in imperishable bronze: "All will be joy-smiths, and their tasks shall be to beat out laughter from the ringing anvil of Life" (1221).

As peaceful and idyllic as this new world order appears to be and as beloved a figure as Percival is, questions remain concerning exactly what kind of gift has been brought to humans and in what sense laughter is beaten out. First of all, unlike fire, this trickster's gift does not benefit *all* the members of the community. That Goliah's world peace is made possible by the exploitative labor of blacks stolen from Africa, Chinese and Japanese coolies, and shanghaied sailors is accepted by this new order of peace, prosperity, and joy. In addition to those already murdered for not accepting Goliah's "invitation," those who cannot or do not fit into this perfect crime-free world order are deliberately disposed of, including "incurable criminals, hereditary inefficients, and professors of Sociology." Indeed, whether or not Goliah's gift of world peace benefits any of the community is questionable, for in this chilling 1907 tale, the trick of Percival brings us a successful Third Reich. Even though Goliah is referred to as a trickster in the text, enough little snippets ripple this text to call into question whether or not Percival/Goliah is actually a trickster. As Goliah demands renouncement of material gain, he operates more in the spiritual realm of a messiah or shaman than in a trickster's.

Still, Goliah does not fit the messianic profile as offered in "The Seed of McCoy." Unlike McCoy, an outsider who is *asked* to pilot and refuses to assume a more authoritative role, Goliah *forces* himself upon the world as mediator. And unlike McCoy, who never requires abandonment of free will and questioning for his piloting, Goliah's iron will allows no questions. This lack of questioning, antithesis of Trickster, is an extremely ironic aspect in "Goliah." For Percival, the most holy knight who led the quest for the Holy Grail and who could have saved the Fisher King and the land, failed to do so because he did not know the right questions to ask. Goliah/Percival is neither messiah, like McCoy, nor trickster. Goliah/Percival might be best understood as a false messiah: an outsider who can con others into believing that he has divine or superpowers by appropriating trickster's methods without transforming into a trickster as Scundoo does. Scundoo is one of the few shaman/priests who is a positive figure in London's works, perhaps because Scundoo uses trickster's method, reliance on wits and cleverness.

Commenting on Ricketts's work, Lewis Hyde notes that "humankind has had two responses when faced with all that engenders awe and dread in this world: the way of the shaman (and the priests), which assumes a spiritual world, bows before it, and seeks to make alliances; and the way of the Trickster (and the humanists), which recognizes no power beyond its own intelligence, and seeks to seize and subdue the unknown with wit and cunning."[12] While the shaman focuses on the ideal, the trickster parodies that ideal, "call[ing] attention to the actual constraints of human life." In effect, trickster inserts himself into the shamanic tradition, becoming an inversion of the shaman. Trickster's ability to invert the shaman leaves open the possibility that a "true" shaman and a "false" shaman could exist, and likewise so could a "true" trickster and a "false" trickster. Hyde concludes that this potential for true and false "calls for a recognition of the complexities of recognition itself."[13]

This call for recognition leads us to such fundamental questions as how do we know and how do we know that we know. Certainly London's stories seem to suggest that he believes that self-sufficiency is an essential aspect of knowledge. Those who willingly or unwillingly give up free will become unable to question and view other possibilities, and what trickster does is present possibilities—the possibility of light where there was none or the possibility of fire in a frozen world. We can have a pilot like McCoy to point out possible landing sites, but we must navigate our own ships.

Interestingly, the only socialist story in which the exploited workers overcome oppression and create a positive new world is "The Dream of Debs," which does not have a shaman, trickster, or messiah figure in it. No shaman mediates a way; no trickster orchestrates a trick to reorder the world. No false messiah, no Goliah, strong-arms the community into an unchosen existence. The workers in "The Dream of Debs" are successful in overthrowing oppression through communal egalitarian efforts. Attending to the distinct differences between trickster and shaman, messiah and false messiah, helps expose Goliah as an ironic antihero even though Goliah seems to express the proper socialist sentiments. Acceptance of Goliah as trickster leads to a simplistic acceptance of totalitarianism, whereas Goliah as shaman or false messiah leads us to a more complex questioning of social order, our roles within that order, and upheavals of it. For London, a man who signed all his correspondence "Yours for the Revolution," seems to warn against shamans, priests, and false messiahs, exhorting his readers never to surrender free will; instead, London encourages his readers to become self-sufficient tricksters—revolutionaries—themselves.

Notes

1. See William E. Lenz, *Fast Talk and Flush Times* (Columbia: University of Missouri Press, 1985).

2. Jeanne Rosier Smith, *Writing Tricksters: Mythic Gambols in American Ethnic Literature* (Berkeley and Los Angeles: University of California Press, 1997), 7.

3. Andrew Wiget, "His Life in His Tail: The Native American Trickster and the Literature of Possibility," *Redefining American Literary History,* ed. A. LaVonne Brown Ruoff and Jerry W. Ward Jr. (New York: Modern Language Association,1990), 94.

4. London's vivid characters, such as Wolf Larsen in *The Sea-Wolf* and Martin Eden, seem to promote individualism rather than socialism, yet both characters die because their individualistic paths leave them isolated and insupportable.

5. For exceptions, see, for example, Earle Labor, *Jack London* (New York: Twayne, 1974), and Earle Labor and Jeanne Campbell Reesman, *Jack London, Revised Edition* (New York: Twayne, 1994). Labor and Reesman examine London's use of mythic patterns in his short stories and novels. See also Jacqueline Tavernier-Courbin, *"The Call of the Wild": A Naturalistic Romance* (New York: Twayne, 1994). Focusing on *The Call of the Wild,* Tavernier-Courbin offers a detailed examination of Buck as the mythic hero. In "Jack London: The Problem of Form," *Realism and Naturalism in Nineteenth-Century American Literature* (Carbondale: University of Southern Illinois Press, 1984), 166–79, Donald Pizer examines London's use of parables and fables. Much more attention has been paid to London's use of myth in his late short stories, particularly his Hawaiian tales; see Jeanne Campbell Reesman, "The Problem of Knowledge in Jack London's 'The Water Baby,'" *Western American Literature* 23 (Fall 1988): 201–14, in contrast to James McClintock, *White Logic: Jack London's Short Stories* (Grand Rapids, Mich.: Wolf House Books, 1978). See also Lawrence I. Berkove, "The Myth of Hope in Jack London's 'The Red One,'" *Rereading Jack London,* ed. Leonard Cassuto and Jeanne Campbell Reesman (Stanford, Calif.: University of Stanford Press, 1996), 204–15.

6. I would like to thank Jeanne Campbell Reesman for her encouragement and the time she spent with me studying the mythic images underpinning and, sometimes, shifting underlying meaning in London's short stories. Her insightful connections always spur me forward.

7. Franklin Walker, *Jack London and the Klondike: The Genesis of an American Writer* (San Marino, Calif.: Huntington Library, 1994), 190.

8. Ibid. 190.

9. My conviction that we should not water down the religious significance of trickster was reinforced by comments made, particularly by Gloria Cronin, during a roundtable discussion led by Jeanne Rosier Smith during the American

Literature Association Symposium on the Trickster, Oct. 11, 1997, at the Cal-Neva Resort, Lake Tahoe, Nevada.

10. All quotations from Ricketts are from Mac Linscott Ricketts, "The Shaman and the Trickster," *Mythical Trickster Figures: Contours, Contexts, and Criticisms,* ed. William J. Hynes and William G. Doty (Tuscaloosa: University of Alabama Press, 1997), 83–96.

11. All quotations from London's short stories are from *The Complete Short Stories of Jack London,* ed. Earle Labor, Robert C. Leitz III, and I. Milo Shepard (Stanford, Calif.: Stanford University Press, 1993).

12. Lewis Hyde, *Trickster Makes This World: Mischief, Myth, and Art* (New York: Farrar, Straus and Giroux, 1998), 294–95.

13. Ibid. 295.

Daring the Free Fall

Sula as Lilith

DEBBIE LÓPEZ

*C*reator and destroyer, seducer of men and murderer of infants, succubus and snakewoman, Lilith is Creation's first female trickster. In pronouncing the ineffable name of God, she is also, arguably, Creation's first female author.[1] With the nineteenth-century rise of feminism, she becomes a pervasive figure in both literature and art. Some of her more haunting twentieth-century incarnations come in the works of ethnic women writers—not surprisingly, given that, as Jeanne Rosier Smith has argued in *Writing Tricksters,* these writers may be seen as employing trickster techniques themselves: "Interpreter, storyteller, and transformer, the trickster is a master of borders and exchange, injecting multiple perspectives to challenge all that is stultifying, stratified, bland, or prescriptive."[2] That Toni Morrison's Sula assumes what some critics have seen as mythic stature is in large part thanks to the author's employment of Lilith as a source for her protagonist. On the other hand, in Sula, the mythical Lilith inhabits one of her most richly human avatars.

Raphael Patai observes in *The Hebrew Goddess:* "No she-demon has ever achieved as fantastic a career as Lilith, who started out from the lowliest of origins, was a failure as Adam's intended wife, became the paramour of lascivious spirits, rose to be the bride of Samael the Demon King, ruled as Queen of Zemargad and Sheba, and ended up as the consort of God himself . . . What she meant for the Biblical Hebrews can only be surmised, but by the Talmudic period (second to fifth centuries C.E.) she was a fully developed evil she-demon, and during the Kabbalistic age she rose to the high position of queenly consort at God's side."[3]

Lilith's legend grew out of what rabbinical commentators viewed as the discrepancy between the two biblical accounts of the creation of woman. Whereas in Genesis 2:22, woman is born of Adam's rib, Genesis 1:27 reads: "Male and Female He created them." Rabbis inferred from the latter that the creation of man and woman was simultaneous and that, consequently, Adam must have had a mate prior to Eve. According to Hebraic tradition, Adam consorted with Lilith because he had grown tired of mating with beasts. Trouble arose when she refused to lie beneath him in sex, arguing that she was his equal, not his subordinate. Their debate is recounted in the *Alphabet of Ben Sira:*

> [Lilith] said, "I shall not lie beneath," and [Adam] said, "I shall not lie beneath but above, for your place is beneath and mine above." She said to him: "Both of us are equal for both of us are of earth." And they did not listen to each other. When Lilith saw this, she uttered the Ineffable Name and flew off into the air of the world.
>
> Thereupon Adam rose in prayer before his Creator and said: "Master of the World! The woman whom You gave me fled from me." Instantly the Holy One, blessed be He, sent three angels after her to bring her back. And the Holy One, blessed be He, said to Adam: "If she wants to return, good and well, and if not, she will have to take it upon herself that every day one hundred of her children should die."
>
> The angels left Adam and went after her. They overtook her in the sea, in the strong waters in which the Egyptians were to drown in the future. They told her the word of God, but she did not want to return. They then said to her: "We shall drown you in the sea." She said to them: "Let me be, for I was not created except for weakening the newborn children . . ."
>
> When [the angels] heard her words, they pressed her to take her, whereupon she swore to them in the name of . . . God that "Each time when I see you or your names or your likeness on an amulet, I shall not harm that child." And she took it upon herself that a hundred of her [own] children should die every day.
>
> Making her home in a cave, she mated with scores of demons, and, finally, with the prince of devils himself. God created Eve, Lilith's more submissive replacement, out of Adam's rib.

Lilith's means of retaliating were inventive and multifarious. As Barbara Walker relates, although Lilith herself appears in just one brief passage in the canonical Bible, for over a thousand years her daughters, the *lilim,* would continue wreaking havoc. Into the Middle Ages, the Jews were still employing amulets to ward off the *lilim,* lascivious succubae who would descend on men in their sleep eliciting nocturnal emissions, which they would then use in creating their own demon brood. For the Greeks, the *lilim* were Empusae, Lamieae, or Daughters of Hecate. Christians called them succubae or harlots of hell: "Celibate monks tried to fend them off by sleeping with their hands crossed over their genitals, clutching a crucifix. . . . To protect baby boys against her, chalk circles were drawn around cradles with the written names of the three angels God sent to fetch Lilith back to Adam. . . . Some said men and babies should not be left alone in a house or Lilith might seize them."[4]

Also known as night-hags, Lilith's daughters were, in spite of that name, famed for their beauty. So captivating were they that, reputedly after one encounter with a night-hag, sex with a mortal woman would never again suffice.[5] In medieval demonology, Lilis, or Lilith, is a famous witch, and Goethe introduces her as such in the Walpurgis night scene in *Faust*. Robert Burton's *Anatomy of Melancholy* introduces both Lilith and Lamia, the shape-changing serpent-woman of Greek mythology. And the Latin Vulgate Bible officially joins the two she-demons by giving "Lamia" as a translation of Lilith.

They are also linked in medieval iconography. Engravings depict Eve posed on one side of Adam, with Lilith on the other. In other medieval works, Adam and Eve stand beneath the Tree of the Knowledge of Good and Evil, while a serpent-tailed Lilith perches in the branches above. This latter configuration directly conflates Lilith with her Greek counterpart, Lamia. When, several centuries later, post-Romantic artists would depict Lilith, they too would most often echo this equation, presenting Adam's first consort either as intimate with snakes or as serpentine herself. Painter/poet Dante Gabriel Rossetti strategically elaborates on this congruency. In his poem, "Eden Bower," the sinuous temptress, Lilith, persuades the snake to let her assume his shape so that she herself may corrupt Eve. For Rossetti, clearly one fall will not suffice—not only is it a woman who first tastes the forbidden fruit; it is also a woman who whets Eve's appetite. Thus a major reason for Lilith's nineteenth-century popularity asserts itself: both in Rossetti's England and in America, rebellious suffragettes were convincing their more docile associates to reject male dominance. Figuratively speaking, Lilith was seducing her sister, Eve.

Bram Dijkstra notes in *Idols of Perversity* the preponderance of snake-women in late nineteenth-century art. He also makes the connection between Lilith, Lamia, and feminists:

Literally hundreds of painted and sculpted versions of Lilith, Salambo, Lamia and assorted other snake charmers came to blend as generic depictions of Woman, the eternal Eve. For this first and, in the eye of the fin-de-siecle male, most perverse of women was also perpetually shown in intimate communication with serpents of virtually every length and girth throughout the forty-year period spanning the turn of the century. . . . The link between Lamia and the late nineteenth-century feminists, the viragoes—the wild women—would have been clear to any intellectual reasonably well versed in classical mythology, since the Lamia of myth was thought to have been a bisexual, masculinized cradle-robbing creature, and therefore to the men of the turn of the century perfectly representative of the New Woman who, in their eyes, was seeking to arrogate to herself male privileges, refused the duties of motherhood, and was intent upon destroying the heavenly harmony of feminine subordination in the family.[6]

For the community of the Bottom, Morrison's Sula would have seemed to fit this she-demon's profile exactly. While she is originally the less aggressive partner in her friendship with Nel, from the moment Sula arrives back from her own self-exile dressed as a femme fatale, she plays the disruptive Lilith to Nel's domestic Eve. When Sula enters Nel's home, suddenly "the dishes piled in the sink [look] as though they [belong] there; the dust on the lamps [sparkles]; the hair brush lying on the 'good' sofa in the living room [does] not have to be apologetically retrieved, and Nel's grimy intractable children [look] like three wild things happily insouciant in the may shine" (96).[7] Nel herself even begins to feel "a little raunchy" in Sula's presence (95).

Like Lilith, Sula is a defiantly independent breaker of gender taboos in part because she has lived in a realm not subject to patriarchal authority. This is most frequently the case with female tricksters. As Lewis Hyde points out in commenting on the relative scarcity of female tricksters, stories about Native American female tricksters, for example, all come from matrilineal tribes: "In short, we find [the] female trickster in the context of female power."[8] Sula grows up "in a house with women who thought all men available, and selected from among them with a care only for their tastes" (119). Patricia Hunt points out that while the Peace women's "address, 7 Carpenter's Road, suggests that this is the road where Christ will be found, . . . [t]he obvious reversal is that Sula does not live in her father's house, but in her grandmother Eva's house."[9] Adamic in her role as namer (of Tar Baby and the Deweys) Eva reigns over a house "built over a period of five years to the specifications of its owner, who kept on adding things: more stairways—there were three sets to the second floor—more rooms, doors and stoops. There were rooms that had three doors, others that opened out on the porch only and were inaccessible from any other part of the house; others that you could get to only by going through somebody's bedroom" (30). And as has frequently been noted, the house's random excess reflects its matriarchal owner's preoccupation with power.[10]

As in Lilith's demesne by the Red Sea, in the Peace household, the normal rules of patriarchal order don't apply: Eve/Eva not Adam/BoyBoy reigns; Eva's daughter, Hannah, can freely admit that she doesn't like her own child; and the matriarch Eva can murder her own beloved son rather than witness his degradation into infantilism. Like Lilith, Eva is at once both powerful creator and destroyer. Her granddaughter, Sula, matches the Lilith model better, except in refusing motherhood. Yet even this seeming exception proves false, as in some versions of the Lilith myth, the she-demon bears no offspring. In fact Sula's refusal of the maternal role reinforces her nature as a trickster, because, though sexually rapacious, tricksters in general are almost never procreative.[11]

With the exception of Ajax, for Sula, as for Lilith, sex is itself a means of surreptitiously asserting authority over one's lovers. The consummate housebreaker, Lilith was considered, sexually, to pose such a threat that, after she had intercourse with a woman's husband, she was thought to share rights of cohabitation. To expel her, the man would actually have to secure a letter of divorce.[12] Though less persistent, Sula is similarly disruptive. Morrison writes that "the fury [Sula] created in the women of the town was incredible—for she would lay their husbands once and then no more. Hannah [Sula's promiscuous mother] had been a nuisance, but she was complimenting the women, in a way, by wanting their husbands. Sula was trying them out and discarding them without any excuse the men could swallow" (115).

Sula feels the "utmost irony of and outrage in lying under someone, in a position of surrender, feeling her own abiding strength and limitless power" (123). Whereas, in most versions of the myth, Lilith has sex with men for the purpose of producing more demon offspring, Sula uses men for the thrill of experiencing a kind of premature death: "a stinging awareness of the endings of things: an eye of sorrow in the midst of all that hurricane rage of joy. There, in the center of that silence was not eternity but the death of time and a loneliness so profound the word itself had no meaning" (123). Here, she seems to be self-consciously exploring aspects of human sexuality that have also been addressed by psychoanalysts—in particular, the idea that "the significance of eroti-cism . . . is that it allows transgression of the most fundamental taboo, that separating life from death."[13] This particular type of transgression is characteristic of tricksters in general. As Cristiano Grottanelli argues: "Nothing can be a great loss to the trickster; this makes the trickster the perfect champion and the perfect scapegoat—as well as the perfect gambler. . . . The trickster has nothing to lose, for the impurity of boundaries is upon him already, and, having nothing to lose, he moves about freely and gets away with anything, using even death as a form of birth, redemption, and promotion."[14]

In her one close sexual relationship—with Ajax—Sula assumes, like Lilith, the dominant position. And it is notable that, as Houston A. Baker Jr., points out, the minute Ajax discerns that she is becoming possessive, his first act is to "[return] to a male dominant position in intercourse and [head] for a Dayton, Ohio, air show."[15] Humorously, Morrison writes, "He dragged [Sula] under him and made love to her with the steadiness and intensity of a man about to leave for Dayton" (134). The humor here also has its pathos. What specifically provokes Ajax's flight is Sula's sympathetic suggestion that he lean on her for sup-port against the injustices of the outside world (133). The self-conscious artifice of Sula's Lilith pose is at its most poignantly apparent here. She emerges, instead, a would-be enabling Eve—less like the Lilith of myth, more like Nathaniel Hawthorne's hapless victim, the lamian Beatrice Rappaccini, whose poisonous nature is in large part the product of her male observers.

Sula also resembles Beatrice in being herself a lamia. The townspeople interpret her birthmark as, alternately, a copperhead (103) and a rattle-snake (104). And like Beatrice, she is perceived as somehow poisonous: "Some of the men, who as boys had dated her, [remember] that on pic-nics neither gnats nor mosquitoes would settle on her" (115).

But the most striking parallel between Sula and both Lilith and Lamia lies in their common role as child-stealers and/or infanticides. Lilith, in particular, is defined by her threat in this regard. The very word *lullaby* originates from two Arabic words meaning "Beware of Lilith!" Parents drew chalk circles around their infants to guard against Lilith; to protect themselves and their children from Sula, the people of the Bottom "[lay] broomsticks across their doors at night and [sprinkle] salt on porch steps" (113). And their superstitious fears are, to some extent, justified, as Sula is a child-stealer in both a literal sense (as the killer of Chicken Little) and a figurative one. Becoming the guardian of Eva, she makes the latter her child, so to speak, and then forces her to live in the nursing home in an infantilized, womblike state of suspended animation. Eventually, the townspeople's condemnation of Sula will culminate when they sense an affinity between her and the town's other trickster outcast, Shadrack. Sula and Shadrack are "two devils" (117). In other words, Sula, like Lilith, eventually becomes the consort of Satan himself. This is even more obviously the case given the most virulent of the rumors circulating concerning Sula. Morrison writes that "it was the men who gave her the final label, who fingerprinted her for all time. They were the ones who said she was guilty of the unforgivable thing—the thing for which there was no excuse, no compassion. . . . They said that Sula slept with white men" (112). For the townspeople, Sula is indeed the devil's mistress.

While, as Jeanne Rosier Smith observes, "we might expect such a figure to pose a threat to community, Morrison shows us that in fact Sula sustains and gives life to her community by giving them a reason to unite. . . . The trickster's amorality sharpens the community's sense of a moral code."[16] The same can be said for Lilith. Lilith's threat makes mothers better guardians of their children and bonds husbands more closely with their wives.

Sula's effect upon the residents of the Bottom is precisely this. Faced with what she perceives as Sula's danger to her son, even Betty, "called Teapot's Mamma because being his mamma was precisely her major failure" (113–14) suddenly becomes a devoted parent. On the other hand, after Sula's death, the community returns to its former careless ways. Teapot's mother resumes beating him.

> Other mothers who had defended their children from Sula's malevolence (or who had defended their positions as mothers from Sula's scorn for the role) now had nothing to rub up against. The tension was gone and so was the reason for the effort they had made. Without her mockery, affection for others sank into flaccid disrepair. . . . Wives uncoddled their husbands; there seemed no further need to reinforce their vanity. And even those Negroes who had moved down from Canada to Medallion, who remarked every chance they got that they had never been slaves, felt a loosening of the reactionary compassion for Southern-born blacks Sula inspired in them. (153)

It may first seem puzzling that this long catalog of Sula's meliorative effects upon the community's domestic relations should conclude as it does. Why should her presence serve to reconcile the breach between freeborn Canadian blacks and African Americans born in or descended from slavery? Why, indeed, raise the issue of slavery at this point in the novel? In part, Morrison is deliberately recalling the novel's opening, which grounds the Bottom's origins in the "nigger joke" played by a white farmer on his slave.

Having promised his slave freedom and a piece of bottom land, the farmer finds himself regretting the second promise. He solves his dilemma by tricking the slave into believing that the infertile, hilly land granted him instead is preferable because in God's eyes, it appears as the bottom. As Houston A. Baker Jr. so astutely observes, "This etiological tale of place naming inscribes the fact and fantasy of capitalism. It is the writing of an American betrayal that can be read as follows in the words of W. E. B. Du Bois: 'But the vision of "forty acres and a mule"—the righteous and reasonable ambition to become a landholder, which the nation had all but categorically promised the freedmen—was destined in most cases to bitter disappointment.' The joke within the Bottom's economics is the deprivation of the 'means of production' that characterized America's relationship to former slaves." [17] More specifically, the novel's larger context invokes the travails that followed participants in the Great Migration from the South. [18] *Sula*, in effect, describes a community's financial and social impotence and isolation.

As self-exiles, Lilith and Sula serve as scapegoats for communities that are themselves in exile. Hence, finally, Lilith's perfect appropriateness as a model for Morrison's protagonist. For as Aviva Cantor observes, "What is particularly intriguing about the Lilith myth is that most of the legends about her developed in Exile, either after the Babylonian Exile (586 B.C.E.) and certainly after the Roman deportations of Jews into captivity (70 C.E.). Lilith appears in the Babylonian Talmud in rudimentary form; her character is developed in the *Zohar* and other medieval mystical works. No scholar has dated the *Alphabet of Ben Sira* but all agree it was written in the Gaonic period, before 1000 C.E." [19]

In other words, Lilith always flourished at times when Jews feared for their very survival—and, not coincidentally, given the patriarchal nature of Jewish society—at times when Jewish manhood seemed threatened. As Cantor goes on to argue, in no other Jewish mythical character do

Lilith's particular "crimes" against humanity coalesce. Only Lilith is simultaneously dangerous to pregnant and birthing women, to infants, and to sexually vulnerable men. All of these threats make her especially menacing to a society in crisis, such as that of the Jews in exile—or that of the Bottom.[20]

The people of the Bottom locate all of their fears in Sula as a means of control and of exorcism, much as Melville's Ahab invests the white whale with all of the evil of the universe in order to eradicate evil. While some of the townspeople's superstitions may seem similarly irrational, the virulence of their hatred nevertheless testifies to the formidability of their struggle for survival. The very nature of myth is, as Sacvan Bercovitch has consistently argued, to explain the discrepancies between life as it is and life as it should be. The people of the Bottom mythologize Sula as Lilith because they need a scapegoat of mythic proportions to justify their misery and to inspire their battle for endurance.

And, after all, as Morrison comments, while "their evidence against Sula was contrived . . . their conclusions about her were not. Sula was distinctly different. Eva's arrogance and Hannah's self-indulgence merged in her and, with a twist that was all her own imagination, she lived out her days exploring her own thoughts and emotions, giving them full reign, feeling no obligation to please anybody unless their pleasure pleased her. As willing to feel pain as to give pain, to feel pleasure as to give pleasure, hers was an experimental life" (118). This "experimental life" is of precisely the sort Barbara Babcock-Abrahams sees as the distinguishing characteristic of the trickster: "As Trickster travels through the world, develops self, and creates for mankind haphazardly, by chance, by trial and error without advance planning, he reenacts the process that is central both to perception and creation, to the constant human activity of making guesses and modifying them in light of experience—the process of 'schema and correction.'"[21] "Artist[s] without art forms," Sula and Lilith are both "dangerous"; but as the negative example of the novel's Eve figure, Nel, demonstrates, sometimes there may be no spiritual progress without first daring trespass.

Notes

1. Sandra M. Gilbert and Susan Gubar argue that Lilith's "history suggests . . . that in patriarchal culture, female speech and female 'presumption'—that is, an-

gry revolt against male domination—are inextricably linked and inevitably dae-monic" (35). *The Madwoman in the Attic: The Woman Writer and the Nineteenth-Century Literary Imagination* (New Haven, Conn.: Yale University Press, 1979).

2. Jeanne Rosier Smith, *Writing Tricksters: Mythic Gambols in American Ethnic Literature* (Berkeley and Los Angeles: University of California Press, 1997), xiii.

3. Raphael Patai, *The Hebrew Goddess* (Detroit: Wayne State University Press, 1967), 221.

4. Barbara G. Walker, *The Woman's Encyclopedia of Myths and Secrets* (San Francisco: Harper and Row, 1983), 542.

5. Walker 542.

6. Bram Dijkstra, *Idols of Perversity: Fantasies of Feminine Evil in Fin-de-Siecle Culture* (New York: Oxford University Press, 1986), 307.

7. All quotations from *Sula* are from Toni Morrison, *Sula* (New York: New American Library, 1973).

8. Lewis Hyde, *Trickster Makes This World: Mischief, Myth, and Art* (New York: Farrar, Straus and Giroux, 1998), 340.

9. Patricia Hunt, "War and Peace: Transfigured Categories and the Politics of *Sula*," *African American Review* 27 (1993): 450.

10. For example, Houston A. Baker Jr. makes this argument: "The house's ceaseless increase is a testimony to its owner's desire for expanded dominion. In a curious way, in fact, it attests the very 'manlove' that we are told is the ruling creed of the Peaces" (140). *Workings of the Spirit: The Poetics of Afro-American Women's Writing* (Chicago: University of Chicago Press, 1991).

11. Hyde 8.

12. Patai 225.

13. Jessica Benjamin, "Master and Slave: The Fantasy of Erotic Domination," *Powers of Desire: The Politics of Sexuality,* ed. Ann Snitow, Christine Stansell, and Sharon Thompson (New York: Monthly Review Press, 1983), 285.

14. Cristiano Grottanelli, "Tricksters, Scapegoats, Champions, Saviors," *History of Religions* 23 (1983): 137.

15. Baker 142.

16. Smith 116.

17. Baker 137.

18. Phillip M. Richards, "*Sula* and the Discourse of the Folk in African American Literature," *Cultural Studies* 9, no. 2 (1995): 284.

19. Aviva Cantor, "The Lilith Question," *On Being a Jewish Feminist: A Reader,* ed. Susannah Heschel (New York: Schocken Books, 1983), 44.

20. Cantor 45–46.

21. Quoted in *Mythical Trickster Figures: Contours, Contexts, and Criticisms,* ed. William J. Hynes and William G. Doty (Tuscaloosa: University of Alabama Press, 1993), 8.

The Trickster Metaphysics of Thylias Moss

JAY WINSTON

Wil_illiam Blake, in a celebrated fragment, describes a strange, perhaps paradoxical, angel:

> As soon as I went an angel came:
> He wink'd at the thief
> And smil'd at the dame
> And without one word spoke
> Had a peach from the tree,
> And 'twixt earnest & joke
> Enjoy'd the Lady.[1]

The contemporary American poet Thylias Moss works in a manner not unlike that of Blake's mischievous angel. Her voice occupies a space "'twixt earnest & joke," embracing both extremes of this seeming dichotomy. Within one short poem, sometimes within one stanza, we find her gravitating between the deadly earnest of a polemic, giving vent to the angry voices of the oppressed and forgotten, and a relentless, "postmodern" irony that recognizes few boundaries, playing and joking with the most sacred of words and ideals in the most devil-may-care fashion.

Moss's poem "Running Out of Choices" can be seen as both exemplar and critique of this paradoxical mode. In the opening stanzas we find the poet tossing aside the signifiers of a wide range of atrocities, from the then-current fighting in Beirut to the murder of Medgar Evers, seeing them all as mere annoyances, words that, because of associations, serve as impediments to her work, "words that get automatic respect / whether or not the speaker has anything to say." Birmingham Sunday, one of the sacred rallying points of the American Civil Rights Movement, like Evers's murder, is, for example, turned into a kind of sick joke:

> For related reasons I can't consider Alabama
> unless I also consider churches and Easter dresses so ugly
> bombs were thrown to eliminate the ugliness
> while the girls were still in them.[2]

In making this "ugliness" into dark comedy, the poet seems to be attempting to negate the greater ugliness inherent in every location to (or from) which she attempts to escape through poetic device, the essential ugliness that seems to stand in the way of the free creativity that she desires. Ultimately, however, the possibility of such escape is denied, even through the detachment inherent in such irony within the poem itself:

> Where can I go without somehow returning to Cleveland,
> Evergreen cemetery, my father, Rebecca Robinson,
> Sis. Winchell who killed
> her husband, Cordia Jackson, my pastor's daughter, murdered
> in the projects I might have lived in had I not been so lucky.[3]

This is an ironic poem, thus, that throws irony into question. These places, people, and things mentioned, central to the self and to the society of the poet, cannot be escaped through rhetorical devices or disaffected poses. An unbound artist's voice, with language free from previous signification, from social, political, and emotional resonances, is not possible.

Such signification might, however, be reimagined. Such reimagining is central to Moss's poetry as she works to, in bell hooks's words "decolonize our minds and imaginations."[4] That is, she is trying not to negate but to liberate signifiers from colonizing, controlling paradigms. In this, her work is very much in tune with Henry Louis Gates Jr.'s conception of the Signifying Monkey, the Yoruba trickster figure working throughout African American writing as a "figure of indeterminacy," ever resisting "the enclosure of negation" and, instead of negating, "wreak[ing] havoc upon the signified."[5] Moss works to counter prevailing narratives not with binary oppositions but with a kind of productive "havoc" in which possibilities are raised up in place of traditional oppositions and oppositionality itself is critiqued.

In a number of poems, particularly "The Wake for the Lost Two Hundred Miles," "Passover Poem," "Tribute to Jesse and Then Some," "The Adversary," "Spilled Sugar," and the prose poem "The Warmth of Hot Chocolate," each of which will be discussed in this essay, Moss reimagines the Christian tradition with its various signifiers, including angels, devils, and, of course, God. While, in doing so, she expresses an often problematic and gleefully paradoxical nonbelief at times, she does not seek to nullify this traditional cosmology. Rather, like William Blake, she reifies its signifiers, but in new and different forms, redefining them in terms that are less stagnant, perhaps less patriarchal (though, interestingly, she never reassigns the gender of her God, preferring to leave his masculinity intact, if reexamined), certainly more open and personal.

She does so, significantly, in a manner that is concerned not only with the personal but with a larger, specifically African American context (Moss describes herself as "both black and Native American,"[6] though the latter does not seem to play as prominent a part in the poems here discussed). As such, Moss is taking part in a metaphysical tradition in African American poetry concerned with the centuries-old problem stated powerfully by James Baldwin: "if one despairs—and who has not?—of human love, God's love alone is left. But God . . . is white."[7] Whereas some, such as Amiri Baraka, and Baldwin himself, have ultimately decided to do away with or replace this Christian God, others, notably Countee Cullen, "wishing he I served were black," have attempted to make peace with him through a kind of reimagining:

> Lord, I fashion dark gods, too
> Daring even to give You
> Dark despairing features . . .
> Crowned with dark rebellious hair . . .[8]

Ultimately, however, as Alan Shucard points out, "Cullen's religious verse only began by struggling against Christianity; it ended by singing in fulfillment of Christianity."[9] Significantly, Cullen follows his metaphysical speculations in "Heritage" with an apology:

> Lord forgive me if my need
> Sometimes shapes a human creed.[10]

Such an apology is the last thing one would expect from Moss. Baldwin wrote: "if a concept of God has any validity or any use, it can only be to make us larger, freer, and more loving. If God cannot do this, then it is time we got rid of him."[11] For Moss, it seems, God *can* do this, but only if one abandons Cullen's dichotomy of rebellion and acceptance and is willing to truly "fashion" the God that is required. In doing so, however, Moss rejects any rigid identity politics, or identity religion, based upon manichean dualisms of black and white. She does not, that is, seek to fashion a "dark god" to counter the "white," preferring instead to "wreak havoc" in the spaces between, "'twixt earnest and joke." In the process, she redefines these polarities, finding liberatory possibilities in such redefinition as a means to, in Ralph Ellison's oft-quoted terms, "change the joke and slip the yoke." [12]

In "The Wake for the Lost Two Hundred Miles," a particularly playful example of Moss's metaphysics, the Holy Trinity is refigured, along with the three monkeys and the three stooges as father, daughter, and gas station attendant. We are given the description of a vaguely spiritual "summer ritual" of father and daughter traveling together:

> The main highways were paved slick as Elvis;
> we avoided those so his wheels could crack gravel,
> build church. [13]

The very movement, connection of car and road is given a sense of holy agency, somehow more real than that to be found on a more traction-free road surface, one created by the same modern paradigm that brings us the "slickness" of popular culture. They stop at gas stations, which are similar to the extent that they make up a kind of repeated litany, made up of the vaguely pagan work of "Joe" the attendant, his ritual checking of parts, "like fetish which it is," and his key, "like an ankh" to the pop machine, as he gets sodas for the three to drink with a ritual lunch:

> A supper of cold beans and a tomato
> sandwich, a three way split and we all
> thought to ourselves: we've got
> the three monkeys, three stooges, even
> the trinity covered. [14]

This ritual, thus, with its allusive, elusive signifiers of spirituality leaves its characters at the level of a kind of secondary trinity of trinities, made up of the profane ignorance of the three monkeys, the violent absurdity of the three stooges, and the traditional sacredness of Father, Son, and Holy Ghost. They are all at once: sacred and profane, earnest and joke. As such, Moss shows her affinity for a folk tradition in which, as Zora Neale Hurston put it, "nothing is too old or too new, domestic or foreign, high or low for . . . use. God and the Devil are paired, and are treated no more reverently than Rockefeller and Ford." [15] Here, though, even the earthly eminence of Rockefeller and Ford is denied to the holy trinity, found eating a simple lunch outside of a gas station. Holiness is, in a sense, separated from a necessary relation to power.

"Passover Poem" arrives at approximately the same point, though coming from the opposite direction. Here God is humanized, re-created in man's image as he "wipes his eyes."[16] He is anthropomorphic not merely in the physical sense, having eyes, but, more important, in an emotional and ultimately existential sense, sharing in the "blur of disbelief" of suffering humanity, along with its sense of hopelessness in viewing injustice and atrocity. Like the "creator" of "Running Out of Choices," this God tries to blink and make it all go away, but it does not work, "death does not pass over." The poem concludes with an expression of pity for a "poor God [who] cannot pass the buck, he made the buck." Here, as throughout the poem, Moss turns to the ironic, punning wordplay that is one of her great strengths ("He looks at a million Latino boys called Jesus. Jesus"), making her God a kind of quintessential tragicomic character, ultimately responsible for all, and unable to divest himself of this responsibility, yet condemned to sit and watch with the impotent blinking of all-seeing eyes. As such, God is, in a sense, reified as a figure of compassion. Yet, rather than the ultimate, transcendent source of compassion, here he is imagined as a recipient of compassion. He shares in human suffering (in the incorporeal form of God the father, rather than as the embodied Christ suffering on the cross) rather than standing apart from it with the power to regulate suffering and consolation.

The reversal is a trope that has been used by earlier African American poets, such as Baraka and Gwendolyn Brooks, though quite differently. Baraka, in "Black Dada Nihilismus," reverses the position of forgive and forgiven, subject and object of compassion, as Moss does, yet ends up, like the God of Revelations, denying forgiveness:

> God, if they bring him
> bleeding, I would not
> forgive.[17]

Brooks, on the other hand, seems far more of a forbear to Moss's own attitude, writing, in "the preacher ruminates behind the sermon:"

> I think it must be lonely to be God
> Nobody loves a master.[18]

Brooks's God, like Moss's, thus would seem to be imagined to fulfill Baldwin's demand that he make us "more loving," if in a manner somewhat opposite to that of the God who "is love." Rather, he might be seen as one who needs our love (though, in Brooks's poem he still is "a master" and is still distant, both categories that Moss throws into question). Apparently disempowered, he is, in a sense, brought close rather than nullified.

Such compassion, however, clearly does not exclude criticism, or demands that this God exercise more compassion. "Tribute to Jesse and then Some," taking its cue from remarks made by Jesse Jackson during the 1988 presidential campaign, plays with the idea of Jesus, Mary, and Joseph as a homeless family. The poem begins by contrasting the loss of dignity of the homeless with the superficial compassion of those who donate shoes to the poor and attend charity luncheons, and that of the welfare system (this written well before the "reforms" of Bill Clinton):

> Welfare is about as charitable as America gets
> with its limbo stick rules of income to make you
> crawl. Then Jesse said it, I heard it with
> my own ears, saw it with my own eyes, and now I'm
> on my way to tell the king that Jesus was born homeless
> to a single mother like her counterparts
> cloistered in the projects, alleys, subway tunnels,
> forsaken buses, tenement nunneries, the order of Mary,
> all of them with God-solicited child again and again.[19]

Like the father, daughter, and gas station attendant compared to the trinity, here the most popularly maligned members of American society, the urban homeless and poor single mothers, are placed on a level with the most exalted family in the Western tradition. This was Jackson's intention. Moss is with him, up to a point, but has her "and then some":

> our father art in heaven so he can't pay child
> support but thy will be done anyway . . .

The God of "Passover Poem," thus, is seen again attempting to pass the buck; his position here is seen to be that of not simply "God the Father" but "God the deadbeat dad," with lines from the Lord's Prayer worked into a cynical excoriation of the absentee parent who nonetheless demands the respect due to a father.

Whereas Jackson merely attempted to make a fruitful connection based upon Christian tradition, Moss here reimagines the signification of that tradition within the specific context of the contemporary American urban poor, for whom the father figure who forsakes his family, as God might appear to have forsaken his, has become the norm. Again, however, as this figure is redefined, his light diminished, he is brought closer, into a far more personal relationship.

In "The Adversary" Moss extends this analysis in looking at the relationship of this humanized, fallible God with Satan, and at the very notion of Satan. Satan, here, becomes not so much the manichean embodiment of evil as God the absentee father's big excuse:

> The problem: God's need for adversary,
> worthy opponent, for just short of [emphasis mine] equal
> . . . for God, all glowing is vain.
> Satan accepts the rest. What rains down,
> the heavenly sewage and trash, the blame
> for holy wars, rescue rages. For every drop of blood.[20]

Clearly far short (intentionally) of any Miltonic "justifying the ways of God to men," Moss demonstrates the essential weakness in traditional Christian dualism, with its various answers to the "problem of evil," in which good is able to retain its luster despite having created evil and allowed that evil to flourish. Moss dismisses this dualism by reimagining Satan as merely God's scapegoat, a means to hide his own fallibility.

And she extends this shattered dualism to that of black and white, traditionally corresponding to notions of God and Satan, good and evil, as well as to racial divisions:

> In heaven Satan was a minority in a neighborhood
> where everyone else was saint. Crosses burned and
> his car, house, clothes, wings; all
> his possessions. And the burning and reburning
> of memories establishes hell.[21]

Satan, thus, like the holy family of "Tribute to Jesse and Then Some," becomes representative of the dispossessed African American, whose "hell" has been created through persecution by those on the "white" side of the classical dualism. His "blackness" only becomes evil in comparison to the notion of goodness inherent in "whiteness," which has been strategically created and is wholly dependent upon the "black" to maintain itself. He is the fabricated evil other, the colonized.

He might be seen, thereby, as a contemporary American counterpart to the idealized revolutionary Satan of the Romantics, characterized by Shelley as

> a moral being . . . Far superior to his god, as one who perseveres in some purpose which he has conceived to be excellent in spite of adversity and torture, is to one who in the cold security of undoubted triumph inflicts the most horrible revenge upon his enemy, not from any mistaken notion of inducing him to repent . . . but with the alleged design of exasperating him to deserve new torments.[22]

Shelley, echoed by Blake, Godwin, and others, reinterpreted, or "signified upon" Milton. Moss, however, goes a step further in her final stanzas. She re-presents this persecuted, apparently righteous devil imagined by the Romantics and, having made him her own (placing him in a contemporary American context as opposed to that of the French Revolution), proceeds to take him apart. He becomes, like the God of "Passover Poem," an object of pity and, more than that, quite the opposite of an effective revolutionary:

> Poor Satan. His authority denied him
> by a nose, a longer, pointed Caucasian nose.
> Where's the gratitude for Satan who is there
> for God no matter what; Satan
> who is the original Uncle Tom.[23]

He is not, in Moss's reimagining, anything resembling the fierce revolutionary of the Romantics. Nor is he any glorified urban militant; rather, in the very opposition in which he, in Shelley's words, "perseveres in spite of adversity and torture," he is the ideal servant. As such, he serves as the ultimate exemplar of what Henry Giroux describes as that "oppositional behavior" that, rather than having any real "radical significance . . . is fueled by and reproduces the most powerful grammar of domination,"[24] as God can maintain his own position of not only power but moral authority only so long as the evil other continues to play his own part. As such, the poem critiques not only the dualisms found in both traditional Christian narratives and Romantic counternarratives but also popular notions of resistance in the contemporary African American community; the violent "gangsta" who gives a sense of moral authority to those he purports to be standing up against.

In "Spilled Sugar" and "The Warmth of Hot Chocolate," Moss goes a step further, questioning not so much the moral but the existential nature of her God. In "Spilled Sugar," the focus is on the mortal, the physical in its encounter with, or creation of, the metaphysical. The poem returns us, in a sense, to the father and daughter of "The Wake for the Lost Two Hundred Miles," though here the tone is far more somber. The poem leaves aside the tragicomic, fallible, anthropomorphic God to deal with human suffering and the relationship of that suffering to a conception of God, a God who is almost impossibly abstract. The father and daughter reexamine this relationship following the death of a wife/mother:

> Neither he nor I will move from the shrine
> of Mother's photo. We begin to understand
> the limits of love's power. And as we do,
> we have to redefine God; he is not love at all.
> He is longing.[25]

This definition, clearly, is one that is situational, anything but static, moving beyond any set cosmology or countercosmology, in the embodied sense as formulated by Blake or by the Thylias Moss of "Passover Poem" or "The Adversary," to a spirituality that recognizes its basis, or perhaps its entire substance, in human need. Again, as in "The Wake for the Lost Two Hundred Miles," there is a sense of parallelism, of ultimate compassion, between "God and Man:"

> He is what he became those three days
> that one third of himself was dead.[26]

God is represented, thus, as an interesting, dynamic kind of emptiness, an emptiness that is personified by need and made parallel to that of the grieving family. The temporarily severed holy trinity, lacking the son, mirrors the trinity of father, mother, and daughter, each feeling the loss of one of its essential parts, a loss that appears to swallow up, to deny wholeness to, the other two-thirds so that the emptiness "becomes" the whole. But, more significantly, it also becomes the "longing" for wholeness. And this longing, unlike love, seems to know no limits, to represent the infinite that is associated with God. God, hence, becomes simultaneously representative of emptiness or incompleteness and of the desire for fullness or wholeness. He is at once negation and the hope for ultimate affirmation.

"The Warmth of Hot Chocolate" plays with this paradox, in what might be seen as Moss's most paradoxically forthright statement of a metaphysics, in which God is pondered and finally left somewhere between belief and nonbelief, existence and nonexistence, "earnest & joke." The prose poem is written in the voice of an "angel," and one that is very much in the tradition of Blake's trickster. This angel herself embodies paradox, as expressed in her opening lines:

> Somebody told me I didn't exist even though he was looking dead at me. He said that since I defied logic, I wasn't real for reality is one of logic's definitions . . . My compliments did not deter him from insisting he conversed with an empty space since there was no such thing as an angel who doesn't believe in God.[27]

Reality, in this argument, is created by logic, as angels are part of a logic that is centered on the concept of God. Nonetheless, within the particular logic of the poem, her existence is self-evident. Within the poem she is looked "dead at" by this "somebody" to whom she is present as object. And at the same time, she exists to the reader as the voice of the poem and hence the arbiter of any "reality" that it attempts to convey (a poetic device perhaps moving the poem itself into the realm of paradox, trick, or joke). She might be seen to exist as void, or longing, like the God of "Spilled Sugar," except for this presence. Hence she is something other, imagined into being by another logic entirely.

Thus, as voice of the poem, this angel is able to work in a kind of free "trickster" space, mediating between being and nonbeing, in which she can play with signifiers including her own. She plays, first of all, with the physical form of the angel, stating that wings actually grow from the scalp, and that an angel generally is unaware of them, and unaware that he or she is an angel at all until "the release of chemical secretions activated whenever [he or she] jump[s] off a bridge" (Moss here appears to be referencing Frank Capra's *It's a Wonderful Life*, hence revealing her cosmology's origins to be based upon popular culture as much as more "sacred" texts; hence blurring boundaries in a manner similar to that of "The Wake for the Lost Two Hundred Miles"). More important, she plays with the sacred status of angels who are "not intrinsically holy, just intrinsically airborne" (which might describe Blake's amoral angel perfectly). The angel, hence, is free from the bindings of standard moral doctrines that constitute "holiness" and, as such, can reimagine this cosmology from within. Like the trickster, she is between all categories, all standards, "a figure of indeterminacy."

The second section of the three-part prose poem looks more directly at this figure of a god who is not believed in yet, who, again, is humanized, fallible, made more "real" even as his very existence is questioned. In this way, Moss pulls together the anthropomorphism of "Passover Poem" and "The Adversary" with the abstraction of "Spilled Sugar." The section begins: "I think God covets my wings. He forgot to create some for himself." More significant than these very human failings described, including those of covetousness (not only a failing but a broken commandment) and forgetfulness, this God, himself the ultimate object of faith, is suspected of *lacking faith* in his own power, or his own infallibility (in the very literal sense of the inability to fall):

> I suggested to God that he jump off a bridge to activate the wings he was sure to have, you never forget yourself when you divvy up the booty, but he didn't have enough faith that his fall wouldn't be endless.[28]

God, thus, is in a state of insecurity, unsure of his own position, his own power, his own "godliness," afraid of the potential to "fall" that he himself created, the "buck" that cannot be passed.

In the third and final section, Moss's angel narrator reveals that she shares this doubt, in lines that seem simultaneously to uphold and deny the very existence of this God as did the "somebody" of the first section in regard to the angel herself:

> I don't believe in him; he's just a comfortable acquaintance, a close associate with whom I can be myself. To believe in him would place him in the center of the universe when he's more secure in the fringes.[29]

This is a God more comfortable than sublime, more personal than transcendent. He is peripheral, rather than central, not a master to be served, but a source of consolation. He is in the background, not above or below but very much on the level of the human, the father, daughter, and gas station attendant. And, like them, he is less than secure in his position, ever afraid of falling.

The belief, or lack thereof, however, reveals a more complex relationship, a kind of power struggle between the personal and the spiritual, or an inextricable mingling between the two, as the basis for this paradoxical relationship:

to trust him implicitly would be a mistake for he then would not have to maintain his worthiness to be God. Even the thinnest, flyweight modicum of doubt gives God the necessity to prove he's worthy of the implicit trust I can never give because I protect him from corruption, from the complacence that rises within him sometimes.[30]

Not trusting in the false dualism described in "The Adversary," the angel seeks to serve as the conscience of a God that depends upon faith for his existence, as this necessary God can only be sustained in his usefulness by a modicum of disbelief. Only by being forced to prove his goodness, his (to return again to Baldwin's terms) ability to "make us larger, freer and more loving," through the threat inherent in this disbelief, will he be good.

In a sense, the positions of God and "Man" as creator and creation, subject and object, are reversed, with the accompanying reversal of power relations and moral authority. God is created to serve human needs, for goodness, for wholeness, for "God," and is here imagined, therefore, as an extremely abstract, extremely ironic construction. Yet, at the same time, he is an important presence, a part of the most personal and emotional of relationships, the undeniable "longing" described in "Spilled Sugar," the comfort for the destitute in "Tribute to Jesse and Then Some." He is not merely imagined passively but comes to exist in a void that is nonetheless filled with "longing," so that the imagining and reimagining in which Moss takes part seems more negotiation than creation, with something that is not yet is.

Moss's concern in these poems is clearly not one of rejecting belief in favor of nonbelief, nor good for evil, nor the profane for the sacred. Marilyn Hacker writes: "Thylias Moss names the black truths behind white lies."[31] I would suggest, rather, that she is attempting to go between and beyond all such dualisms as "black truths" and "white lies." She is concerned with the possibilities that may come up through juxtaposing seeming opposites, of bridging "the distance from Africa to Andover . . . the distance between black and white," as she writes in "Interpretation of a Poem by Frost."[32] Thus, in "Tribute to Jesse and Then Some," the Pied Piper of Hamlin is associated with smokers of crack pipes, "so many pipers in the neighborhood";[33] in "There Will be Animals," Little Red Riding Hood is juxtaposed with Dachau. Innocence and experience are blended, the lines between categories dissolved.

She is not, however, to use Jorie Graham's terms, "dream[ing] of a unified field" in which, no longer opposed, everything fits together in a manner that the mind can grasp. Nor is she, like Blake, setting up any classifiable countercosmology against that of a dominant church. Rather, her interest appears to be in opening up fields, to liberate those signifiers that have become trapped in stagnant and/or destructive paradigms of meaning. Instead of seeking, after Blake, a "Marriage of Heaven and Hell," by redefining, or refixing, those terms, Moss wants to throw such signifiers into flux, so that rather than "marrying" them, she leaves them free and single, open to possibilities.

As such, Moss is working with something similar to Gerald Vizenor's concept of "trickster hermeneutics." Vizenor's concern is with trickster stories in which one finds "characters that liberate the mind and never reach closure."[34] The same can be said, I think of Moss's "trickster" poems, in which both author and characters (as in Vizenor's work) play the trickster role. There are no endings, only openings.

Thus, Moss finds ironic wonder in Wonder Bread, joy in Joy dishwashing liquid.[35] In "Birmingham Brown's Turn," Moss ponders various stereotypes found in popular culture, acknowledging, "I realize that Birmingham Brown is supposed to be an insult," but tries to find possibilities beyond that insult:

> . . . And anyway, what if
> the world—knowing how crazy it is
> documented to be—is traveling upside
> down; what if Birmingham is on the
> top? The night sure treats him
> royally . . . [36]

That is, the stereotype, based upon old, destructive categories, might be better used, reified as its position is reversed—or at least the possibility raised that its position might be seen as reversed, or in some other way than that which is the accepted signification—rather than discarded. Hence, she is doing with the worst stereotyped manifestations of the duality of black and white in racial terms what she does with dualities of good and evil, God and man. Not content simply to disavow them and move on, she attempts to find new, perhaps liberatory possibilities, new readings.

In "Approaching Venus' Flytrap During a Hungarian Film: A Subtitle," Moss complains:

> *... There are subtitles*
> *to make me doubt my ears, discourage*
> *my own interpretations, fuck up*
> *the possibilities of truth.*[37]

In this, I think, we can see Moss's agenda in a nutshell: to "un-fuck up" the possibilities of truth in language, in racial categories, and, in the poems I've discussed, in religion. She does not deny context. In fact, she often works within what appear to be the bleakest of contexts. Rather, she attempts to find new ways in which different signifiers can be interpreted within those contexts, discovering ways in which they might become things that one may use rather than be used by. Subject/object dualities are thrown into flux, turned into forms of dialogue.

In this, I see a corollary to bell hooks's concepts of "decolonization" as mentioned above. Moss, like hooks, is interested in overthrowing those truths, or those interpretations, which have been given a hegemonic capital "T." She wants to deny the colonial biases of a dominant culture often indifferent and/or hostile to those who have been inculcated in its often disempowering ideals, liberating signifiers as a means of liberating minds and lives. Hooks's concern is that of:

> transforming the image, creating alternatives, asking ourselves questions about what types of images subvert, pose critical alternatives, and transform our worldviews and move us away from dualistic thinking about good and bad. Making a space for the transgressive image, the outlaw rebel vision, is essential to any effort to create a context for transformation.[38]

Thus, despite the specifically race and gender bases of the problems of the issues of colonization that she describes, hooks is not attempting to take part in any binary opposition of "black truths" against "white lies"; rather, she wants to get away from such "dualistic thinking." This is exactly Moss's point in—much as she might criticize and attempt to deflate her "God"—her refusal to, like Blake and Shelley, take the part of Satan.

"We do more than resist," writes hooks, "we create alternative texts that *are not solely reactions* [my emphasis]."[39] Moss, in her metaphysical poems, is attempting to do much the same thing with the signifiers of Christian thought, not to "solely react," by embracing the "other" side of a colonizing dichotomy but to create alternative texts in a liberatory space somewhere in the freer air between its rigid polarities. And it is from such a space that the work of transformation, subversion, transgression, liberation, can be continued. Hence, the Western, patriarchal God is reified but in a sense that he is no longer the master or colonizer. His signification is to be renegotiated in a manner that is beneficial to both God and mortal, in which God is allowed to exist, but only if he proves himself to be useful.

This is not to say, however, that Moss's agenda in these poems is purely one of minority politics. Like Blake, she is also concerned with that apparently more color-blind aspect of traditional Christianity that seems to be a denial of life itself, which Blake described as "binding with briars my joys and desires."[40] Her very playful use of Christian signification in "The Warmth of Hot Chocolate" and "The Wake for the Lost Two Hundred Miles" would seem to imply a theology based as much upon ideals of joy and desire as upon any rigidly political ideal of liberation (not that joy and politics necessarily need to be mutually exclusive; as Moss herself says in an interview with Sean Thomas Dougherty, "for me the ideal is how to exist with these darker parts and yet be able to have the joy, to have the bliss, to have that as well").[41] While her poems have strong political resonances and potentials, and certainly make no effort to stand outside of political "realities," to place Thylias Moss in a ghetto of "topical verse" would be, I think, to do her a disservice. In fact, I would say that her very trickster nature would keep her from being caught on either side of a dichotomy of political and personal, or earnest and joke.

What is perhaps most important to Moss's metaphysical reimagination is that it be done with a sense of humor, ever emphasizing the "joke" in "slipping the yoke." Cornel West writes (in reference to what he sees as the humorlessness of W. E. B. Du Bois) of "the distinctive black tragicomic sense and black encounter with the absurd."[42] Moss, unlike West's version of Du Bois, makes this encounter with the absurd quite comfortably, choosing to encounter it on its own terms, but adopting, or adapting, those terms for herself, to her own uses. She finds a kind of empowerment, if limited, in irony, in paradox, in humor, in recognizing the grave seriousness of situations yet choosing, for the moment, not to take them too seriously, to see what other possibilities there are and what can be done with them. In this regard, she might be said to take hooks's "decolonization" a step further, to the point that even oppression and atrocity, the points that most political movements rally against, might be played upon, reimagined.

The reimagination with which she is concerned is perpetually dynamic, ever undoing and reconfiguring itself. Thus, her counter cosmologies, or counternarratives, might be seen as anticosmologies, antinarratives. Yet, ultimately, she denies nothing. She does not, like Baraka, attempt to nullify the concept of the Christian God. Nor does she, like Cullen, attempt to see past his apparent failings. Nor, finally, does she imagine, like Blake, a "truer" version to counter the prevailing one. Rather, she looks at what is there and tries to find different perspectives, different ways in which it might be imagined. If there are failings to be seen, she embraces her God for those failings, finding him thereby a more compassionate figure, inspiring as well as dispensing (and holding back) compassion, one with whom one may more easily negotiate. And, of course these failings include also his failure to truly exist, as an omni-compassionate good parent or at all. We are left with paradoxes, unanswered questions, varying possibilities where before there was dogma. Clearly, these negotiations are not ended. Rather, they resist closure at every point. Moss leaves open all answers, "wreaking havoc," only with limitations, the "subtitles" that "fuck up the possibilities of truth."

Notes

Sincere thanks to Mara Amster, Betsy Huang, Jim Longenbach, and Anne Zanzucchi for feedback, encouragement, etc.

1. William Blake, *The Portable Blake,* ed. Alfred Kazin (New York: Penguin, 1978), 125.

2. Thylias Moss, *Small Congregations: New and Selected Poems* (Hopewell, N.J.: Ecco Press, 1993), 55.

3. Moss 57.

4. bell hooks, *Black Looks: Race and Representation* (Boston: South End Press, 1992), 178.

5. Henry Louis Gates Jr., *Figures in Black: Words, Signs and the "Racial" Self* (New York and Oxford: Oxford University Press, 1987), 49, 236, 238.

6. Sean Thomas Dougherty, "Interview: Thylias Moss," *Onthebus* 4, no. 5 (1992): 298.

7. James Baldwin, *The Fire Next Time* (New York: Dell, 1962), 46.

8. Countee Cullen, *On These I Stand: An Anthology of the Best Poems of Countee Cullen* (New York and London: Harper and Brothers, 1947), 28.

9. Alan R. Shucard, *Countee Cullen* (Boston: Twayne, 1984), 35.

10. Cullen 28.

11. Baldwin 67.

12. Ralph Ellison, *The Collected Essays of Ralph Ellison,* ed. John F. Callahan (New York: Modern Library, 1995), 100.

13. Moss 85.

14. Ibid. 86.

15. Zora Neale Hurston, *The Sanctified Church* (Berkeley, Calif.: Turtle Island Press, 1981), 56.

16. Moss 40.

17. Amiri Baraka, *Transbluesency: Selected Poems, 1961–1995* (New York: Marsilio, 1995), 97.

18. Gwendolyn Brooks, *Selected Poems* (New York: Harper Perennial, 1963), 8.

19. Moss 121.

20. Ibid. 25.

21. Ibid. 25–26.

22. Percy Bysshe Shelley, "A Defense of Poetry," *Critical Theory Since Plato,* ed. Hazard Adams (Orlando: Harcourt, Brace, Jovanich, 1992), 524.

23. Moss 26.

24. Henry Giroux, *Theory and Resistance in Education* (South Hadley, Mass.: Bergin and Garvey, 1983), 103.

25. Moss 81.

26. Ibid. 81.

27. Ibid. 23.

28. Ibid. 23.

29. Ibid. 24.

30. Ibid. 24.

31. Ibid., back cover blurb.

32. Ibid. 116.

33. Ibid. 122.

34. Gerald Vizenor, *Manifest Manners: Postindian Warriors of Survivance* (Hanover, N.H.: Wesleyan University Press, 1994), 14, 15.

35. Moss 145.

36. Ibid. 104.

37. Ibid. 63.

38. Hooks 4.

39. Ibid. 128.

40. Blake 111.

41. Dougherty 298.

42. Cornel West, "Twilight Strivings in a Twilight Civilization," *The Future of the Race,* by Cornel West and Henry Louis Gates Jr. (New York: Knopf, 1996), 58.

"Stop Making Sense"

Trickster Variations in the Fiction of Louise Erdrich

CLAUDIA GUTWIRTH

"*I* never really done much with my life, I suppose. I never had a television."[1] In these flat, rather oddly juxtaposed sentences, Lipsha Morrissey, the narrator of the title chapter of Louise Erdrich's first novel, *Love Medicine* (1984), and a key figure in her fourth, *The Bingo Palace* (1994), challenges the conventional notion that television is at best incompatible with—at worst adversarial to—accomplishment.[2] The oblique angle of the challenge and the relative irrelevance of the convention provide an immediate clue as to Lipsha's role in these texts. A polytropic figure, Lipsha provides Erdrich with the means to play on our notions about the trickster. His characterization, in turn, invites us to examine issues that intersect with what might be called a trickster problematic.

Lipsha is a member of the contemporary generation of two Chippewa (Ojibway) families, whose intertwined history is detailed, from a variety of viewpoints, in Erdrich's *Love Medicine, Tracks* (1988), and *The Bingo Palace*.[3] Together, these novels comprise the saga of four generations of the Kashpaw and Nanapush/Pillager clans.[4] Central to a full appreciation of these stories, and of Lipsha himself, is an awareness of the central role of Nanabush, or Nanabozho, in traditional Chippewa oral narratives. Lack of such knowledge doesn't diminish Erdrich's work, which is resonant enough to stand on its own (as its popularity attests) but a familiarity with Nanabozho illuminates the novels' connection to a tribal context and their interconnections with one another.

In traditional Chippewa stories, the figure of Nanabozho was an emissary of Kitche Manitou, the Great Spirit.[5] A teacher, helper, and healer, but also a buffoon, Nanabozho possessed the ability to transform himself. As we learn from ethnographer Basil Johnston, author of *Ojibway Heritage,* a standard text of Chippewa history, and of the *Ojibway Language Lexicon,* which Erdrich cites as the source for the Chippewa terms in *Tracks,* Nanabozho, "at will and need . . . could become a corporeal being of almost any species."[6] He is a paradoxical figure:

> On the one hand, he was a supernatural being possessing supernatural powers; on the other . . . he was the son of a mortal woman subject to the need to learn . . . [he] was essentially an incorporeal being . . . Though transformation seemed complete in a physical mode, it was never complete in the incorporeal sense. It was this aspect that made Nanabush a human, most unlike an incorporeal being.[7]

According to Johnston's account of oral descriptions of Nanabozho, he possessed the human qualities of "courage, generosity, [and] resourcefulness" along with the "human limitations of ineptitude, indecisiveness, inconstancy, [and] cunning."[8]

Alternately wise and foolish, Erdrich's Lipsha is the son of outlaw-hero Gerry Nanapush, and grandson of Lulu Nanapush. Lulu is possessed of healing powers. Lipsha, too, is depicted as a healer of sorts (he has inherited "the touch" from Lulu), but one who bungles his most important "cure": an attempt to turn his adoptive grandfather, Nector Kashpaw, away from his marital infidelities. When Lipsha decides to feed his grandfather turkey hearts (those of the more appropriate geese, who mate for life, having proven difficult to obtain), the wheels of disaster are set in motion, resulting in the choking death of Grandpa Nector. Although he acknowledges his adoptive grandmother's role in the tragedy, Lipsha blames himself for his mishandling of the "love medicine," which, he tells us, is "something of an old Chippewa specialty" but "not for the layman to handle. . . . Before you get one, even, you should go through one hell of a lot of mental condensation" (*LM* 241).

The significance of the trope of "mental condensation" will shortly become evident. But first, we should note that having—and bungling—the powers of a healer, along with his Nanapush lineage, gives Lipsha the credentials of what anthropologists—and, more recently, literary scholars—have conventionally termed the Chippewa trickster figure.[9] Paul Radin, in his seminal anthology, *The Trickster: A Study in American Indian Mythology,* points out that although the etymology of the Winnebago word *wakdjunkaga* (which has been translated as "the tricky one") is unknown, the word has been associated with terms for other such figures in the literatures of several Native American tribes.[10] Depending on the tribe, the figure called trickster appears variously as coyote, Old

Man, raven, bear, and wolf, and in other guises. The story-cycles featuring these figures have many elements in common. Like Lipsha's story of the "love medicine," many of them are cautionary tales. In traditional Chippewa narratives, the trickster, Nanabozho, is figured as a hare.

To call Nanabozho a trickster is perhaps inevitable but is also problematic. The concept of the trickster is, appropriately, tricky: in different times and places, this figure evinces heroic and even godlike qualities, yet is also a deceiver, a bungler, and a source of comedy. Anthropologist Barbara Babcock has observed that "the distinctive feature of trickster . . . may well be [the] ability to confound classification." [11] This ability shows up the academic preoccupation with classification, forcing those of us who confront trickster to confront and contend with our own practices of categorization as well. [12] Trickster's ability to confound established or conventional cultural categories such as hero, fool, rogue—even human and animal, male and female—means that the trickster and his literary manifestations can cause us to question the validity of a perspective that places these categories in opposition. [13] Insofar as trickster "represents a plurality that cannot be classified in conventional terms," [14] s/he is also an apt figure for the cross-cultural hybridity of many Native Americans.

What some researchers have seen as tricksters' resistance to definition stems from the multiplicity of behaviors and characteristics ascribed to them in various times and places. [15] The ability to resist being defined by others is an important means of reserving one's power in the world, particularly in a situation in which naming can become a means to manipulation or erasure. In *Tracks*, a novel of the Turtle Mountain Chippewas' struggle for survival in the 1900s, the narrator, who identifies himself simply as Nanapush, reserves the right to use his name, "an important one" (32), only in special circumstances. He tells Lulu, his spiritual granddaughter and a central character in *Love Medicine* as well, "Nanapush is a name that loses power every time that it is written and stored in a government file. That is why I only gave it out once in all those years" (32). Nanapush, the sole member of his clan to survive the tuberculosis epidemic that decimates the tribe in 1912, resists definition by the white authorities who come to negotiate with the remaining members of the tribe for their land. The only time he speaks his name to an official record keeper is on the occasion of Lulu's baptism, in response to the priest's question "The father's name?" (61). Even in this circumstance, however, he remains undefined, for the priest does not know that the name Nanapush has given is his own.

Nanapush tells Lulu about the origins of his name:

> My father said, "Nanapush. That's what you'll be called. Because it's got to do with trickery and living in the bush. Because it's got to do with something a girl can't resist. The first Nanapush stole fire. You will steal hearts." (33)

As Nanapush "speaks" his name and its story to Lulu, the text of *Tracks* articulates it as well, and in the process contradicts his assertion that he "only gave it out once" (32). For here it is, inscribed in the text, given out to us. *Tracks*—whose very title connotes inscription—manifests an ambivalence toward writing, a necessary evil in the struggle against white domination and the loss of collective memory resulting from the death of tribal peoples. Later in the novel, Nanapush laments the tribe's inevitable collusion with textuality:

> I began to see what we were becoming . . . a tribe of file cabinets and triplicates, a tribe of single-space documents . . . A tribe of pressed trees. A tribe of chicken-scratch that can be scattered by a wind, diminished to ashes by one struck match. (225)

This passage alludes to the necessity of the tribe's participation in the textual practices of white culture in order for it to maintain a semblance of autonomy and to document its claims to ancestral lands. But that very writing itself seems counter to an identity that derives in part from an oral heritage. The archival impulse is Western. Once a version of a story or other oral performance is transcribed, it is fixed, fossilized. The latter part of Nanapush's description, however, foregrounds the ephemerality of writing—the trick we play on ourselves when we assume that the past can be preserved in text, and that text itself is preservable. By extension, this passage also exposes the fantasy aspect of assuming that access to the past—through textual traces or otherwise—is possible.[16]

While reluctantly conceding the necessity of the written, Nanapush maintains allegiance to the oral tradition. He tells us that he survived the sickness that claimed his family by talking: "I saved myself by starting a story . . . Death could not get a word in edgewise, grew discouraged, and traveled on" (46). On another significant occasion, he saves Lulu, whose feet have frozen, partly by talking, his words becoming first "the string between [them]" and then a healing water: "I talked on and on until you lost yourself inside the flow of it, until you entered the swell and ebb and did not sink but were sustained" (167). Here we see Nanapush as healer, which ties him to pan-tribal tradition.[17] Yet Nanapush also feels the burden of bearing tribal memory. A sole survivor, he has "had to squeeze so many stories in the corners of my brain. They're all attached, and once I start there is no end to telling because they're hooked from one side to the other, mouth to tail" (46). Unable to pass on these stories to his children, he tells them, through the medium of the novel, to anyone who will listen.

In *Tracks*, Nanapush alternates with one other narrator in telling the story of Fleur Pillager, his spiritual daughter and Lulu's mother. Fleur, whose bear tracks are evidence of a transformative power that links her with the Chippewa trickster figure, is also connected to the spirits and animals of the surrounding environment.[18] One of only two survivors, along with her cousin Moses, of the epidemic that destroys the Pillager clan along with that of Nanapush, Fleur has a special relationship to the manitous, those "other-than-human-persons" who in varying degrees people the landscape of all three novels.[19] She is described repeatedly, from a variety of perspectives, as being in communication with Misshepeshu, whom Nanapush calls variously "the lake monster" (8), "the lake man" (35), "the water thing" (175).[20] Continually associated with bearlike qualities, Fleur lives in a cabin at the far end of Matchimanito lake, a place that has explicit connections with Anishinabe tradition.[21]

Unable to accept that her own spiritual power is not stronger than the force of the white man's laws, Fleur loses her land to loggers at the end of *Tracks*. This loss occurs largely through Fleur's and Nanapush's betrayal by Margaret and Nector Kashpaw. With only enough money to cover the white man's taxes on either Kashpaw or Pillager land, Nector and Margaret opt to save the former, for it is potentially more valuable in monetary terms. Nanapush, who is more fully alive to the spiritual value of land, "the only thing that lasts life to life" (33), comments that "no one thought to ask for a receipt" of this transaction, which goes undiscovered until the spring brings "the shouts of men, faint thump of steel axes" (191, 206).

The betrayal of Pillager/Nanapush by the Kashpaws sets up the motif of intrafamilial conflict that is carried through in *The Bingo Palace*, which depicts Lipsha's rivalry with Lyman Lamartine, a grandson of Fleur and son of Lulu.[22] The shift in the balance of power from Nanapush/Pillager to Kashpaw is signified by Lyman's plans to build a casino on Fleur's land—the same land she loses at the end of *Tracks,* but later regains, appropriately, through trickery and expert card-playing, in an episode detailed in *The Bingo Palace.*[23] Much of the latter is narrated by Lipsha, Fleur's great-grandson, whose exploits are often a source of comedy.

Narratives that appear in the storytelling traditions of several Native American tribes feature an "unpromising hero," who is generally

> an orphan raised by an old woman, sometimes his grandmother. Although it eventually becomes apparent that he is the son of a powerful spirit, he demonstrates no power at the beginning and is considered a person without significance. Having been given certain tools by an old woman the unpromising hero often embarks upon a journey that represents a series of trials. After successfully overcoming these trials, he returns to his people as a culture hero.[24]

This passage seems virtually to describe Lipsha, abandoned by his mother—who later dies, leaving him an orphan—and raised by his grandmother Marie, a detail that emphasizes his connection to folkloric tradition. *Love Medicine* details some of the seriocomic trials that Lipsha undergoes—his bungling of "the touch," his wrongheaded decision to join the army, and finally his successful assistance to his father, Gerry Nanapush, in the latter's escape from white prison authorities. *The Bingo Palace* picks up Lipsha's story where the earlier text leaves off.

Perpetually in search of a love medicine—this time one that will gain him the undivided attentions of Shawnee Ray Toose, a woman he describes as the tribe's "hope of a future" (13, 19) and the focus of his rivalry with Lyman—Lipsha makes a reluctant pilgrimage to his great-grandmother Fleur's, in a chapter of *The Bingo Palace* at the exact center of the novel. Here the tone is serious. The walls of Fleur's cabin, Lipsha discovers, are inscribed with writing; stacks of papers reach to its ceiling and even the tablecloth is "covered with pen lines" (135). This suggests that Fleur herself has become an archivist, but the significance of this transformation is never spelled out. Silence, in this world, is just as important as talking, and tracklessness can be an asset, helping one to resist an enemy's pursuit.[25] Furthermore, Lipsha's discovery of the writing on Fleur's walls gives us a clue as to how to read the text. Lipsha is able to "pick out familiar patterns" and aware that "I am reading a set of words, a sentence" but for him this sentence is merely "something that loops toward the window, which makes no sense to me and which I can't understand" (135). While this signifies the difficulty of passing on a heritage to those whose assimilation by the dominant culture, however partial, may prevent understanding of tribal history, it also suggests that understanding is reductive, and may therefore be beside the point. In fact, we can read this passage, and by extension the novel as a whole, as a critique of the need to understand, to interpret or make sense of things—that is, to establish a definitive or univocal meaning.

The Bingo Palace concerns Lipsha's struggles to understand not only the signifying practices of writing, specifically Fleur's, but also the qualities of another perplexing medium of signification: money. Lipsha begins by playing bingo in pursuit of a coveted object, a front-wheel drive van with "every option you can believe" and room enough to be "a starter home, a portable den" (63) (as such, an appropriate vehicle for the always-moving coyote/bear/Nanabozho).[26] Lipsha tells us "I don't know it right away, but [the van] is the prize that will change the order of my life" (62).[27] The van, whose winning is guided by the magical intercession of Lipsha's late mother, June Kashpaw, is ultimately Lipsha's vehicle for the rescue of his father, Gerry Nanapush, once again, as in *Love Medicine,* on the lam after an escape from prison. It thus serves as a unifier of the family. In pursuit of this prize, Lipsha comes to terms with his mother's attempt to drown him as an infant, and discovers his personal power.

Soon after he begins to covet the van, however, Lipsha finds himself playing bingo for cash, and he senses that something important has been lost in the process. While Lipsha's pursuit of the van is unequivocal, his thoughts about the pursuit of money are ambivalent. Unlike his Uncle Lyman, who, being "half Kashpaw" through his father, Nector, has "money sense" (*LM* 281), Lipsha sees money at first as "insulation"—a means to keep away want, rather than an end in itself (*BP* 95). Yet he also sees it as a means to obtain more money, for he realizes that "insulation buys insulation" (*BP* 95). Just as, in Lacanian discourse, the signifier refers only to other signifiers, forever barred from the signified, money ultimately refers only to itself, even more than to what it can buy. It is to this aspect of money that Lipsha maintains an attitude of skepticism, aware of its ambiguous value.

One of Lipsha's strengths is that "money doesn't make any sense" to him (*BP* 100). The Kashpaws' appreciation of money, on the other hand—along with money's tendency to appreciate in Kashpaw hands—is perhaps overdetermined by their family name. Whereas Lipsha sees money as "dead stuff," to his Uncle Lyman it is "alive," something that grows, "reproduces" (101). When Lipsha makes a joke in this context about "the facts of life" we learn that Lyman's stance toward money signifies trouble, for "Lyman has no humor about this" (101). Yet, while listening to Lyman's plans for accumulating even more capital than he has already obtained from his bingo palace, Lipsha detects "a secret in his face": Lyman "doesn't believe that what he is doing is completely as simple as making money" (103).

Lyman, the businessman and tribal politician who schemes to develop Fleur's—and the tribe's—sacred ground into a casino of the type now flourishing on many Indian reservations throughout the United States, falls under the spell of blackjack when he goes to Vegas for an Indian Gaming Conference, and he ends up blowing not only his winnings, accumulated in his first six hours at the tables, but also the "loan from the Bureau of Indian Affairs that had just come in to finance the tribal gaming project" (*BP* 93). Eventually, he hocks his late father's peace pipe, an item of special significance, and gambles away that money too. Lyman's susceptibility to the fascination of gambling illustrates the evils of an activity about which the novel as a whole equivocates. If even the clear-headed Lyman, who never comes under the spell of the bingo whereby he earns much of his money, can succumb to the casino, where the sun never shines but it is perpetually day, how damaging will be the place he plans for the reservation, not only to the tribe's history but also to its future? Is economic gain worth cultural loss? Ironically, it is Lipsha, following the comic trials and tribulations of his dual quests for a love medicine and a vision, who provides the beginnings of an answer, when he finally attains "a little vision" in the chapter of the same name:

> It's not completely one way or another, traditional against the bingo. You have to stay alive to keep your tradition alive and working. (*BP* 221)

He questions this just a few lines later:

> I can't help but wonder, now that I know the high and the low of bingo life, if we're going in the wrong direction, arms flung wide, too eager. The money life has got no substance, there's nothing left when the day is done but a pack

of receipts. Money gets money, but little else, nothing sensible to look at or touch. (221)

Lipsha concludes, however, with a comment that reveals his awareness that Fleur may not be, after all, a passive witness to the transformation of her land: "I can't help think that Fleur Pillager has made the best of what gives here by tapping Lyman for the long term" (221). If Lipsha is right, Fleur herself has an active role in Lyman's eventual success.

Unlike Lipsha, who during his vision quest achieves a glimpse of what the revenue from gambling may cost the tribe in spiritual terms, Lyman rationalizes that

> Gambling fit into the old traditions, chance was kind of an old-time thing . . . Money was the key to assimilating, so Indians were taught. Why not make a money business out of money itself? (LM 326–27)

Lyman is partly right. Games of chance have a place not only in today's rush to cash in on the opportunities for profit afforded by casinos but also in Chippewa tradition. The Chippewa origin myth celebrates Nanabozho's successful defeat, through trickery, of "the great gambler, with whom he battles over the destiny of his people," as Jeanne Rosier Smith reminds us in her recent book, *Writing Tricksters* (79). In Lipsha's family the ability to play poker—as well as to cheat by crimping cards—is well established, a heritage that is passed from Fleur to Lulu, from Lulu to Gerry, and from Gerry to Lipsha himself. What Lyman fails to realize is the difference between "people in a powwow tent, playing at the hand games, an old-time guessing event . . . hands and songs and spells . . . conjuring of the bones" and a modern casino where "Chippewas . . . take money from retired white people" (LM 326–27). He seems never to consider the potential damage to tribal identity that may result from a "future based on greed and luck" (328).[28] One of the dilemmas posed by casino gambling and highlighted here is that those involved play for money, and not for the sake of play itself.

Although *The Bingo Palace* doesn't fully endorse Lyman's perspective—it continually weighs the casino's potential for cultural damage against the possibility of economic benefit to the tribe—the novel seems finally to acknowledge the necessity of revenue, just as Nanapush ultimately concedes the necessity of his people's becoming a "tribe of pressed trees" and "chicken-scratch" (T 225). Through Lipsha's "little vision," Erdrich seems to be saying that the gambling enterprise is a necessary risk, one whose long-term gains may offset its short-term losses: by securing economic survival for the tribe, the casino offers the possibility of its cultural continuance. The tribe will do so by using "the luck that temporary loopholes in the law bring to Indians for higher causes, steady advances" (BP 221).

In the Native American context, survival and writing may themselves be seen as evidence of tricksterism. Following centuries of decimation, living to tell the tale of a family's heritage takes skill, cunning, and luck, all qualities attributed to folkloric tricksters at one time or another. Hermes, the ancient Greek trickster, was a messenger; all storytellers, insofar as they are the bearers of communications, are thus in some sense tricksters. Furthermore, the adaptation from an oral tradition to a written one indicates a transformative skill of the kind ascribed to tricksters. Louise Erdrich, a writer who is part Chippewa, part Cree, part of the American mainstream but close to her Native heritage, may be seen as such a figure: a messenger between the worlds of Chippewa tradition and the dominant culture.

There is a long history of debate over whether the term "trickster" is appropriate in the Native American context. Much writing on trickster manifestations in the literatures of Native America—and under "literatures" I include those narratives traditionally classified as mythology and folklore—seems haunted by the fact that in these literatures there is often a figure who possesses the dual attributes of trickster and culture hero. Because such figures are depicted as participating in the creation of the world, as having the capacity for self-transformation and rebirth, and as demonstrating greedy, instinctual, transgressive and often rapacious appetites, depending on the tale, chant, song, or ritual at hand, we find a concern among researchers to delineate in these narratives a process of evolution/devolution from trickster to culture hero (or even savior) and back.[29] Perhaps most famously, Karl Kerényi, in an essay included in Radin's book, is concerned to differentiate the Winnebago trickster from his famous cousin in Greek mythology.[30] He disqualifies the Native American trickster from divine status on the grounds that he is merely a literary hero—Kerenyi calls him "the creator of a literature"—while a god, such as Hermes, is "the creator of a world."[31] (Kerenyi's failure to recognize literature's role in the creation of the world is perhaps material for another paper.) Other researchers of Native American trickster tales have been troubled by their blending of animal attributes along with human and godlike qualities in one figure, who is by turns cunning, foolish, and heroic.

On a more general level, there have been objections to the concept of the trickster itself, on the grounds either that it is too broad to be useful for purposes of classification, or that its use implies a cross-cultural approach that may tend to occlude constitutive differences among diverse peoples, in the process confirming the hegemony of the dominant culture.

Erdrich's Nanapush fiction engages explicitly and implicitly with each of these issues. Though her use of the Nanapush name points to a strictly Chippewa heritage, Erdrich's writing figures her characters in ways that link them with a pan-tribal Native American tradition, and beyond. Lipsha's great-grandmother, Fleur, laughs a "bear laugh" and, as we have seen, leaves bear tracks behind her when she walks in the snow (*BP* 273–74); Lipsha, according to one narrator, "shoots across the road like a coyote" (*BP* 7) and elsewhere expresses sympathy for the "Wiley Coyote" [sic] of the Road Runner cartoons (*LM* 344). His father Gerry's ability to wiggle out of the stickiest of situations figures him as a hare: in one of his many escapes from the police he is shown "squeezing himself unbelievably through the [window] frame like a fat rabbit disappearing down a hole" (*LM* 209).

In addition, details of Erdrich's characterizations of the various members of the Nanapush clan suggest a purposeful alignment of these tricksterlike figures with those of Greek and Judeo-Christian mythology. Lipsha's maternal grandfather is alternately called "Old Man Pillager" and Moses. Like the Hermes of Greek mythology, who reverses the tracks of the cattle he has stolen from Apollo and walks backwards to avoid the god's detection, this Moses walks backwards from boyhood on, as a result of his mother's efforts to protect him from vengeful spirits (*LM* 74–75).[32] As Hermes charms and then slays the many-eyed Argus, so Fleur causes the tornado that destroys the off-reservation town of Argus, an event that is recalled in *Tracks*.[33] Pauline Puyat, the conarrator of that novel, is herself an Argus-like figure: a witness to the action who feels responsible for not saving the young Fleur from a gang rape, she spends her life conjuring up a series of self-inflicted trials as penance for standing by at the scene, and later locking the rapists in a meat freezer as the tornado hits.[34] Gerry's ability to escape detection parallels that of

Hermes: both leave undetectable tracks at key moments in their respective narratives.[35]

These sorts of details indicate Erdrich's engagement with what I have called a trickster problematic.[36] Her characters, like most of us, do not fit into neat categories; most are of mixed—Indian and European—descent. Erdrich's blending of literary traditions in the characterization of these figures is perfect for trickster, who in the most general sense is a liminal figure, a border crosser who, in Radin's words, "possesses no well-defined and fixed form."[37] The use of the name Nanapush allows Erdrich to play in her novels with the debate among anthropologists over whether or not it is correct to call such figures as coyote and bear in Native American tales "tricksters." The term "Nanapush" becomes, in Erdrich's work, a kind of intertextual marker for a figure who may, in fact, be more complex—or, as is equally possible, simpler—than his cousins in other literary traditions, from ancient Greece to North America and elsewhere.

Lipsha himself is attuned to Greek parallels in the story of his rivalry with his half-uncle Lyman for the affections of Shawnee Ray. "Reading," he tells us

> is my number-one hobby, and I have browsed a few of the plays of the old-time Greeks. If you read about a thing like Lyman and me happening in those days, one of us would surely have to die. But us Indians, we're so used to inner plot twists that we just laugh. (*BP* 17)

In its broadest sense, the term "trickster" functions as an index to the comic, a trope of laughter and play.[38] Knowledge of trickster texts and contexts foregrounds the comic elements of Erdrich's novels, in which humor and tragedy are intertwined. It also helps us to come to terms with Lipsha, whose contradictory qualities and malapropian language might otherwise lead us to judge him as inconsistent and therefore to dismiss his point of view as unreliable or his characterization as flawed. Knowing about "tricky Nanabozho" (*LM* 236) we know that Erdrich is not only making fun of Lipsha and having fun with him but also employing him as narrator in a playfully serious fashion.

A sense of fun informs Lipsha's use of language in *Love Medicine*. Lipsha's numerous verbal retropings therein include a description of his brother's hotheaded episodes as "his frequent leaves of sense" (*LM* 342) and his expression of perplexity, "I was in a laundry then" (*LM* 234), where laundry is a substitution for quandary.[39] Such wordplay is also prominent in *The Bingo Palace*. While fasting during the vision quest that is central to that novel's action, Lipsha's strongest visions are, appropriately, of fast food—specifically, hot dogs and ice cream from the Dairy Queen. Aware that these visions aren't "the real thing" Lipsha comes think of the whole process as "my getting nowhere fast" (*BP* 200). Ultimately, however, he succeeds, envisioning the imminent transformation of his family's ancestral land into the casino Lyman is planning:

> Where Fleur's cabin stands, a parking lot will be rolled out of asphalt. Over Pillager grave markers . . . blackjack tables. Where the trees that shelter brown birds rise, bright banks of slot machines. Out upon the lake that the lion man inhabits, where Pillagers drowned and lived . . . the great gaming room will face with picture windows. (219)

Disturbed by the image of blackjack tables and slot machines where the family graves once stood, Lipsha asks the skunk-deity who brings the vision to "change the channel"—as if having a vision were akin to watching television (which may, after all, be our modern equivalent of second sight). Of course, he has never had a television, which is probably just as well.[40]

Lipsha's verbal playfulness returns us to the trope of "mental condensation," a process that, as we saw earlier, he recommends to anyone who might be planning to fool with a love cure (*LM* 241). We might at first be tempted to read this phrase as simply another of Lipsha's mangled idioms, with "condensation" a mistaken substitute for concentration. Psychoanalytic theory, however, provides us with another way of reading Lipsha. In psychoanalytic discourse, condensation is an essential aspect of the functioning of the unconscious. It is also a way of describing the metaphorical operation of language.[41] As the trickster figure is problematic in its ubiquitous variety, the figure "trickster" is emblematic of language. With its multiple, often contradictory meanings, the term "trickster" is a trope of condensation—that is, a metaphor for metaphor, a figure for language itself. Metaphor is derived from the Greek word meaning to cross over, to carry across, activities that characterize tricksters as various as Hermes and coyote.[42]

As trickster frustrates our passion for classification, traversing the always already artificial boundaries between categories, Lipsha himself calls into question our mania for making sense. "You've got to listen to me," he tells his beloved Shawnee Ray, "even though I am making no sense. In fact, because I am making no sense, you should listen harder" (*BP* 112). We are stuck with language, which aspires to definition, to the setting of borders, even as it evokes the indefinability of a phenomenon such as trickster. As Lipsha suggests, the only remedy is to make ourselves receptive to things that don't make sense: the playful, the multiple, the incoherent. The presence of trickster reminds us to stop making sense, both as a way to avoid the violence that the imposition meaning often entails, and as a means of embracing language's inherent capacity for overdetermination.

Lipsha's significance, his status as a culture hero of sorts, is signaled in the final pages of *The Bingo Palace*. The day after the blizzard that intervenes during Lipsha's rescue of his father, Fleur leaves her cabin for the last time, "thinking of the boy out there. Annoyed, she took his place" (272). The latter detail suggests that Fleur has reversed her earlier practice of sending others to die in her stead, saving Lipsha, whom we have just seen freezing, possibly to death, in a stuck car. The text forestalls our easy certainty, however, for the suggestion is elliptical and easy to miss.

Upon Fleur's departure, we learn that

> She didn't take the written walls, she didn't take the storehouse facts. She didn't take the tangled scribe of her table or the headboard, the walls, the obscured and veiny writing on the tamped logs and her bed . . . No, all of the writing, the tracked-up old cabin, she left for the rest of us to find. (272)

The narrative here merges the multiple perspectives of the two earlier novels into a communal one, thus lifting the burden of stories from the individual and shifting it to the community, renewed in numbers since the time of *Tracks*. There is a suggestion in this passage that the three novels themselves may be the result of Fleur's inscribed legacy, although she herself never speaks directly in these texts.

Like the coyote who ambles along, eliciting our laughter without asking for our analysis, Erdrich invites us to resist the closure that the end of a text seems to bring, in favor of an unending stream of narrative. As the communal voice says of Fleur at the end of *The Bingo Palace*:

> She doesn't tap our panes of glass or leave her claw marks on eaves and doors. She only coughs, low, to make her presence known. You have heard the bear

laugh—that is the chuffing noise we hear and it is unmistakable. Yet no matter how we strain to decipher the sound it never quite makes sense, never relieves our certainty or our suspicion that there is more to be told, more than we know, more than can be caught in the sieve of our thinking. (274)

Notes

1. Louise Erdrich, *Love Medicine* (New York: Harper Collins, 1993), 230.

2. I use the date of the first edition of *Love Medicine* here, to show its original chronological relationship to Erdrich's other texts. However, all page references are to the expanded edition of 1993. Where abbreviations are necessary, *Love Medicine* will be cited as *LM, Tracks* (New York: Henry Holt and Company, 1988) as *T,* and *The Bingo Palace* (New York: HarperPerennial, 1995) as *BP.*

3. "Chippewa," a variant spelling of Ochipwe (in turn a variant of Ojibwe) is white America's official name for the tribe. Anishnaabe/Anishinabe (pl. Anishnaabeg) is the older name that tribal peoples use. I have chosen to use the name Chippewa throughout, except when quoting or paraphrasing the work of researchers and critics who use one of the other names for the tribe. For information on names and orthography, see Theresa S. Smith, introduction to *The Island of the Anishnaabeg* (Moscow: University of Idaho Press, 1995), and Nancy J. Peterson, "History, Postmodernism and Louise Erdrich's *Tracks,*" *PMLA* 109 (Oct. 1994): 991n8.

4. These three texts are in fact part of a tetralogy that includes Erdrich's second novel, *The Beet Queen* (1986), which I have chosen not to treat in this paper.

5. This figure is also known by the various names Nanabushu, Manabosho, and Wenebojou, among others (cf. Smith, *Island*). Given the evolution of Ojibwe-Ochipwe-Chippewa, the sound-values of b/p seem similar, at least to non-Chippewa auditors of the Chippewa language.

6. Johnston, *Ojibway Heritage* (New York: Columbia University Press, 1976), 159.

7. Ibid. 160.

8. Ibid.

9. For recent literary studies of Erdrich's adaptation of the Chippewa trickster figure, see especially Jeanne Rosier Smith, *Writing Tricksters: Mythic Gambols in Ethnic American Literature* (Berkeley and Los Angeles: University of California Press, 1997), chap. 3; and Catherine M. Catt, "Ancient Myth in Modern America: The Trickster in the Fiction of Louise Erdrich," *Platte Valley Review* 19, no. 1 (Winter 1991): 71–81. For more general discussion of the Native American trickster, see Andrew Wiget, "His Life in His Tail: The Native American Trickster and the Literature of Possibility," *Redefining American Literary History,* ed. A. LaVonne Brown Ruoff and Jerry W. Ward Jr. (1990; rpt., New York: Mod-

ern Language Association, 1993), 83–96; Gerald Vizenor, ed., *Narrative Chance: Postmodern Discourse on Native American Indian Literatures* (Albuquerque: University of New Mexico Press, 1989); Brian Swann and Arnold Krupat, eds., *Recovering the Word: Essays on Native American Literature* (Berkeley and Los Angeles: University of California Press, 1987); and Jarold Ramsey, *Reading the Fire* (Lincoln: University of Nebraska Press, 1983).

10. This association is presumably based on the similar roles and behaviors of the figures in their respective narratives, rather than an etymological connection through or to trickery. Radin's discussion of terms in *The Trickster: A Study in American Indian Mythology* (New York: Schocken Books, 1972) is worth quoting at length, for he reminds us of the ways in which etymological distinctions can become blurred. He writes: "The Winnebago word for trickster is *wakdjunkaga*, which means *the tricky one.* The corresponding term for him in Ponca is *ishtinike*, in the kindred Osage, *itsike* and in Dakota-Sioux, *ikto-mi.* The meaning of the Ponca and Osage words is unknown, that of the Dakota is *spider.* Since all these three stems are clearly related etymologically, the question arises as to whether the Winnebago rendering, *the tricky one,* does not really mean simply *one-who-acts-like-Wakdjunkaga,* and is thus secondary. In no other Siouan language is the stem for *tricky* remotely like *wakdjunkaga.*" Radin 132, italics in original.

11. Barbara Babcock-Abrahams, "'A Tolerated Margin of Mess': The Trickster and His Tales Reconsidered," in Andrew Wiget, ed., *Critical Essays in Native American Literature* (Boston: G. K. Hall and Co., 1985), 167.

12. The term *trickster* as applied to Native American texts, whether transcribed oral narratives, songs and other ceremonial literature, or recent prose fiction, thus offers a problematic that illuminates critical approaches to these texts, perhaps to a greater degree than it does the texts themselves. How he or she handles the "trickster" is particularly revealing of a researcher's or critic's concerns, assumptions, and goals. There has been much recent commentary on the use of the trickster as a strategy of opposition or resistance to oppression. However, I have not been able to find a discussion of the origins of the use of the term "trickster" as a means of identifying certain figures or features of literary texts. The OED cites the appearance of the term as early as 1711 but does not comment on its application to literature. Presumably, the trickster figure began to be identified in literature in the late nineteenth century, when the practice of ethnic and racial categorization, and of anthropology, came into vogue.

13. As Arnold Krupat points out in the introduction to his *Ethnocriticism: Ethnography History Literature* (Berkeley and Los Angeles: University of California Press, 1992), in the zone of cross-cultural contact "oppositional sets like West/Rest, Us/Them, anthropological/biological, historical/mythical . . . often tend to break down" (15). He argues that "culture and cultural difference . . . like

racial or gender difference, is better conceptualized in dialogical rather than oppositional terms" (19).

14. Jay Cox, "Dangerous Definitions: Female Tricksters in Contemporary Native American Literature," *Wicazo-SA Review* 5, no. 2 (Fall 1989): 17.

15. In the introduction to their recent compilation, *Mythical Trickster Figures: Contours, Contexts, and Criticisms* (Tuscaloosa: University of Alabama Press, 1993), editors William J. Hynes and William G. Doty note a few: "an ambiguous and anomalous personality," the tendency to act as a "deceiver/trick-player," "shape-shifter," "situation-invertor," "messenger/imitator of the gods," and "sacred/lewd bricoleur" (34). They add that "anyone attempting to study tricksters faces significant methodological issues . . . at one extreme one finds colleagues trained in Jungian psychology talking about *the* trickster as a universal archetype . . . At the other extreme some anthropologists have called for the elimination of the term "trickster" altogether because it implies that a global approach to such a figure is possible" (4).

Hynes and Doty are careful to acknowledge their own cross-cultural comparative perspective (26), a perspective I believe Erdrich shares.

16. Peterson, who quotes this passage at greater length, comments that "Nanapush deconstructs the West's reverence for the written word as a stabilizer of meaning and tradition" (989). Such an activity is certainly appropriate to a trickster figure.

17. In "Life and Death in the Navajo Coyote Tales," for example, Barre Toelken discusses the healing powers of coyote, noting that "in a ritual, an allusion to a well-known line, or speech, or action of Coyote will summon forth the power of the entire tale and apply it to the healing process under way" (Swann and Krupat 390). The Navajo coyote figure bears a close resemblance to the Chippewa figure of the hare, and, as we will see, Erdrich alternates between them, making direct and indirect references to both.

18. Pauline Puyat, who alternates with Nanapush in narrating *Tracks,* remarks that "we followed the tracks of her bare feet and saw where they changed, where the claws sprang out, the pad broadened and pressed into the dirt" (12). This motif of transformation recurs several times in *The Bingo Palace.*

19. Smith, *Island* 7, quoting A. Irving Hallowell.

20. Smith, *Island,* discusses the manifestations of this being in both traditional and modern Ojibwe culture. She reports that "Mishebeshu [sic] means literally Great Lynx" and that among present-day Ojibwe in Ontario, the creature is "thought of as both a huge water cat and a serpent" (97, 99).

21. According to Smith, *Island,* Matchimanitou is a "generic term for a group of malevolent beings that includes Mishebeshu [sic]" (200). Erdrich's characterization of Misshepeshu differs, however. Pauline calls him "the gold-eyed creature in the lake, the spirit which [the people] said was neither good nor bad but

simply had an appetite" (*T* 139). Pauline describes Fleur as "the hinge" between Misshepeshu and the Chippewa people (*T* 139).

22. Untangling the familial relationships gets tricky here. Lyman is Nector's son by Lulu. According to *Tracks,* Nector's brother Eli may very well be Lulu's blood father; in any case, he accepts that role. Lipsha's father, Gerry Nanapush, is Lulu's son by Moses Pillager, Fleur's cousin. Lyman is therefore Lipsha's half-uncle as well as his rival.

23. The chapter of *The Bingo Palace* entitled "Fleur's Luck" depicts the latter episode, but its timing in relation to other events in that novel is unspecified. We can assume, however, that the card game occurs sometime after the events of *Tracks,* and sometime before the beginning of those that concern Lyman's plans for the development of Fleur's land.

24. Nora Barry and Mary Prescott, "The Triumph of the Brave: *Love Medicine*'s Holistic Vision," *Emerging Voices: Readings in the American Experience,* 2nd ed., ed. Janet Madden and Sara M. Blake (Fort Worth: Holt, Rinehart and Winston, 1993), 558–59.

25. At the end of the novel, Lipsha and Gerry elude capture by prison authorities when the snow covers their tire treads during a blizzard (*BP* 259).

26. Many tales depict these figures in transit, traveling, on the road and in between (cf. Wiget, "His Life in His Tail" 86).

27. As Wiget says of the trickster of several tribal narratives, Lipsha "fixes his mind on a single goal, but the means required to achieve this goal will effect a radical transformation of his personal identity" (ibid. 88).

28. Greed and luck are trickster attributes as well, but trickster tales generally demonstrate the negative consequences of the former and the ephemerality of the latter. See, for example, the Cheyenne story "The Eye-juggler," in which Coyote's covetousness for the power of distance vision results in a comic but ultimately instructive comeuppance, as retold by Barry Holstun Lopez in *Giving Birth to Thunder, Sleeping with His Daughter: Coyote Builds North America* (New York: Bard/Avon: 1990), 64–65.

29. Ron Messer, in "A Jungian Interpretation of the Relationship of Culture: Hero and Trickster Figure within Chippewa Mythology," *Studies in Religion-Sciences Religieuses: A Canadian Journal/Revue Candienne* 11, no. 3 (Summer 1982), 309–20, summarizes some of these approaches, which make recourse to theories of cultural development in an attempt to reconcile the presence of seemingly contradictory qualities, such as foolishness and heroism, in one being. Thus, for example, in the late nineteenth century Franz Boas "claimed that the trickster's heroic qualities emerged only as a consequence of the development of civilization" (309). Such a view of course rests on the assumption that the trickster's foolish/bungling/deceitful/instinctual qualities are "inferior traits" as compared with those of a hero who brings cultural artifacts to humankind. When

Jung calls the trickster "a psyche that has hardly left the animal level" (quoted in Messer 317, from an essay included in Radin's *Trickster*) this implies a hierarchical perspective on the relationship between man and other beings that is, as we will see, problematic. Working within a Jungian framework, Messer doesn't challenge these assumptions, but his overview illuminates their presence in trickster studies. From a more critical perspective, Barbara Babcock discusses the work of researchers who characterize trickster figures in terms of "degeneration" from "an originally high and noble deity" (164); she summarizes, too, the arguments of those who view the culture hero as having evolved from the trickster. Rather than concurring with either of the evolutionary/devolutionary perspectives, she concludes that "the ambivalence and the contradictions with which Trickster's tales abound . . . express the generative situation of ambivalence and contradictions that the very basis of culture engenders" (165–66).

30. More recently, Lewis Hyde has taken the opposite tack. In *Trickster Makes This World: Mischief, Myth, and Art* (New York: Farrar, Straus and Giroux, 1998) he aligns figures from several Native American storytelling traditions— Coyote, Hare, Raven, and others—with Hermes and other figures from a variety of cultural contexts, focusing on their analogous functions and characteristics.

31. Radin 190, 191.

32. "The Hymn to Hermes," *The Homeric Hymns,* trans. Charles Boer (Dallas: Spring Publications, 1993), 23.

33. For the classical reference, see *The Metamorphoses of Ovid,* trans. Mary M. Innes (London: Penguin, 1955), book 1, pp. 45–48.

34. Ultimately Pauline rejects her Chippewa heritage for the Catholic religion and accepts the name assigned to her by the Church when she becomes a nun. Thereafter she is Sister Leopolda, who reappears in the darkly comic "Saint Marie" section of *Love Medicine.*

35. Boer 42–43; *BP* 259.

36. Smith, *Writing Tricksters,* brings the concept of a "trickster aesthetic" to bear on her discussion of the narrative strategies and themes of a group of texts by ethnic American women writers. The notion of a trickster aesthetic seems to me to be related to that of a trickster problematic.

37. Radin xxiv.

38. As Kenneth Lincoln points out in his extended examination of the figure in *Indi'n Humor* (New York: Oxford University Press, 1993), trickster allows for the elaboration of the comic element in these texts. Lincoln's discussion of trickster figures in *Love Medicine* organizes them according to the comic typology delineated by Northrop Frye's *Anatomy of Criticism,* enabling an awareness of the novel's humor as well as its seriousness.

39. Laundry, here, becomes an apt metaphor for quandary, for Lipsha's pre-

dicament begins when he witnesses a moment of passion between Lulu and Nector that happens in the laundry room.

40. Lipsha would prefer to see, as he puts it, "some horses who split the sky with their hooves . . . a bear, an eagle" (*BP* 220). Here, Erdrich uses Lipsha to tweak our stereotypical images of Indians, who are so often romanticized for their supposed connections with a "natural" or "animal" realm.

41. For Freud's discussion of the role of condensation in the unconscious process of dreaming, see *The Interpretation of Dreams*, trans. and ed. James Strachey (New York: Avon, 1965), chap. 6, "The Dream-Work," 311–85. Jacques Lacan's famous articulation of the connections between language and the unconscious—"the unconscious is structured in the most radical way like a language"—appears in his essay, "The Direction of the Treatment and the Principles of Its Power," *Ecrits: A Selection*, trans. Alan Sheridan (New York: Norton, 1977), 234.

42. In a different context—that of the Freudian transference—Joel Fineman explores this aspect of the functioning of language and discusses the etymology of "'metaphor,' *metaphorein*" (105). His essay, "Pas de Calais" in *On Puns: The Foundation of Letters*, ed. Jonathan Culler (New York: Basil Blackwell, 1988, 100–114), helped to crystallize my reading of the figure of trickster in this way. The structure and function of metaphor in the production of meaning receives extended treatment in Lacan's "The Agency of the Letter in the Unconscious or Reason since Freud" (*Ecrits* 146–78), a text Fineman elucidates.

In a discussion of trickster behavior, Lewis Hyde notes that "Trickster is polytropic, which in its simplest sense means 'turning many ways' (though the Greek *polutropos* is also translated 'wily,' 'versatile,' and 'much-traveled')" (52). Lipsha's turns of phrase highlight the linguistic dimension of the concept of polytropism.

Turning Tricks

Trafficking in the Figure of the Latino

MARÍA DEGUZMÁN

Miguel Arteta's recent film *Star Maps* about a young Chicano who dreams of a film career and supposedly hawks Hollywood star maps on street corners but whose actual job is that of a polysexual trickturner in his father's family business, a prostitution ring, recalls the obscene side of the trickster figure—one that, of course, has long accompanied the figure of the trickster characteristically associated with, among other forms of outlawry, deceit and forbidden eroticism. Prostitution may be theorized as trade not only in sexual favors but moreover in roles presumably scripted "cleverly" enough on the part of the "trick" to engage a client's or "john's" desires and to satisfy the demands of fantasy by passing a performance off as "real." This trade between trick and john is generally one of unequal exchange on any number of interlocking levels, from socioeconomic to ethnic hierarchies. The trick attempts to negotiate representational power in a situation in which he or she is being commodified and consumed according to the john's desires, desires born out of social difference as well as inequality. The "trick" both as person and act within prostitution highlights an essential fact about tricksters, regardless of specific cultural context, and that is that they embody a set of survival tactics designed to hoodwink not so much an individual, though they may certainly do that, as the usually binaristic categories (mainstream vs. marginal, truth vs. lie, authentic vs. inauthentic) conscripted in the service of an exploitative system. The social phenomenon of prostitution reminds us that "tricksters" "figure" as ciphers of a *system*.

Beyond the deceit and the forbidden eroticism, the obscenity of the trickster figure is not that of the trickster as figure but of the trickster as a figure implicated in a system involving the eroticized exploitation of difference. The film *Star Maps* showcases what might be unsightly to mainstream U.S. consumption of the Latino as a flavorful figure bringing the genuine arts of living to Anglo-America—*namely, the dominant culture's john-like investment in an illusion of authenticity.* This essay examines the way in which an illusion of authenticity is played out in relation to the figure of the Latino in two novels by gay male writers, *City of Night* (1963) by the Scottish-Texas-*Mejicano*[1] John Rechy, and *Mala Noche* (Bad Night) (1977) by the self-proclaimed gringo Walt Curtis. The narratives of both novels depend on hustling, Rechy's in a guilt-ridden fashion, Curtis's full of Pier Pasolini tenderness for the Mexican migrant-worker boys whose company he seeks out in Portland, Oregon. Both novels revolve around an illusion of authenticity in relation to the figure of the Latino, but to seemingly diametrically opposed ends, each novel throwing the other in bolder relief like the flip side of the same coin. An exploration of *City of Night* and *Mala Noche* together reveals the two halves of an ironic picture of the Latino as trickster in the United States. The picture that emerges puts our own roles "on scene," turning the trick such that we see our own desires reflected in the dynamics of "ob-scene" trafficking in ethnicity, in the figure of the Latino.

About Rechy's novel, Chicano literature scholar Juan Bruce-Novoa argued in 1990: "What . . . distinguishes *City of Night* from the novels chosen for the [Chicano] canon is the lack of a narrow focus on ethnicity. Rechy does not convert ethnicity into a problem, nor even a necessary context."[2] As if following suit and more determinedly, articles published by Ricardo Ortiz (1993) and Rafael Pérez-Torres (1994) both claim that in *City of Night* and Rechy's other early fiction "ethnic questions are almost simultaneously invoked and covered up" and even "silenced."[3] Bruce-Novoa, Ortiz, and Pérez-Torres eagerly write about sexuality in the works of Rechy, "one of the most prolific of Chicano novelists,"[4] but are compelled to apologize for his reticence on matters of ethnicity. I contend, however, that such analyses have capitulated to simplistic binarisms—assertion/denial, uncovered/covered, articulation/silence. Beginning with the first sprinkled references to "El Paso," "Mexico" (13), and "Mexican" (14) to the last "I returned to El Paso" (379), ethnicity and its construction are central to *City of Night,* only it appears as both the visible and the invisible, the marked and the unmarked.[5]

City of Night is a confessional odyssey of the narrator as a restless young man who leaves his home in El Paso to seek his destiny in five U.S. cities: New York, Los Angeles, San Francisco, Chicago, and New

Orleans. In these cities, he works as a hustler around Times Square in New York City, Pershing Square and Hollywood Boulevard in Los Angeles, the Arcade on Market Street in San Francisco, the Park between Dearborn and Clark in Chicago, and the French Quarter in New Orleans. The chief trick in *City of Night* is the hustler-narrator's turning of his Latino identity into a *transparency*—like the glasscase in his mother's house:

> Even now in my mother's living room there is a glasscase which has been with us as long as I can remember. It is full of glass objects: figures of angels, Virgins of Guadalupe, dolls, tissuethin imitation flowers, swans; and a small glass, reverently covered with a rotting piece of silk, tied tightly with a faded-pink ribbon, containing some mysterious memento of one of my father's dead children . . . when I think of that glasscase, I think of my Mother . . . a ghost image that will haunt me—Always. (14)

The narrator as character represses, rather than expresses, his El Paso Latino identity when asked about his "origins" by his clients, whom he leaves musing: "[A]re you from L.A.? No? . . . —you look like you could be. . . . [A]re you really from the South? New Orleans maybe—" (25). Transparency is the mask by which he makes himself over into a mirror image of other people's sex fantasies (32) and role-plays a "dontgiveadamnyoungman," a "pleasehelpmesir," and a "perrenialhustler" (32) but not a Latin lover or some such ethnic stereotype. This transparency is double-edged, slippery. The narrator's refusal to mark himself in terms of skin color, accent, or some distinguishing physical signs for the reader or in terms of origins for his clients would seem merely to be a protective move. However, keeping his "true" identity to himself allows him to pass unmarked, to be whomever his "scores" want him to be and, furthermore, to be for his readers an everyman, a powerfully representative fellow.

On the narrative level, however, the narrator periodically reminds his readers that he longs to return to El Paso, to his Mexican mother "standing before the glasscase in the living-room" and to "the statue of Christ under that most beautiful sky in the world" (180). In other words, readers are permitted to consume the narrator as hustler who, while passing and making passes, has a Latino's southern heart, which in this case means a pure and vulnerable heart of glass for which the glasscase is, like writer Tennessee Williams's glass menagerie, a poignant symbol of home, mother, and innocence for a prodigal son. One may well begin to wonder if a metafictional contradiction does not lie at the heart of this showcasing of the narrator's El Paso "origins" to demonstrate how genuinely sensitive he is despite his admitted pretense of playing tough guy. Linguistically speaking, it is ironic that the name "El Paso"—meaning, in Spanish, "The Pass"—serves as a line drawn in the sand against all the undifferentiated passing. The repeated self-authenticating disclosures on the narrative level may begin to ring untrue through recurrent invocation, tinsel-townishly maudlin rather than moving. Furthermore, the disclosures may seem like a series of tropes of home, hearth, and sacredness threatening to become stereotypes—Latino-identity as figured by a shawled Mexican woman (24), a colorful Mexican blanket (50), the Virgins of Guadalupe (14), processions of people (*penitentes*) marching and chanting up the mountain in El Paso to the statue of Christ (315). The trick becomes how to keep the self-authenticating disclosures within the artful register of the melodramatic, rather than the meretricious register of the maudlin, and to take advantage of the stereotype to elicit emotion rather than bored indifference.

The maneuver that the novel makes to insure the desired weight and gravity of the narrator's self-revelations against the reader's possible cynicism is to turn *Latinidad,* tricksterlike, into the opposite of what it has meant until part 4, the last major section of *City of Night*—and that is home, colorful brightness, religious devotion, purity, and authenticity. The action of this last section is located in New Orleans during Mardi Gras. It is in New Orleans that non-Anglo ethnicity, including *Latinidad,* takes on the "dark" (here I borrow one of the most frequently used adjectives in this section of the novel) tones of promiscuity, paganism, and prodigality beginning with the mention of the "swarthy-skinned" gypsy woman (288) who at first tries to tell the narrator his fortune and then attempts to enlist him to work for her as a hustler and whose touch he resists as if it were a contamination. New Orleans during Mardi Gras, "this rotting Southern city" (285), is itself described as the repository of "blackness": "Like flotsam from the world's seas, the vagrants of America's blackcities washed into New Orleans" (309). The fact that "black," "blackness," "dark," and "darkness" function symbolically in an almost Manichean metaphysical fashion does not preclude their performance as both obvious and implicit markers of other ethnicities besides Anglo, as in the following phrase—"a *dark* cluster of young Negroes"

(335, italics mine). In a way not previously apparent in the rest of the novel, in part 4 of *City of Night,* darkness is racialized whilst allegorized as the expanding night of the soul in a tale of the journey from innocence to experience, the loss of innocence. Similarly, "Latin-ness" in relation to New Orleans is conveyed not in terms of glasscases full of figurines of pureness and light (flowers, angels) but as the masklike opacity of hispanicity as promiscuity and miscegenation—"bodies passing to other hands, hands to other bodies. . . . *Spanish gauchos, squaws, Arab princes!*" (335). This sequence—"Spanish gauchos," "squaws," and "Arab princes"—italicized in the text so that it leaps off the page like Mardi Gras revelers in the streets, hearkens back to none other than a famous nineteenth-century formula. This formula, incantationally linking Spanish, Indian, and Arabic (and/or Moorish), was the hallmark of a British, French, and, later, Anglo-American imperialist representational mode—Orientalism. During the nineteenth century, Orientalizations of Spain and all things Spanish, including, of course, Mexicans, South Americans, and, speaking in contemporary terms, "Latinos," characterized the novels of Anglo-American imperial identity.[6]

The effect of both the somewhat negative racializations of New Orleans and the conventionalized making of the city's famed *criollismo* or creolization is to make the tropes of *Latinidad,* of the narrator's Chicano "Mexican-ness," seem trustworthy and true, not trite. In comparison to such old stereotyping, the elements of the narrator's El Paso "origins"—the Mexican woman in a shawl, the colorful blanket, the Virgen de Guadalupe, the *penitentes*—gain luster, seem authentic and pure in all senses of that word, not tainted and trumped up. To use Rechy's own language, these elements, which might strike some readers as stereotypical, are thus ennobled, transmuted, through juxtaposition with potentially offensive associations, into "noble stereotypes."[7] Whereas in New Orleans even the memory of his Mexican mother's love for him comes back to him in murky, "darkened" figures—"the ferocious love of my mother from which I had fled leapt on my consciousness like a *dark* [italics mine] animal" (312), his Latino identity from El Paso, though troubled and tragic, stands out more than ever transparently enshrined, pure and purifying, like the glass figurines in the glasscase: "Occasionally I will remember during those teeming French Quarter days . . . things forgotten for long returning as phantom-memories . . . the processions in El Paso . . . the statue of Christ look[ing] down, pityingly" (315).

Ethnicity, rather than "being one element in the protagonist's background"—neither asserted, nor denied—as Juan Bruce-Novoa claims (135), plays a central part that is hard to grasp because it is not deployed in quite the expected manner. It appears as transparency, which authenticates while not *physically* marking the protagonist, thus allowing him to pass, some might say "in-authentically," as an "American" everyman, an effect vitally important for the narrator as protean hustler and to Rechy's allegorically epic bildungsroman aspiring to the status of the Great "American" Novel. Most surprising, however, is that although *City of Night* would seem consciously to eschew *authenticity*, trading the personal for the impersonal as in the alternation between chapters individuated by characters' first names as titles and those anonymously called "City of Night," the novel is heavily invested *in* authenticity or its illusion. The hustler-trickster is authenticated through the figures of "the Latino." Conversely, "the Latino" acquires authenticity against the vast panorama of inauthenticity.

In contrast to *City of Night,* Walt Curtis's *Mala Noche* hotly and unequivocally pursues authenticity in and through the Mexican migrant boys whom he loves. This chapbook novella attempts to separate the pursuit, the objects of this pursuit, and the expression of "authenticity" from any specter or shadow of its opposite, from inauthenticity in the form of trickery of any sort—deceit, deception, exploitation, betrayal, substitution, ambiguity, or anonymity. If in *City of Night* the hustler-narrator trans-lucifies (my term for his act of transparency) his Latino identity for his clients at the same time that he spotlights it for his readers, the street poet laureate of Portland and narrator of *Mala Noche* seeks to confirm that the presumed authenticity of the Latino boys Pepper and Johnny and the other *olividados* and *invisibles* he desires is more than an illusion in the sense of a trick or staged "effect." Though admitting that his love for the Latino boys may well have been unrequited and that they may simply be catering to his fantasy of love and friendship in exchange for a place to sleep, food, or money, he wants to believe that they *like* him and he views them as a source of *true* life, unspoiled by U.S. culture.[8] For instance, Raul, the boy with whom the narrator falls madly in love after Pepper and Johnny are deported back to Mexico, is described as "a miracle of freshness and otherculture naiveté" (93), that is, until the boy no longer reciprocates the narrator's affections. The narrator does not want to think of himself, or have others think of him, as merely the trick, the dupe of "tricky Mexicans." Thus, he declares emphatically, "They are not criminal, particularly manipulative, at all. Not sinister, not that sexual . . . Christ, they are just trying to survive in a racist society. Not speaking the language" (49). And yet the narrator clearly labors under the burden of feeling betrayed when the boys do not reciprocate his love and desire or do so for only a short time: "I'd heard a Mexican macho saying, 'If you fuck with the bull you get the horn!' . . . This image . . . became the subtitle for the blow-by-blow diary of my friendship with them" (26).

So as if to compensate for the "ambiguity" (to borrow Curtis's own term) about his sexual and emotional relationship to these boys and theirs to him (45, 47) he joins his predecessors—Jack Kerouac, Allen Ginsberg, William Burroughs, Malcolm Lowry, and Herman Melville, the latter among the Tahitians[9]—to equate the Mexican boys and Mexico itself with the very "chispa de la vida" (135)—the hot source of life itself, like "the sun and dirt" (156) and like "the milk and sperm" summed up in the Spanish word "leche" of human response (115). At stake is not simply an assessment of the Mexican boys and of Mexico but of *Mala Noche* itself as not just cheap porn (202) but art—the art of having captured "real life" (24) by having touched it and appreciated it in all its grime, poverty, and glory, through the bodies (and hearts) of these boys. Integral to this project is the portrayal of Mexicans and thereby Mexico as providing that combination of elements sacred to an artist on the cutting edge or "border": "These people, despite their poverty, seem more human and emotionally responsive than most Americans" (137). In a new epilogue to the recent reprint of the chapbook, Curtis proudly relays Pauline Kael's comments about the film version of *Mala Noche* (a collaboration between Curtis and Gus Van Sant): "She wrote: '*Mala Noche* has an authentic grungy beauty'" (201). "*Authentic* grungy beauty"—emphasis on the authentic—is both what Curtis sees in the Mexican boys and what he would like his readers to see in his book.

Although *fantasy* remains an acknowledged factor, the aim—one might say the metafantasy—is to shed fantasy in favor of the *real* thing as in: "I finally get to be close to Johnny up close, *no fantasies,* really touching and seeing him close" (41). Contrary to the opinions of hostile critics who, for example, have seen in Curtis's story only "'a sick black-humored circle of exploitation . . . Walt wants their bods and they want his cigarettes, food, crash pad, and car!'" (202), *Mala Noche* repudiates all such connotations of "trick." If Pepper, Johnny, and Raul are tricksters, the narrative works diligently to represent them as *survivors* and touchstones for a deadened and uncaring Anglo culture, not as hustlers morphing into the shape of any gringo's desires. An "illusion" of authenticity assumes a different meaning and function in *Mala Noche* than in Rechy's *City of Night*. Instead of soon-to-be broken dreams or lost paradises, *ilusión* comes to signify the potential of life against the odds—an antidote to the dominant culture's falsification of values and to the narrator's modestly compromised position as a white man, cashier of a grocery store in Portland's Skid Row area, selling wine to "stupefied men down on their luck, out of work" (22).

Both *City of Night* and *Mala Noche,* despite their differences, trade on the "authenticity" of the Latino and *Latinidad* vis-à-vis Anglo dominant culture. To this extent, they perpetuate a myth, an illusion, which like any other myth or illusion, serves to assuage, as the narrator of *City of Night* tells us, "savage contradictions within this legend called America" (280)—savage contradictions, for instance, like pressures to pass in the dominant culture's terms and the fact of multilevel tiers of exploitation despite pledges to the ideals of equality and justice for all. On the other hand, to the extent that the articulations of ethnicity and sexuality, expressions of desire and constructions of *Latinidad,* are inextricably imbricated in both works, *City of Night* and *Mala Noche* do not allow readers to consume the Latino and *Latinidad* as separate from an economy of desire, fantasy, *ilusión*. The "Latinos" in these novels—the hustler-narrator of *City of Night* with his heart of glass in El Paso and the Mexican boys Pepper and Johnny of *Mala Noche*—may turn tricks, but are they what we want when we look for a "Latino trickster," a figure to allegorize the cultural work of Latina/o literature in the United States? "Latino trickster" has both an ethnographic and anthropological ring to it. Such a term for the work of Latino literature and culture suggests an interest in "Otherness," an "Otherness" that through resistance and mischief teaches "us" something about "our" culture. Both *City of Night* and *Mala Noche* raise this question: For whose benefit is the trick, the illusion of authenticity? The trickster, although potentially associated with lying, cheating, deception, hiding, and various kinds of inauthenticity, is primarily understood as an authentically folklorish figure from the imaginative survival lore of a people in peril or in some kind of danger. To call someone a "trickster" points up his or her trickiness, subversiveness, at the same time that it unmasks and contains him or her as just that—a trickster—thus granting her/him a specific, classifiable, and almost venerable role to play in society. What role might the "trickster as Latino" and the "Latino as trickster" be playing in the U.S. Imaginary in the wake of Proposition 187, NAFTA, English-only legislation, and the marketing of Latino literature in and beyond the academy walls?

The figure of the Latino, especially as male-gendered, despite negative stereotyping by the dominant culture, provides the opportunity for bracketed or "fictional" identification with the outlaw. *Mala Noche* hardly disguises this kind of identification. Walt Curtis states in a piece entitled "The Other Side," one of several afterwords to his chapbook *Mala Noche:* "Mexico is our shadow, our lawless side, the escape valve. Crooned about in all the country-and-western songs. Land more primitive than our own. Mexicans are errant children, an instinctive and spontaneous breed, passionate and simple race" (199). This passage frames the outlaw not as a dangerous bandit with the potential to seriously disrupt the social order but as a young *picaro* bringing the genuine arts of living or as a carrier of arcane knowledge or traditions that offer an almost quaint version of extreme unction from the tedium, boredom, or "falsity" of the dominant Anglo-American culture's way of life.

It is no accident that both *City of Night* and *Mala Noche* present Latinos, and specifically Mexicans, within a framework of confession. The conjunction of confession and Latinos operates on two levels in *City of Night.* The narrator's entire narrative is framed on both ends by a confession of his having lapsed from his Mexican mother's religion, Catholicism. In the very first chapter he tells readers, "Soon, I stopped going to Mass. I stopped praying" (17). The last chapter ends in "the Lenten city" (377) of New Orleans not merely during Mardi Gras, but on Ash Wednesday itself, the day of atonement in his Mexican mother's religion. Such a relation between figure, the Latino, and narrative mode, confession, could be limitingly read as the result of an overdetermined cultural association of Mexicans with Catholicism. After all, the narrator of *Mala Noche* declares during his odyssey in Mexico, "Theologically I am opposed to Catholicism, but the esthetics and human emotion of the religion move me" (136). The conjunction of the figure of the Latino and the confessional mode in these works has a more ecumenical basis than the tendency to link Mexicans with Catholicism. That broader basis is guilt, the guilt of those who pass into the dominant culture or in some way belong to it vis-à-vis "pobre Méjico," so far from God and so close to the United States. What trafficking in the figure of the Latino, and specifically the Mexican, in *City of Night* and *Mala Noche* affords both the narrators and possibly the writers themselves is either the memory of or the hope for absolution, absolution from guilt, a guilt that is not merely individual but deeply cultural—the guilt accrued living in El Norte. Thus, the narrator of *Mala Noche* describes his journey to Mexico as "a pilgrimage" (137):

> Like Malcolm Lowry, the great British Columbian novelist, who wrote so magnificently of Mexico in his major novel *Under the Volcano*, I wanted to come face to face with my life. Just as his self-destructive, drunken, and autobiographical character the Consul had. Even if I risked my life. André Gide, quoting Jesus Christ, wrote, "You must lose your life in order to find it."
>
> Christ wasn't talking about gaining the next life, or immortality. He wasn't saying that one should reject this life. But one must free himself or herself of present fetters. Do something different, in order to discover the possibilities of living. Of course, theologians will argue about this! I know existentialism is out of fashion today. But I believe it's true. That's why I came to Guanajuato." (137)

Similarly, the narrator of *City of Night* goes or returns at the end of his narrative, like the prodigal Son, if not to Mexico proper, then to one of the cities or rather border towns closest to it besides Brownsville and Laredo: "And I returned to El Paso" (379). This move of turning Mexico and Mexicans into touchstones for both personal and cultural absolution may not seem much different from the combination of sentimental, historical novels, travel literature, and folklore such as *Ramona: A Story* (1884) by Helen Hunt Jackson, *Land of Little Rain* (1903) by Mary Hunter Austin, *The Blood of Conquerors* (1921) by Harvey Fergusson, or *Coronado's Children* (1930) by J. Frank Dobie. Absurd as it may at first seem to put these two works by gay male writers Rechy and Curtis in league with what has been categorized as southwestern/western regional writing, this deployment of the figure of the Latino signals a continuity. That is, the figure of the Latino can be seen as a device in narratives motivated by guilt and the device is an old trick, although newer and more surprising in 1963 and 1977 than today in the wake not only of the Chicano/a movement and the rise of Chicano Studies, but, with respect to *Mala Noche,* of Proposition 187 and NAFTA as well. Both *City of Night* and *Mala Noche* have been republished since their original publication dates: the former in 1984 by the Grove Press and the latter in 1997 by BridgeCity Books. The new editions of both works contain pieces of apologetics attempting to bring them up to date precisely, one might argue, so that this device may not come off as a well-worn trick that can no longer pass for "real." The 1984 version of *City of Night* is prefaced by an introduction in which Rechy implicitly counters, with numerous references to his "half-Mexican" roots, those critics who accuse him of burying his Chicano identity:

> From childhood, I had wanted to be a writer. My mother was Mexican . . . I learned Spanish first and spoke only it until I entered school. . . . [I]n midteens . . . I began an autobiographical novel entitled—oh, yes—*The Bitter Roots*. It was about a half-Mexican, half-Scottish boy, doubly exiled in many ways. (x)

Similarly, *Mala Noche* demonstrates a concern that it may currently be received as the creation of an out-of-touch gringo whose work, rather than promoting cultural and historical understanding between, for example, Anglos, Chicanos, Native peoples, Mexicans, queer, bisexual, and straight, female and male, manages, instead, to offend everyone. A passage from the acknowledgments reads, "Finally—even tho my writing in moments might seem racist, sexist, and disrespectful, I honor Latino culture and the Mexican and Indian peoples." Finally, a passage in an afterword piece entitled "Will Mexico Have Another Revolution?" which Curtis refers to as "a sort of update and historical perspective" (187), addresses NAFTA head on: "It's 1997, not 1977, as I make these comments. Since the signing of NAFTA in 1994, the peso's been devalued! Carlos Salinas de Gotari fled the country—the architect of NAFTA!" (187). These lines gesture to an attempt to extricate his chapbook from the fast and hot commodification not only of Mexican workers in the United States but of the very figure of the Mexican in particular and of the Latino in general. As readers and consumers, we may do as we please with these apologetics. They implicate us as much as they implicate their writers. If we do not believe that old dogs can learn new tricks, tricks that will fool us out of seeing them as such, then we might inquire how their perhaps by now old tricks contribute to our understanding of ethnicity in "American," or more accurately, U.S. literature.

On the one hand, *City of Night* presents us with a trans-lucification of "minority" identity such that this identity serves both to *locate* and thus to "authenticate" at the same time that it allows the narrator to *become ubiquitous,* to pass as a representative any-and-everyman. *Mala Noche* involves an Anglo narrator who wishes to shed his dominant or hegemonic ethnicity and absorb, as if by osmosis, the authenticity he associates with the Mexican migrant worker boys and *pobre Méjico* so close to the United States. The narrator longs to pass into the world of the Mexican migrant worker boys he loves and be accepted by them. This longing is part and parcel of the desire that his wholehearted involvement with them may divest him of any suspicion of being a cannibalizing pseudo-border-*artista* that his modestly privileged position as an Anglo male might provoke in his readers.

On the other hand, despite the authentication projects of both novels, ethnicity manifests itself as a construct, a product of conscious retrievals or acquisitions. While such a model does not in itself present a particular challenge to current paradigms of ethnicity within the field of ethnic studies, both novels traffic in a particular ethnicity as a touchstone building block in a process of ethnic reconstruction and the reconstruction of ethnicity. The concurrence of appeals to authenticating "essence" and to performative self-construction in these works leads us as readers and theorists to the crossroads between ethnic studies and queer studies. I say "queer studies" despite Rechy's emphatically stated dislike of the term as unredeemably offensive to someone of his generation, because regardless of such objections, "queer," unlike the terms "gay," "homosexual," and "Trojan"—the latter suggested half in jest by Rechy himself—conveys not merely same-sex object choice, but the activity of putting something taken for granted into question.[10] The word "queer" has a long and rich history, not merely as a noun, a pejorative synonym for homosexual, but as a verb and an adjective. From the end of the eighteenth century onward, "queer" was actually employed as a verb—"to queer"—meaning to question, to puzzle, to put in doubt. The doubt or question connoted by the phrase "to queer" pertained to the mundane and the material (dis)ordering of things but also to the philosophical and the metaphysical. In the wake of gay liberation, "queer" gestures to another or rival order of things. "Queer" as a verb and as an adjective marks a resistance to conventional social structures and business as usual.[11] Moreover, the word "queer," as adjective and verb, serves well to signal the close relation that exists between questioning the presumed order of things and turning tricks, or tricking the system. Unlike other terms, such as "gay," "homosexual," or "Trojan," it begins to communicate the effect of both of these novels upon a heterosexist paradigm of ethnicity. In neither novel is ethnicity primarily a matter of biological ancestry or descent; rather, to borrow Goethe's phrase, it is a matter "of elective affinities," or in the case of *City of Night,* of elective alienations. Although both novels associate Latino ethnicity with authenticity, ethnicity is not so much a question of physical heredity as of actions, objects of desire, and symbols. Moreover, in both novels ethnicity applies as much to the dominant culture as to the subordinated ones, the outsiders, the "minorities." Both *City of Night* and *Mala Noche* imply that, like being "Mexican," to be "Anglo" is to be ethnic. In *City of Night* this "Anglo-ness" is none other than *Latinidad* made transparent or scrubbed clean. In *Mala Noche* it is an identity ("gringo") desanitized and paradoxically validated through contact and identification with the dirt, poverty, and spunk of the Mexican boys.

Ethnicity as elective affinity encompassing both dominant and subordinated groups while being produced in their interplay is not merely the incidental by-product of work by self-identified gay novelists, one Anglo-Chicano passing as Anglo and the other Anglo wishing to pass as Mexican. To the contrary, these narratives produce and advance ethnicity as affinity rather than biology (even in the case of Rechy's narrator and his Mexican mother) to the extent that both transfigure and/or trade blood ties for other forms of connection. Each of the novels cites the well-worn trope of brothers in arms, soldiers in the same foxhole, and enemies on the battlefield to signal the extrafamiliar, homosocial form of consanguinity between men who shed blood together or shed each other's blood. However, despite this tendency to lean on old, "familiar," one might say socially validated tropes of extrafamiliar blood ties between men, what is new and different about these novels is their tricking of the consanguinity model not of war (an impossibility, perhaps, given that it is an activity based on the shedding of blood), but of biological kinship and specifically biological kinship in terms of ethnicity.

Displacing blood ties or biological kinship in *City of Night* is an expanding network of disconnected persons linked together from the narrator's perspective as memories of cities, strangers in those cities, and these strangers' confessions. A number of critics have maintained that Rechy's work has been excluded from the Chicano canon because it does not reinforce or honor the code of *la familia*—monogamy, loyalty, homage paid to the household saints, praise for *la abuelita*'s cooking, and so forth. This refusal to conform to the code of *la familia* so conceived only partly explains the exclusion of Rechy's work from the Chicano literary canon. Actually, *City of Night* with its repeated references to home and mother in El Paso does not entirely eschew the conventions of this code. In fact, in this instance it fulfills them with emotion so deep that one is tempted to abandon a reading of these disclosures in terms of a series of tropes. Frankly, homophobia is probably most responsible for the exclusion of *City of Night* from the Chicano canon and for the marginal position granted to it in the general canon of "American" literature. Critics have also reasoned that its exclusion is owing to its supposed lack of interest in ethnic questions, and its abandonment of the code of *la familia* is viewed as one symptom of this indifference. However, to equate a refusal to conform to the code of *la familia* with the absence of ethnicity as a factor in the work is to misread ethnicity as primarily a matter of consanguinity or to privilege consanguinity—not merely marriage, but marriage inasmuch as it signifies the biological mingling of genetic material in the physical reproduction of children—as the chief motif of any narrative in which ethnicity is central.

The displacement of blood ties in *City of Night* is effected through an expanding network of remembered cities, strangers, and confessions culminating in the encounter with the Anglo Jeremy Adams, "a well-built, masculine man in his early 30s, with uncannily dark eyes, light hair" (345). This expanding network model is for most of the novel diametrically opposed to the code of *la familia* and to blood ties, except in this last encounter entitled "Jeremy: White Sheets." The title highlights the symbolic function of color or its seeming absence (as "white" is often treated) without directly underscoring the color to be the marker of Jeremy's "Anglo" ethnicity. Nevertheless, the name "Jeremy Adams" and the color coding of the entire encounter with the phrase "white sheets" only thinly disguises the fact that what takes place in this chapter is a meeting between a half-Latino man and an Anglo man, that is, between people of ostensibly different ethnic backgrounds. Significantly, the Anglo man's eyes are described as "uncannily dark" in relation to his "light hair" (345). The eyes, the contrast between them and his coloring, provide the lure, the locus of relation with Jeremy or the desire for one on the narrator's part. The reader is led to wonder if Jeremy's eyes are dark like the narrator's and if what is implied is that, in this respect, the half-Latino narrator and the Anglo Jeremy might be considered brothers. In other words, the last encounter between men in *City of Night* tricks the consanguinity model of ethnicity by flickeringly mimicking a biological model of relations. This move is highly effective in that it manages to co-opt rather than merely oppose the code of *la familia* and ethnicity as biology rather than affinity. Not surprisingly, the narrator's encounter with Jeremy takes him back to suppressed memories of his mother's love for him and his own traumatized love for his father "emerging . . . out of the ashes of . . . early hatred" (347).

In *Mala Noche* a sweet, tricky supplantation of blood ties takes place through the narrator's creation of a temporary or not so ephemeral alternative family among the Mexican boys he cares for as well as desires. To frustrate the notion of ethnicity as blood ties the narrator seizes upon and emulates a kinship feature of the Mexican culture that surpasses biological kinship. The narrative tells us:

> Two Mexicans, who are so close as Raul and Nico are, call each other "carnal." Which means more than brother. More than "blood." They are like two soldiers on a battlefield, sharing the same foxhole. They protect each other and share everything. It isn't a sexual relationship, either. Or, at least, they don't think of it as so. Maybe that's being a little too dramatic. But that's close to the truth. It's *La Raza*. (108)

Carnales—"carnals" translated literally—has strong resonances of "biology" and "blood ties." The term connotes a fleshly bond between two people and as such suggests that it is based on consanguinity, the sharing of the same blood, as with blood brothers. Yet, the narrator is quick to point out, "carnales" means "more than brother," "[m]ore than 'blood'" (108). The relationship between the Mexicans Raul and Nico is not merely a surrogate form of brotherhood. It bests brotherhood. The relation between "carnales" is understood to be super-consanguineous, in two senses of the word "super"—"exponentially" and "beyond." To the extent that carnal connotes blood ties raised to the *n*th power, the term operates within a system of consanguinity. However, to the extent that it implies a relation "beyond" literal brotherhood, it transcends, does not depend on consanguinity. It is this latter non-consanguineous, better than consanguineous opportunity that the narrator would like to partake of with the Mexican boys, only giving physical expression to the denied homosexuality latent in the term "carnales" designating so intimate a bond between two men. Despite being a gringo, in this way the narrator can share in bonds tested through a trial of fire, a fire missing from U.S. Anglo culture even as it places the Mexican migrants under a line of fire (arrest, deportation, and so on). Striving to achieve a "carnal" relation (in all senses of those words) with the Mexican boys, the narrator tricks the kinship system of his ethnic group with that of another ethnic group. This tricking or deft substitution of one kinship system with another comprises the ethnicity transformation act of *Mala Noche*. This trick, of course, fails to overcome certain circumstances—such as poverty, lingering cultural misunderstandings, *la migra* or the immigration police, and the fickleness of the young boys who quite literally cannot afford to be loyal or to stay in one place but must do what they can to survive in a society bent on arresting, deporting, even killing them. The narrator as trickster trying to play tricks on the kinship system gets his feelings bruised and beaten as surely as the Mexican boys suffer hunger, thirst, hard labor, and the blows and bullets of the police—hence, the title *Mala Noche*, bad night. And yet, the courage to trick brings the narrative into being, makes possible the story.

City of Night and *Mala Noche* not only traffic in the figure of the Latino to achieve authenticity but do so in a way that tricks the consanguinity paradigm of ethnicity, as it applies both to self-construction and identification between self and other. The importance of this stratagem especially within the genre boundaries of confessional autobiography (despite the odyssey-like, epic-fantasy qualities of *City of Night*), of the picaresque novel or novella, and of first-person narrative in general cannot be overemphasized. It is precisely these genres that traditionally in their reception have been equated with realism—the fictional recreation of lived experience and a recognizable social order—and have served, if not intentionally, then unwittingly as a blueprint for further lived experience at the cultural junctures where life imitates art and models of ethnicity are extracted from literature. Yet even if categorized as romances and adventures (after all, the republished version of *Mala Noche* is entitled *Mala Noche and Other "Illegal" Adventures*), at quite the opposite spectrum from realism, the importance of this tricking of the consanguinity model of ethnicity cannot be underestimated as what remains after the tricksters have been identified and the trick has been explained is a certain utopian hope that a non-consanguineous construction of ethnicity stemming from unofficial and unsanctioned, one might say queer, cross-cultural identification can present a not entirely contained challenge to the dominant culture's ob-scene trafficking in ethnicity, in the figure of the Latino.

Notes

1. "Texas Mejicano" is John Rechy's preferred designation for his ethnicity according to Rechy himself ("The Outlaw Sensibility in the Arts: Liberated Ghettos and Noble Stereotypes," lecture, Harvard University, Cambridge, Mass., Dec. 11, 1997).

2. Juan Bruce-Novoa, "Canonical and Non-Canonical Texts," *Retrospace: Collected Essays on Chicano Literature and History* (Houston: Arte Publico Press, 1990), 135; hereafter cited in parentheses in the text.

3. Ricardo L. Ortiz, "Sexuality Degree Zero: Pleasure and Power in the Novels of John Rechy, Arturo Islas, and Michael Nava," *Journal of Homosexuality* 26, no. 2/3 (1993): 115; Rafael Pérez-Torres, "The Ambiguous Outlaw: John Rechy and Complicitous Homotextuality," *Fictions of Masculinity: Crossing Cultures, Crossing Sexualities,* ed. Peter F. Murphy (New York: New York University Press, 1994), 224.

4. Ibid. 224.

5. John Rechy, *City of Night* (New York: Grove Press, 1963), 9; hereafter cited in parentheses in the text.

6. See my own study of romances of Anglo-American imperial identity by William Gilmore Simms, Nathaniel Hawthorne, and Oliver Wendell Holmes in my chapter on the way in which Orientalization as an Anglo-American representational mode or practice transformed Spaniards, Moors, Africans, Jews, Gypsies, and Native Americans, the Old World and the New, colonizer and colonized, into tropes of doomed racial mixing, "Imperial Visions: Moor, Gypsy, and Indian" in "'American' In Dependence: Figures of Spain in Anglo-American Culture" (Ph.D. diss., Harvard University, 1997), 77–115.

7. Rechy, "Outlaw Sensibility."

8. Walt Curtis, *Mala Noche, and Other "Illegal" Adventures* (Portland: Bridge-City Books, 1997), 36; hereafter cited in parentheses in the text.

9. A line in *Mala Noche* compares the Mexican coastline with Tahiti: "the Mexican coastline is like Tahiti" (139).

10. Rechy, "Outlaw Sensibility."

11. María DeGuzmán, "What Are We Queering For?: Strategies of Self-in-Evidence" (paper presented on the panel "Critical Taste: Rethinking Aesthetics and Cultural Studies" at the annual conference of the College Art Association, Toronto, Canada, 1998), 3.

Where Are the Women Tricksters?

LEWIS HYDE

All of the standard tricksters are male. There are three related reasons why this might be. First, these tricksters may belong to
patriarchal mythologies, ones in which the prime actors, even oppositional actors, are male. Second, there may be a problem with the standard
itself; there may be female tricksters who have simply been ignored. Finally, it may be that the trickster stories articulate some distinction between men and women, so that even in a matriarchal setting this figure
would be male.

It is often said that the well-known tricksters are not male but androgynous or at least of indeterminate sexuality. Victor Turner says, for
example, "Most tricksters have an uncertain sexual status: on various
mythical occasions Loki and Wakdjunkaga transformed themselves into
women, while Hermes was often represented in statuary as a hermaph-
rodite."[1] This seems to me to overstate the case. The classical hermaph-
rodite, for example, is born of the union of Hermes and Aphrodite; to say
the figure represents Hermes is an insult to Aphrodite.

The other cases are a little more complicated. The Winnebago trickster once disguised himself as a woman, married the son of a chief, and
bore three sons.[2] Loki once transformed himself into a mare in heat so as
to distract the stallion that was helping to build the wall around Asgard.
Not only that, but this stallion and mare mated, and Loki thus bore a
foal, the eight-legged horse, Sleipnir.[3] There is also one obscure reference
to Loki's having eaten the half-cooked heart of a woman and by that
becoming sufficiently female as to give birth to monsters.[4]

These are the best, and I think the *only,* examples of tricksters being
both male and female. They do not, however, seem to me to indicate
"uncertain sexual status." In both cases *a male figure* becomes briefly female and then reverts to being male. The male is the ground, the point
of departure. In the Winnebago case, in fact, the sex-change episode
ends with Wakdjunkaga losing his disguise and saying to himself "Why
am I doing all this? It is about time that I went back to the woman to

185

whom I am really married. [My son] must be a pretty big boy by this time."[5] As Radin points out, this is the only mention of Wakdjunkaga having a family; the narrator is underlining trickster's framing maleness, within which there has been an episode of femaleness.

The best we can do, I think, is to modify my opening assertion: the standard tricksters are male, some of whom on rare occasions become briefly ᶠᵉmale.

As for trickster being part of patriarchal mythology, I'd like to approach the topic from the other side, by way of a possible female trickster figure, Baubo. In Greek Eleusinian mystery religion, Baubo was a woman (sometimes a queen, sometimes a nurse) who managed to make Demeter laugh in the midst of her grief and anger over the loss of her daughter Persephone. Demeter's bitter sadness had caused fertility to withdraw from the world; the corn seed would not germinate in the ground. Whoever could break her grief was also, therefore, the bringer of spring and fertility. And how did Baubo make Demeter laugh? By lifting her skirts and exposing her pudenda, a shameless and im-pudent act by definition.[6] Baubo was also associated with the dirty jokes, the obscene badinage, women made during Demeter's fertility rites. During the Eleusinian festival of Demeter, ribald remarks were called out on the "bridge of jests" between Athens and Eleusis. (Such joking is a common feature of fertility festivals, meant to arouse the earth and humans alike.)[7]

In any event, we have here a female figure of great antiquity, a female flasher as it were, whose shamelessness is linked with fertility and the return of the dead, all of which are part of the trickster's mythological territory.

But in fact we have very little *story* about Baubo. The earliest record occurs in the seventh century B.C.E. *Homeric Hymn to Demeter* where Baubo is called Iambe and where the critical interaction between her and Demeter is described with restraint: "careful Iambe . . . moved the holy lady with many a quip and jest to smile and laugh and cheer her heart."[8]

The standard commentary on this hymn, while explaining that in "the Orphic version" of the story "Baubo by an exposure caused Demeter to smile," allows that "the epic dignity of the poet of the hymn" has erased that shameless image, a circular remark since the *Hymn* acquires its "epic dignity" exactly by such erasures.[9] We know the fuller "Orphic version" of the story from Clement of Alexandria, a Church father who cites the crucial lines from an ancient Orphic poem ("she drew aside her robes, and showed a sight of shame"), but not without a prefatory apology: "[the] Athenians and the rest of Greece—I blush even to speak of it— possess that shameful tale about Demeter."[10]

Thus with both the poet of the *Hymn to Demeter* and Clement of Alexandria we not only hear an old story that features a shameless female reversing a moribund situation, we get to witness the old story in the process of losing its details. Cases such as this (or of Sheela-na-gig, another female flasher whose image appeared on churches in Ireland up into the Middle Ages) suggest that there may have been a tradition of female tricksters that disappeared over the centuries during which Zeus worshipers and Christian "fathers" were shoring up their dignity. There has, of course, been much speculation in recent decades about gender relations in the prehistory of mythology. A remark by Charlene Spretnak in regard to Demeter's story is typical: "It is likely that the story of the rape of the Goddess [Persephone] is a historical reference to the invasion of the northern Zeus-worshipers, just as is the story of the stormy marriage of Hera, the native queen who will not yield to the conqueror Zeus."[11] Spretnak takes the *Hymn to Demeter* to be a retelling of much older stories about Isis and Gaia, a retelling in a new context where Zeus is the high god and Baubo has become "careful Iambe," and it is getting harder and harder to remember what exactly she did to make Demeter laugh.

The Baubo case suggests that perhaps the traditional literature on tricksters hasn't cast a wide enough net, that there are female figures out there, we just need to look more widely to find them. My own reading has turned up two or three, but before I speak of them I should say that my own sense of the category "trickster" calls for a mythic figure with an elaborated career of trickery. I say this because it is not hard to think of women who have pulled a trick or two; lying, stealing, and shameless behavior are not masculine essences. But one or two episodes do not make a trickster.

Maxine Hong Kingston once suggested to me that the Chinese woman who pretended to be a warrior so that her father would not have to go to war, Fa Mu Lan, was a trickster. I'm skeptical; her ruse is certainly a trick, but it's the only one; she's not like the Monkey King whose deceptions fill a hundred chapters. Similarly, there has been some attempt to describe certain women in the Hebrew Bible as female tricksters. Rachel tricks Laban, for example, when she and Jacob are leaving Laban's house

(Gen. 29–31). They leave without announcing their departure, and as they go Rachel steals the teraphim, the household idols. She prevents Laban from searching for the missing goods by telling him "the way of women is upon me" (Gen. 31:35). From this event one critic concludes: "She is the trickster who dupes the one in power! She is a trickster by means of role reversal."[12] Again, I'm not convinced. She has a trick, surely, but there is no elaborated career. These are examples of female trickery, not of female tricksters.

As for female tricksters, there are several, one of which I'll comment on. There is Aunt Nancy of African American lore, though she is actually a version of Ananse, the Ashanti spider trickster, and the corpus of tales about her is small.[13] There is Inanna, the "deceptive goddess" of ancient Sumeria.[14] There is a figure from the Chiapas Highlands of Mexico called Matlacihuatl (also known as *Mujer Enredadora,* the Entangling Woman). She has what looks like a mouth at the back of her neck, but it turns out to be a vagina. If a man seduces her, *he* becomes pregnant, not she.[15] And finally—the case I want to expand on—in the American Southwest there is a female Coyote trickster.

Reading through hundreds of Native American trickster stories, Franchot Ballinger found about twenty that had a female Coyote, almost all of them from two Pueblo Indian groups, the Hopi and the Tewa. In these settings the female Coyote exists alongside the male Coyote, and the majority of the stories are still about the latter. Nonetheless, she does exist, and she differs from her male counterpart in several ways. She is as hungry as he, but she is not driven by his insatiable sexual desire. The male Coyote occasionally has children, but they are usually incidental to the tale. The female Coyote's children play a more significant role, as Ballinger explains:

> Sometimes [the story] opens with a reference to her hunting food or carrying water for her children. Sometimes when she decides that she wants something that is not rightfully hers (for example, pretty spots, a song, an improved scheme for hunting), she wants it (as least ostensibly) for her children. In other stories, her children are active participants in the events that demonstrate or reveal their Trickster mother's foolishness, lack of self-control, or unnatural desires.[16]

Finally, Ballinger found no stories in which the female Coyote is a culture hero. She is not known as a thief of fire, a teacher of dances, or an inventor of fish traps.[17]

As for why the female Coyote stories appear in these settings, Ballinger suggests that it is a consequence of the ways in which power and gender are connected in Hopi and Tewa life.

The most obvious fact we should note about stories with female Tricksters is that they are *all* from tribes that were or are yet matrilineal and/or matrilocal. In most, and maybe all, of the tribes I've named, women have traditionally had significant *de facto* or official authority and power. For example, among the western Tewa and the Hopi, women traditionally control the economic system and the home which is at the core of that system. Women own the houses, the fields, and the fruits of cultivation through their clans, with the clan mothers having final say in matters of distribution. Furthermore, strong ties among mothers-daughters-sisters create a solidarity of opinion which in turn carries much authority. Among the Tewa, it is the women who have traditionally cared for family ritual possessions.[18]

In short, we find this female trickster in the context of female power, a fact that, in the end, supports the idea that the canonical tricksters are male because they are part of patriarchal mythology.

At this point it could be asked why, if tricksters are disruptive and oppositional, they wouldn't be female *especially* in patriarchy. The answer might be a version of Sacvan Bercovitch's point about how ideologies contain dissent. Any system does well to figure its problems in terms of its own assumptions. If power is masculine, best to have the opposition be masculine as well. In the history of Greek religion there was once a cunning goddess named Metis. Zeus ate her. So much for the really threatening opposition. Later Zeus fathered Hermes and by one reading of the *Hymn,* as we saw, Hermes becomes Zeus's faithful-unfaithful servant, not an opponent. This manner of containing dissent does not itself belong to patriarchy; surely a matriarchy would do the same thing. Having a female Coyote in the Hopi tradition may be a good way to protect women's powers from fundamental change.

Be that as it may, having considered the female Coyote stories, it should be said that they are not so much a gateway into an ignored territory as the exception that proves the rule. Unless the problem lies with unrecorded tales, even among the Hopi and the Tewa, the male Coyote is the primary trickster. Furthermore, if in North America there are fewer than two dozen female trickster stories, then the Native American trickster is primarily male. Finally, these stories come from groups where significant forms of power belong to women, but here too they are an exception. There are many matrilineal Native American groups—the Tsimshian and the Tlingit on the North Pacific Coast, for example—and in all of them the trickster is male.[19] We do have two clear cases in which a female trickster is associated with matrilineal decent, but the latter is not a sufficient cause of the former. In North America, where significant forms of power belong to women, the trickster is still usually male.

Which brings us to the final line of inquiry into the roots of this gendering. Perhaps some part of this myth is about men, as the myths about Isis or Gaia or Demeter are about women. Perhaps the gendering of trickster derives from sex differences.

There are several ways in which this might be the case. First of all, at least before the technology of birth control, the consequences of the kind of on-the-road opportunistic sexuality that trickster displays were clearly more serious for the sex that must gestate, bear, and suckle the young (it makes sense that the Hopi mute trickster's sexuality to get the female figure). Second, these might be stories about non-procreative creativity and so get attached to the sex that doesn't give birth. It should be noted that trickster's fabled sex drive rarely leads to any offspring. Tricksters do not make new life, they rearrange what is already at hand.

Finally, this mythology may present a (non-Oedipal) narrative about how boy children separate from their mothers. John Stratton Hawley's remarks about Krishna and his mother set me to thinking in this line. Hawley argues that in the Hindu culture that gave rise to the butter thief stories, the nurturing of boy children involves an intimacy between the sexes that tends to erase sexual polarity; this erasure produces a later problem for boys when it comes time to claim their separate sexual identity.[20] On the one hand there is a strong bond between Krishna and his mother, Yasoda. "Her consistent desire is that Krishna remain in her world, remain a child," and to a large extent, he does.[21] On the other hand, he wants to be free of her. The butter thief stories enact the doubleness, the ambiguity, of this simultaneous dependence-independence. "Although his appetite is large enough to make him totally dependent on all the women surrounding him, he remains totally independent. At no moment does he become bound by obligation."[22] Hawley at one point contrasts Krishna with Siva, a male deity who avoids dependence by containing himself, by self-restraint. Krishna, on the other hand, gets it both ways, which requires trickery. "Siva's method involves a radical curtailment of activity—ascetic stasis—whereas Krishna's is a product of his constant, lithe, even crooked movement. It is that irrepressible activity of both body and mind, rather than an inner concentration, that renders him invulnerable to the claims of the women who would domesticate him."[23] Invulnerable, but not distanced. His trickery allows him to be connected-not connected to the female sphere.

This part of the myth *does* seem to be about male psychology, then, about that charming male type who can be maddeningly present and not present to women.[24] It's a type not confined to India. Hawley's formulation is all the more striking because something similar appears in other contexts. In West Africa, one of Legba's early problems is to get his mother Mawu into the distance, and he does so by creating a separation that he then proceeds to bridge. The Signifying Monkey stories, too, especially the parts in which the Monkey plays the dozens, involves coming to a balanced or poised understanding about "mamma," one that simultaneously takes her seriously and doesn't take her seriously. Hermes may steal Apollo's cattle, but it is his mother Maia who first catches him at it and tries to discipline him. He refuses to display any need for her but promises to take her with him when he becomes the Prince of Thieves.

In sum, there is at least one place where the trickster material is about issues particular to young men, and in that case there should be no mystery why the protagonist is male. Even in situations where women hold significant power, a story about men negotiating their connection to women will be a story with a male protagonist. That said, it isn't clear why the opposite is not the case as well: women may be the same sex as their mothers, but from all I've seen, mother-daughter relationships are just as fraught with ambiguity and with tensions over connecting and not connecting. The fact that that tension has not found mythic elaboration in trickster tales probably brings us back to the earlier point, that most of these stories belong to patriarchal religions.

Notes

1. Victor Turner, "Myth and Symbol," *International Encyclopedia of the Social Sciences,* ed. by David Sills (New York: Macmillan and Free Press, 1972), 580.

2. Paul Radin, *The Trickster: A Study in American Indian Mythology* (New York: Schocken Books, 1972), 21–24.

3. Jean I. Young, trans. *The Prose Edda of Snorri Sturluson: Tales from Norse Mythology* (Berkeley and Los Angeles: University of California Press, 1966),

66–68; Lee M. Hollander, *The Poetic Edda,* 2nd ed., rev. ed. (Austin: University of Texas Press, 1962), 62.

4. Henry Adams Bellows, *The Poetic Edda* (New York: American-Scandinavian Foundation, 1923), 231; Hollander 139.

5. Radin 24.

6. There is a similar motif in Japan. After Susa-nö-o's attacks, the sun goddess Amaterasu hides in a cave, the world grows dark, and the seasons stop. To draw her from the cave, a playful goddess (Ama No Uzume) dances by the door, exposing her breasts and genitals. The other gods laugh, which arouses the sun's curiosity, and she begins to emerge. Wing-tsit Chan et al., *The Great Asian Religions: An Anthology* (New York: Macmillan, 1969), 232–33; Merlin Stone, *Ancient Mirrors of Womanhood,* 2 vols. (New York: New Sibylline Books, 1979), 2:129.

These two examples add a corollary to the idea that tricksters revive high gods by debasing them. If the high one is a goddess, it may take a female trickster to do that work.

7. Winifred Milius Lubell, *The Metamorphosis of Baubo* (Nashville: Vanderbilt University Press, 1994), passim.

8. Hugh G. Evelyn-White, trans., "Homeric Hymn to Demeter," *Hesiod: The Homeric Hymns and Homerica,* ll. 200–241, Loeb Classics (Cambridge, Mass.: Harvard University Press, 1914), 303.

9. T. W. Allen, W. R. Halliday, and E. E. Silkes, *The Homeric Hymns,* 2nd ed. (Oxford: Clarendon Press, 1936), 150–51.

10. G. W. Butterworth, trans., *Clement of Alexandria,* Loeb Classical Library (Cambridge: Harvard University Press, 1919), 41.

11. Judith Plaskow and Carol P. Christ, eds., *Weaving the Visions: New Patterns in Feminist Spirituality* (San Francisco: Harper and Row, 1989), 72–73.

12. Naomi Steinberg, "Israelite Tricksters, Their Analogies and Cross-cultural Study," *Reasoning with the Foxes: Female Wit in a World of Male Power,* ed. J. Cheryl Exum and Johanna W. H. Bos (Atlanta: Scholars Press, 1988), 7.

13. Lawrence Levine, *Black Culture and Black Consciousness* (New York: Oxford University Press, 1977), 110.

14. Carole Fontaine, "The Deceptive Goddess in Ancient Near Eastern Myth: Inanna and Inaras," *Reasoning with the Foxes: Female Wit in a World of Male Power,* ed. J. Cheryl Exum and Johanna W. H. Bos (Atlanta: Scholars Press, 1988), 84–102.

15. Lawrence E. Sullivan et al., "Tricksters," *The Encyclopedia of Religion,* ed. M. Eliade (New York: MacMillan, 1987), 15:51, citing Hunt.

16. Franchot Ballinger, "Coyote, She Was Going There: Prowling for Hypotheses about the Female Native American Trickster" (unpublished talk given at MLA, Dec. 28, 1988). Most of the tales Ballinger found are in Ekkehart Malotki and Michael Lomatuway'ma, *Hopi Coyote Tales: Istutuwutsi,* American

Tribal Religion Series 9 (Lincoln: University of Nebraska, 1984), and Elsie Clews Parson, *Tewa Tales* (New York: American Folklore Society Memoirs, 1926).

17. Here we should acknowledge how much the anomalies of collecting can affect the evidence. The absence of published stories does not mean there are no such stories. A collector of tales must suspect something exists and be interested in it before he or she is likely to find it, and even then, if the tales are sacred, they may be withheld, or withheld from certain people. When women anthropologists went to the Trobriand Islands they heard many things that Malinowski never heard.

18. Ballinger.

19. William C. Sturtevant, gen. ed., *Handbook of North American Indians* (Washington: Smithsonian Institution, 1978–), 7:212 and 274.

20. John Stratton Hawley, *Krishna, the Butter Thief* (Princeton, N.J.: Princeton University Press, 1983), chap. 9.

21. Ibid. 128.

22. Ibid. 295.

23. Ibid. 296.

24. Trickster is a nonheroic male, by the way. If by "hero" we mean someone who muscles his way through the ranks of his enemies, whose stamina and grit overcome all odds, who perseveres and suffers and wins, then trickster is a nonheroic male. Nor is he that ascetic male, the one who develops the muscles of self-restraint, mastering himself instead of others. The lithe and small-bodied escape artist, he doesn't win the way the big guys do, but he doesn't suffer the way they do either, and he enjoys pleasures they find too risky.

Constitutional Allegory
and Affirmative Action Babies

Stephen Carter's Talk of "Dissent"

HOUSTON A. BAKER JR.

One of the best stories of the trickster in Afro-American lore concerns a slave who claimed he could foretell the future.[1] As it turns out, the reason the slave could tell the future was that he had secretly arranged peepholes and monitoring devices during his service as a "house slave" among white folks. Overhearing and overseeing their comings and goings, he was always on top of their agendas and could "predict" what they were going to do. Well, it seems the slave was convincing enough in his prophecy that his master was willing to wager a substantial sum with a neighboring plantation owner. The two planters agreed to secret something under a large pot and have the slave through his psychic abilities "see" or identify the secret. The big day arrives; the event is public; the slave is in a truly tight place. After stalling, delaying, scratching his head and a lot of mumbo jumbo, he concedes, saying: "Well, he run a long time, but they *cotched* the ole coon at last." The slave's master is delighted. The pot is raised and out scampers a raccoon. Of course, the slave's and master's victory turns upon words being spoken in one way and taken or interpreted in another. In short, the "trick" of the slave ultimately resides not only in his abilities at scouting out the Big House but also in his words seeming to mean something they don't. A confession is taken for a revelation.

In her engaging study titled *Writing Tricksters,* the scholar Jeanne Rosier Smith comments as follows: "Tricksters are not only characters, they are also rhetorical agents. They infuse narrative structure with energy, humor, and polyvalence, producing a politically radical subtext in the narrative form itself."[2] This seems apt, with one caveat: Tricksters may, finally, produce texts that are less "radical" than preservative, or even conservative. After all, their centrality in world cultures depends, as

Smith notes, on their ability to manipulate the sacred lore and myths of a people, preserving in narrative guise "community."

It is to one brand of rhetorical, conservative, trickster agency that I wish to draw attention, namely, United States black neoconservatism. My focus is an influential book authored by the Yale Law School professor Stephen Carter and titled *Reflections of an Affirmative Action Baby*.[3] Professor Carter's rhetorical strategies are not without precedent in the contemporary culture of black neoconservatism, whose high priest was once Shelby Steele, currently a fellow of the right-wing Hoover Institute. In fact, Steele is the first contemporary master of an allegorical mode of "tricky speech" that can easily be mistaken for what it is decidedly not.

In his book *The Content of Our Character: A New Vision of Race in America*,[4] Steele quite shrewdly employs the mythology and rhetoric of biblical Christianity to write a seductively ahistorical story of black life in the United States. His appropriation of a Western sacred text—a Great Book as it were—for his metaphorical black talk gained almost immediate sympathy from American audiences. Such audiences value Grand Narratives that can be interpreted to forecast or prophesy the rise and triumph of the West and its "civilizing" mission. Sacred textual triumphalism is often accompanied by a utopianism that implies that the "good life" is attainable by all who would but believe in and honor the injunctions and spirit of the text. Those who follow the sacred text and lead likable American lives will prosper on earth. Dr. Martin Luther King Jr. is thus read by Steele as a Christian martyr—a saint whose eyes and spirit were turned always upward to a putatively "universal" heaven, which ordained that *race,* or black collective liberation, should be a secondary enterprise. For Steele, King honored the full spirit of the sacred text from which Steele derives his allegory. Participation of the many—*e pluribus*—conjoined in a sacred biblical cause is the Christian democratic ideal of Steele's utopian American marketplace: paradise regained. One of his most passionate charges is not surprisingly leveled at what he calls the exclusionary, separatist "party line" of the Black Power Movement.

The totalitarianism suggested by the phrase "party line" is precisely what Steele intends. He defines Black Power, Black Nationalism, and, for all we know, lower-class black American life as committed to an authoritarian agenda. Big black brothers rush helter-skelter across the land, ruthlessly silencing, exterminating, and excoriating those who do not toe the "party line." Thought police and captains of conformity exhort and enforce a strict black uniformity of belief. This is a vision of Stalinist ideological cohesion. It is a policed "party line" that not only forecloses possibilities for common ground (whether sacred or secular) between blacks and whites, but also runs directly counter to the ideals of another sacred Western text, namely the Constitution of the United States of America.

It is not Shelby Steele, however, who constructs an allegorical "marketplace of ideas" using the Constitution as foundation, but Professor Stephen Carter. Before analyzing Carter's intellectual labors it might be useful to say that Black Power—comprehensively read—does not seem guilty of the narrow, provincial, authoritarian, xenophobic line of thought and work charged by Steele. In its manifestation as *Black Cultural Nationalism,* one of the principal ends of Black Power was global outreach. It worked in scholarly, creative, political, historical, and, yes, "mythical" ways to construct *blackness* as a sign for world and diasporic diversity. It sought to reclaim and make known the voices of Africa, the Caribbean, Mexico, Latin America, and, indeed, all historical and geographical regions of the Americas where blacks have migrated. Never before, in so brief a span of American academic time, had there occurred the type of recovery, revised pedagogy, accelerated cultural distribution and scholarly research that was motivated by *Black Cultural Nationalism* during the 1970s and 1980s.

Presumably, it was this global extension of range under the sign *blackness* that enabled black world populations beyond the United States to apply *blackness* as an analytical category to an array of social configurations. *Black British Cultural Studies,* for example, and the now defunct use of *black* as a British sign for coalition politics offer examples of the utility of United States Black Power's influence. The scholar Paul Gilroy's energetic studies *There Ain't No Black in the Union Jack* and *The Black Atlantic* are only recent illustrations of how capacious and open to global inscription Black Power's writings of *blackness* have been. Rather than a xenophobic *racial* totalitarianism, Black Power and *Black Cultural Nationalism* represented provisional efforts by activists and scholars alike to provide new evidence and methods in order to include new geographies for scholarship in the field of cultural studies.

The publicity and activism of Black Power and Black Cultural Nationalism opened academic and professional doors and markets for travelers like Shelby Steele, whose "racial" prerogatives seem not to have troubled him until quite recently. Steele even admits in *The Content of Our Character* to a temporary, but passionate, flirtation with Black Power. However, the arrival of well-capitalized American neoconservatism in the 1980s produced quite another kind of talk from Steele. He seems to have awakened to the discovery of Black Power as a "party line" when new funding became available. It is, however, the work of the black neoconservative Yale Law School professor Stephen Carter that lifts the "party line" hauntings of Black Power to allegorical heights of world demonic forces—a conformist censoriousness that forestalls the triumphal entry into American public and professional life of black, smart, reasonable, competent, dissenting black "intellectuals" like, well, Stephen Carter.

The frozen instant that equals purest nostalgic beauty for Stephen Carter would seem to be our country's first Congress's passage of the First Amendment: "Congress shall make no law respecting an establishment of religion, or prohibiting the free exercise thereof; or abridging the freedom of speech, or of the press; or the right of the people peaceably to assemble, and to petition the Government for a redress of grievances." These words resonate with virtually symphonic overtones of New World freedom. Like all words, however, they are abstract—statements of principle, declarations designed for specific circumstances, utterances shaped by varying interests. Anyone who freezes them into a tableau of disinterested revolutionary white male intellectualism is a broker of nostalgia, pure and simple.

James Madison's original project for the First Amendment was to prevent the federal government from establishing a national religion, thus interfering with citizens' civil rights or their "full and equal rights of conscience." Madison and others sought to guarantee that government did not use religion as justification for thought suppression. Despite Judeo-Christian predispositions, Madison and others knew that a "general" statement would be more likely to secure consensus and ratification of the Constitution than a more elaborated code of prohibitions and sectarian considerations concerning religion. Implicit among the founders, nonetheless, was a "general" notion that Christianity *would* be well encouraged by the states.

New World overtones of freedom translate, in the instance of the First Amendment, as a radical proliferation of meanings and intentions. The same may be said with respect to the First Amendment's provision of "freedom of speech." Conservative nostalgia strives to interpret the First

Amendment's free speech provision as implicitly filled with Madisonian and libertarian "original" grandeur. Such a clean and aesthetically satisfying vision of the amendment is simply not enough. Indeed, the First Amendment was not uneqivocally *meant* to guarantee *anybody's* right to say whatever he or she pleased, so long as it did not present *clear and present danger* to civil society. Had such been the case, hate and love speech alike could be launched into the world with impunity; politicians and governments could be vilified at will; summons to violent overthrow of existing authority could be dispatched without punishment. No, what the specifics of "free speech" meant to the founders was freedom from "prior restraint"—defined as that pre-Revolutionary necessity for newspapers and journals to pass inspection by licensers and censors.

This historical view of free speech as pragmatic openness is more sobering than the conservative's boast of free-range libertarianism. Various provisions on "sedition" and "espionage," McCarthyism within our recent memory, and an image of the Black Panther leader Bobby Seale bound, handcuffed, and gagged in an American courtroom reveal that implicit in the assumptions of the founding fathers was at least the thought that not *all,* or indeed *any* speech was inherently "free"—existing in rarified ether, liberated from dictates and demands of power and the effects of cultural and financial capital.

Uneven development in various sectors of the United States population, and uneven degrees of "freedom," made some speech "free" and other forms of talk rigidly subject to both "prior" and "consequent" restraint. The uneven and differential effects of "free" might be suggested by summoning that old chestnut that no citizen is "free" brazenly to shout "Fire!" in a crowded theater. On the other hand, the black writer Amiri Baraka boldly, and perhaps quite accurately, asserts in one of his most powerful essays of the 1960s that were he to stand on a corner in downtown Manhattan—regaled in all his blackness—and loudly and repeatedly proclaim "I'm a *free* man!" he would be dead or in prison by nightfall. The nobility of the ideal of "free" speech—completely "open" public discursive assemblies—in a fully participatory marketplace of American ideas is, at best, an allegorical revery where blacks, women, Native Americans, Asians, Mexican Americans, and non-property-owners in the United States are concerned.

Time, litigation, judicial tests, trials, and tribunals have, of course, left a mixed record with respect to the First Amendment in American jurisprudence. There is much in this history that is edifying and honorable. Still, the fact remains that there have always been among the populations of the United States those who were more "free" to speak than others. And any visualization of a frozen moment in time when Chief Justice Oliver Wendell Holmes's ideal was the actually existing reality for *all* is but nostalgia. In his dissenting opinion in *Abrams v. United States*, Justice Holmes asserted:

> But when men have realized that time has upset many fighting faiths, they may come to believe even more than they believe the very foundations of their own conduct that the ultimate good desired is better reached by free trade in ideas—that the best test of truth is the power of the thought to get itself accepted in the competition of the market, and that truth is the only ground upon which their wishes safely can be carried out. That at any rate is the theory of our Constitution.[5]

Even Justice Holmes, in his shrewd dissent, acknowledges that no matter how exactly "free" his own personal standards may be, freedom of speech—conceived as fair, truthful, marketplace competition available to *all*—is "theory." Unlimited openness of speech in a marketplace of *truth* is a thing of allegorical revery.

Now if Shelby Steele is the author of the founding popular psychology and Christian-visionary allegory of black neoconservatism, Stephen Carter is the black disciple who elaborates the conservative doctrine of the "natural aristocrat" in terms of First Amendment counters to the Black Power "party line." What we have already set forth concerning the First Amendment suggests the strategic lines available for Carter's work. His *Reflections of an Affirmative Action Baby* is a polemic against affirmative action's affront to a black natural aristocracy. The book begins autobiographically and traces, with finger-thumping conviction and often stirring eloquence, how affirmative action *hurts*.

Born in the valley of the shadow of Cornell University, Stephen Carter was the smartest kid in his class. And through all his days, he has been unfailingly annoyed by traditional civil rights and Black Power agendas that confuse his individual, undeniable, unmistakable "smartness" with the color of his skin. This confusion is a direct outgrowth of a "party line." The cardinal point of Carter's book is that affirmative action is an ineffectual system of *racial preferences* based on skin-color entitlements and nothing more. Product of a "party line," affirmative action has brought disastrous consequences to middle-class "smart" men of color like Stephen Carter and Shelby Steele.

Affirmative action, in Carter's account, was spawned by American racial dynamics that have traditionally produced unhealthy states of civil society. Oppressed by discrimination, black Americans have been driven to intolerant, racially defensive majoritarianism that demands special preferences as recompense for years of unpaid suffering and exploited labor. Yet, when such compensation is offered in the form of affirmative action, Carter believes it results in quite unnerving behaviors on the part of white people. Whites assume—and sometimes blatantly state in public—that blacks who have benefited from affirmative action are not as "qualified" as whites who are, *mutatis mutandis,* hired, admitted, and professionally promoted on the basis of *merit alone.*

Darn it! We hypothetically hear Carter exclaim, *I am individualistically the smartest kid in the class, and I would be seen as a man of merit, if only there were no black party line and its affirmative action offspring. Ah, how much more comfortable and great I would feel if affirmative action were dead!* Carter's book is heavy with such autobiographical angst. It details the author's *personal* embarrassment, his discomfort in the face of affirmative action. At times, it appears the author's *personal* discomfort alone prompts his recommendation that America eradicate affirmative action. He repeatedly tells us that he suffers near-paranoid distraction at the thought that white people might give him an "A" not because he has *merited* it but because of the dark color of his skin. His paranoia troubles him, perhaps more than "merit anxieties" trouble others. Could it be that living large in America places a special burden on Stephen Carter?

Reflections sketches for us the calm material fullness of its author's life: suburban residency (245), academic scholarships and professional degrees, Christmas parties for black Yale law students to show his "solidarity," special status as one of a minute population of black authors in the United States. Surely, these trappings qualify their bearer to track the monstrous offspring of a black "party line" to its lair and slay it utterly? Affirmative action must die. It confuses folks about who Stephen Carter comfortably and smartly is: a man of achievement, a man of *class* difference. Carter wants America to know he is well heeled and an independent thinker. He will never be a mere "follower" of any colored gospels. His "beautiful" life—complete with the self-bestowed privilege of dissociating from the interests of black Yale law students whenever principle demands—reinforces his assumption of his own black natural aristocracy. He writes:

> The black conservatives, so-called, are quite comfortable in their tenured academic positions and other posts, which is, after all, what academic sinecures are for. Despite the name calling of their critics, they will not be silenced. Nor should they be. A central message of freedom for even hated and hateful speech—a message missed equally by those on the right who would ban flag burning and by those on the left who would ban racial epithets—also holds true in this case: silencing debate solves no problems; it simply limits the range of possible solutions. (139)

The constitutional allegory thus commences.

Carter elides his personal politics of black neoconservatism with an idealistically nostalgic championing of "free" speech. Properly understood, Carter's conviction that he occupies class and occupational positions as a result of *merit* alone serves allegorically to assure us that First Amendment counters to Black Power's "party line" have been successful. Individualism—that is, a black neoconservative *I/them* distinction—is represented as (somehow) an earnest of First Amendment efficacy.

The anti-affirmative-action baby is America's best First Amendment metaphor. The *collective* interest of the black majority should bow knees in reverence to such an icon. The black *collective* should salute, sing the *Te Deum*, view St. Stephen as the apotheosis of dissent. Less exaltedly, black Yale Law School students should humbly commend Professor Carter's "free" ideological leanings when he writes as follows:

> My sympathies generally run toward freedom, and I would oppose efforts to regulate racism that is reflected in simple speech, even when the racist views are insulting, offensive, or painful. For example, I would fight, forcefully if unhappily, for the right of students to express the view (in the classroom or in the dining hall or on wall posters, signed or unsigned) that black people display a tendency toward criminality or are intellectually inferior. Cruel and insupportable such views might be, but they are plainly speech. (171)

Stunning! Yet, black law school students might be stumped about Professor Carter's relationship to the specifically *black* cultural capital that landed him his job at Yale.

How could black students find anything of benefit to their self-interest in Carter's public defense of white racism? Under interrogation, would Carter simply tell black students to put up anti-white posters? Would he defend the white racist posters as healthy "debate"? Would he define counter posters as one in a range of "possible solutions"? Is a sense of "local" responsibility with respect to black Yale students part of his professional role? We are compelled to believe Carter's response would be "No."

I believe one way of reading Carter's hypothetical sanctioning of public white supremacist advertisements in Yale's law school is as clear, personal, elitist abdication of "local" responsibility. I say "abdication" because it seems to me black professors with a sense of the realpolitik of the American academy of the 1990s, can fall back on libertarian notions of "free" speech only by refusing to see the battle actually at hand for blacks. Speech, in the racial climate of the twenty-first-century academy, is scarcely as "free" to some as to others. First Amendment "fairness" is scarcely the rule—of ethics, policy, or intellectualism—when, for example, an act of "hateful speech" issues from a black Nation of Islam advocate precisely in academic halls.

In the first quarter of 1994, a loathsome, bombastic speech by Khallid Abdul Mohammed was delivered in an academic venue. The speech became the target of a media-inspired and richly financed white campaign to compel every living black soul in the United States to condemn "hate speech." Battles rage even into the twenty-first century as an ethnically specific, economically overdetermined, white initiative to shut down black-uttered "hate speech" in the United States grows in intensity. The designated enemy for this white realpolitik is the space, place, leadership, and following of that black *religion* represented by the Nation of Islam.

Alternatively, and on a more secular and popular front, the politics of white suppression directs its attack against expressions of rap music such as the black performer Ice Cube's denunciation of Asian retailers in black urban communities. Neither religion nor the academy, it would seem, *in actually existing American reality,* protects the supposedly "hateful" speech of black folks in America. While Stephen Carter is willing busily to champion white supremacist "black bashing," there are aggressive public forces at work in the United States that do not offer even a moderate pretense to guarantee rights of blacks to "Jew bashing," "police bashing," or "retail exploitation commentary."

This unprincipled shiftiness of white American standards of "merit," "excellence," "rights," and "debate" seems not to trouble Carter. He appears to feel that by championing what he *personally* considers fair and legitimate modes of behavior he is in touch with reality. For example, he surely believes he is buttressing a non-relativistic American norm of First Amendment "free" speech when he asserts that he *personally* would condone the installation of white racist posters throughout the Yale Law School. Such implicit anxiety and confessional angst amount, I think, to an abandonment of Yale black law students, willy-nilly, to white racist caprice.

Black students petitioned the Dean of Yale Law School for an extra-classroom means of registering their problems and discomfort with instances of "hate speech" (or, better perhaps, "racial harassment") in Yale Law School classrooms. Professor Carter immediately made it known that he *personally* thought the students' request ludicrous. After all, other students feel free to take issue with professors *in* the classroom. Why shouldn't black students feel and act the same way? Black students responded by saying they felt constrained in classroom situations because white law school professors represent a "power base" that forecloses all possibility of a fair hearing for black student dissent. "Nonsense!" suggests Carter. Black students need to grow up. Yet, Carter himself—after a moving and passionate rehearsal of the sufferings of black intellectual dissenters who refuse a "party line"—cries: "But the dissenters [black neoconservative talkers] lack a black power base from which to intimidate their opponents" (172). Extraordinary! Carter's chagrin at his *personal* situation is not only hypocritical but manifestly jejune.

What in heaven or on earth might persuade the black American majority to offer themselves as a "power base" for the dismantling of affirmative action? Affirmative action, we do recall, was *not* instituted principally to guarantee admission to elite law schools for the "smartest" black middle-class kids on the block. It was instituted as a system—a proposed remedy—for years of discrimination against the black American majority. During the past three decades, affirmative action has been vigorously effective, providing jobs and job training for thousands of black people in the United States.

Why would black people, who indisputably suffer the highest unemployment rates in the nation, want to empower Stephen Carter to shut down whatever vestiges are left—in belief or practice—of affirmative action?

Does it seem at all rational for Professor Carter to solicit a *black* power base when the whole philosophical bent of his talk is precisely disempowering to the *black* student population of the institution where he wields greatest local influence? If his talk—in its "local" instances—is contrary to black emotional, intellectual, and group interests, why would he dream of securing a black majority "power base" for his views? My answer is that Carter dares to dream because he, like Shelby Steele, misreads—nostalgically allegorizes—black American history.

Specifically, Carter holds that the leadership of Dr. Martin Luther King Jr. was discontinuous with the Black Power and Black Nationalist Movements. He even implies, quite strongly, that were Dr. King alive and well in the 1990s, he would—in the name of black Christian morality—reject economic benefits of affirmative action. Such an inference seems in no way informed by an awareness of King's real and adamant calls, in his post-March-on-Washington years, for economic justice.

In his essay "The Dangers of Misappropriation: Misusing Martin Luther King, Jr.'s Legacy to Prove the Colorblind Thesis," Professor Ronald Turner notes that in a 1965 interview Dr. King was asked whether a "proposal for a multi-billion dollar program providing preferential treatment for Blacks or any other minority group was fair." The great civil rights leader responded as follows:

> I do indeed [feel it is fair]. Can any fair-minded citizen deny that the Negro has been deprived? Few people reflect that for two centuries the Negro was enslaved, and robbed of any wages—potential accrued wealth which would have been the legacy to his descendants. *All* of America's wealth today could not adequately compensate its Negroes for his centuries of exploitation and humiliation. (120)

Professor Turner concludes as follows: "One cannot fairly derive a colorblind principle from King's total message and philosophy. Such a derivation could only be achieved by omissions, distortions, simplification . . . and an overall lack of familiarity with King's views" (123).

The institutionalization, flourishing, and global work of Black Power also seems a zone of ignorance for Professor Carter. However, he seems no less optimistic about the American future than Shelby Steele, if only "integration shock" and Black Power's "party line" can be eradicated. Carter avers that "systematic subjugation of black people as a group" is an "oppression that is passing into history" (82). *Whew,* one thinks.

Nevertheless, oppression has left a "frightful legacy." The legacy that concerns Carter, however, is not what one might expect—the poverty, disadvantage, and mass imprisonment of blacks. No, for Carter the most awful legacy of American white racism is a monolithic black civil rights agenda—a "party line" blatantly out of touch with merit-based, dissenting, free-speech black intellectuals. *Whew,* one thinks.

In the present assessment of Professor Carter's tricky rhetorical agency, we should, I believe, suspend judgment for a brief reflective moment. Let us, for an instant, grant Carter his premises. For Carter, the allegorical ideal is the *intellectual*. He writes:

> part of the responsibility of the intellectual is to try not to worry about whether one's views are, in someone else's judgment, the proper ones. The defining characteristic of the intellectual is not (as some seem to think) a particular level of educational or cultural attainment, and certainly not a particular political stance. What makes one an intellectual is the drive to learn, to question, to understand, to criticize, not as a means to an end but as an end in itself. An intellectual believes in criticism in the purest sense of the word, and understands that to be a critic is not necessarily to be an opponent; an intellectual, rather, is an observer willing and able to use rational faculties to distinguish wisdom from folly. (6)

The first Emperor Napoleon—and many thousands now gone—have been aware that the etymology, history, and day-to-day incarnations of the word "intellectual" bear almost no resemblance to the allegorical archetype sketched by Professor Carter. Modern thinkers (from, shall we say, Marx, Nietzsche, Carlyle, Du Bois, and Sartre to Hannah Arendt) who have turned attention to the character of the *intellectual* have understood that any noble Enlightenment claim to "pure" and "disinterested" *reason*, on the part of any human being, is the signal for rational men and women to break out the steel helmets. As Ralph Ellison, in one of his more self-revelatory moments stated: When someone begins to proclaim that the violent erasure of emotion, affect, and everyday life is "disinterested intellectualism," then history is about to boomerang. Such proclamations always forecast the neutron-bomb interpellations of *ideology*—

hard at work and ready to detonate. Nevertheless, Professor Carter's allegorization has as its hero the fiercely individualistic, apolitical, black, "free"-speech-championing, smart kid. So "smart," in fact, that he is prone to misreadings of intellectual history like the following comparison that appears in *Reflections of an Affirmative Action Baby*.

Carter insists that *Booker T. Washington is to a Traditional Civil Rights Agenda what W. E. B. Du Bois is to Stephen Carter*. Here, allegory and a trickster's rhetorical sleight-of-hand combine as we read:

> The argument that dissenters from orthodoxy not speak for the black community is an old and vicious form of silencing. It was used to shattering effect in the age when Booker T. Washington was the only black intellectual whose views mattered. (119)

Washington is portrayed by Carter not only as an "intellectual" (though he in no way conforms to the author's own definition) but also as a thinker who symbolized a "civil rights agenda" concerned with the collective welfare of the black majority. This portrayal contains more than one false note, as almost any student of black American history knows. But . . . undaunted, Carter continues his comparison by misreading Du Bois. Much like himself, Carter asserts, Du Bois was a "dissenter," a black intellectual who believed a pure black rationality could be employed "not as a means to an end, but as an end in itself." This characterization of W. E. B. Du Bois is so surprisingly misinformed that it might prompt a savvy freshman English instructor to gloss the margins with: "You might want to read *The Souls of Black Folk*."

Du Bois's lifetime dedication was to sociointellectual activism. His chosen mode, from student days at Harvard to final labors in Ghana, was unceasing social activism, civil rights agitation, and an always radical "political" stance. Carter's effort to suture the Sage of Great Barrington to his own narrow, anxious, black conservative personalism represents either profound ignorance or base intellectual dishonesty.

Other than problematic homologies, then, what does Professor Carter put forward in his project of ameliorating, if not "curing," the curse he believes affirmative action has brought to the lives of middle-class black professionals in America? His recommendations are twofold.

First, he calls for the complete dismantling of the affirmative action apparatus in the United States. Second, he calls upon America to educate and promote a cadre of black professionals who are so excellent, so proficient, so productive that white America will concede they are "too good to ignore." One might charitably say, these recommendations are grounded not only in *nostalgia* but also in peculiar yearnings for absolutist standards. For, in the final analysis, Carter seems to abandon the Constitution altogether and joins Shelby Steele in the biblical pulpit. Which is to say, *Reflections*' recommendations seem to require at least an Old Testament God, the implicit axiology of the book being not far removed from stone tablets placed in the hands of Moses. An *absolute* standard of judgment and evaluation—independent of human foibles and Hobbesian self-interest—is Carter's foremost holy wish. However, his trickster polemics never begin to make remotely clear how *excellence* (a Lordly excellence, an excellence free from secular bias) can exist. Nor do his self-righteous posturings ever suggest how this *excellence* can be apolitically, ahistorically, unemotionally, disinterestedly conceived. The only way I think for the world to accord with Carter's wish is not through intellectualism or rational dissent, but divine ordination. *Excellence,* becomes in the allegory of Stephen Carter transubstantial with God—and his natural black aristocrats on earth. Now if this is not what Professor Carter intends I am at a loss to understand his recommendations. For certainly the smartest kid knows corporate America—in recent years and under the direct scrutiny of affirmative action—has paid huge sums in "reparations" to black employees. This same corporate America—and most recently Denny's and Texaco—has freely admitted that black employees have been denied, on the basis of skin color alone, entry, promotion, and mobility. *Excellence,* in actually existing American corporate reality, seems quite easily *ignored.* Just as "freedom" of speech for the Nation of Islam and gangsta rap have been put on hold. If, commonsensically, we accept that Stephen Carter understands American corporate and expressive economics, then it appears what our trickster Yale professor really wants to alleviate are his personal symptoms of black-conservative-lamentation syndrome (BCLS). "Woe is me! I am smart, smart, smart . . . but white people only see me as black, black, black. Woe is me!"

Finally, I believe Professor Carter can only comfortably occupy the stage of the "good life" as the smartest kid in the class when he encourages a national campaign to eradicate affirmative action. The disappearance of affirmative action will obliterate all his, and other black neoconservatives' formless little fears that race is the only purchase they have on America's attention. The shrewd homologies and "just so" stories of *Reflections of an Affirmative Action Baby* are, ultimately, only spiritedly personal tales of neoconservative racial anxiety. *Problems des riches.*

That Carter invokes the Constitution of the United States to allegorize his *personal* role in sending poor black folks up in smoke probably would not have surprised James Madison, or Chief Justice Holmes. They knew, all too well, the vagaries of men's "free" deployment of speech. Furthermore, one suspects they understood how "tricky" matters can become when one is a rhetorical agent given to comfortable and comforting predictability in the white master's house. But we all, I think, should be grateful that alternative—if equally allegorical—free wordplay allows us to *cotch* the coon at last.

Notes

1. The tale is indexed as "The Prophet Vindicated" in Langston Hughes and Arna Bontemps, eds., *The Book of Negro Folklore* (New York: Dodd, Mead, and Co., 1958), 73–74.

2. *Writing Tricksters: Mythic Gambols in American Ethnic Literature* (Berkeley and Los Angeles: University of California Press, 1997).

3. New York: Basic Books, 1991. All citations refer to this edition.

4. New York: St. Martins, 1990.

5. *The Constitution of the United States of America, Analysis and Interpretation, Annotation of Cases Decided by the Supreme Court of the United States to June 29, 1972.* United States. 92nd Congress, Second Session. Senate Document 92-82. P. 945.

Selected Bibliography

Note: The selections in this bibliography were chosen for their relevance to literary scholarship on American literature and in support of the particular issues raised in *Trickster Lives,* but they also compose a helpful reading list for anyone working on the topic of trickster. There is, however, a major portion of trickster literature that is not represented here: the hundreds of editions of trickster stories for children. It is remarkable just how many titles there are for child and young adult readers; even a cursory look at the many texts in print calls for serious study of the popularity of trickster for children.

Abrahams, Roger D. *Deep Down in the Jungle: Negro Narrative Folklore from the Streets of Philadelphia.* Chicago: Aldine, 1970.

Ammons, Elizabeth. "Introduction." In *Tricksterism in Turn-of-the-Century American Literature: A Multicultural Perspective,* edited by Elizabeth Ammons and Annette White-Parks. Hanover, N.H.: University Press of New England, 1994, vii–xiii.

Andzaldúa, Gloria. *Borderlands/La Frontera: The New Mestiza.* San Francisco: Aunt Lute Foundation, 1987.

Atwood, Margaret. "Masterpiece Theater." Review of *Trickster Makes This World: Mischief, Myth, and Art* and *The Gift: Imagination and the Erotic Life of Property* by Lewis Hyde. *Los Angeles Times Book Review,* 25 January 1998, 7.

Babcock-Abrahams, Barbara. "'A Tolerated Margin of Mess': Trickster and His Tales Reconsidered." *Journal of the Folklore Institute* 11, no. 3 (1975): 147–86.

Baer, Florence E. *Sources and Analogues of the Uncle Remus Tales.* Helsinki: Academia Scientiarum Fennica, 1980.

Blaeser, Kimberly M. "Trickster: A Compendium." In *Roots and Indestructible Seeds: The Survival of American Indian Life in Story, History, and Spirit,* edited by Mark A. Lindquist and Martin Zanger. Madison: University of Wisconsin Press, 1994, 47–66.

Bright, William. *A Coyote Reader.* Berkeley and Los Angeles: University of California Press, 1993.

Bruce-Novoa, Juan. "Canonical and Non-Canonical Texts." *Retrospace: Collected Essays on Chicano Literature and History.* Houston: Arte Publico Press, 1990.

Christenson, Abigail. *Afro-American Folk Lore.* New York: Negro Universities Press, 1969.

Combs, Allan, and Mark Holland. *Synchronicity: Science, Myth, and the Trickster.* New York: Marlowe and Co., 1995.

Cox, Jay. "Dangerous Definitions: Female Tricksters in Contemporary Native American Literature." *Wicazo-SA Review* 5, no. 2 (Fall 1989): 17–21.

Dijkstra, Bram. *Idols of Perversity: Fantasies of Feminine Evil in Fin-de-Siècle Culture.* New York: Oxford University Press, 1986.

Dorson, Richard M. *American Negro Folktales.* Greenwich, Conn.: Fawcett, 1956, 1967.

Doty, William G. "A Lifetime of Trouble-Making: Hermes as Trickster." In *Mythical Trickster Figures: Contours, Contexts, and Criticisms,* edited by William J. Hynes and William G. Doty, 46–65. Tuscaloosa: University of Alabama Press, 1997.

Erdoes, Richard, and Alfonso Ortiz, eds. *American Indian Trickster Tales.* New York: Viking, 1998.

Gates, Henry Louis, Jr. *Figures in Black: Words, Signs, and the "Racial" Self.* New York: Oxford University Press, 1987.

———. *The Signifying Monkey: A Theory of Afro-American Literary Criticism.* New York: Oxford University Press, 1988.

Grottanelli, Cristiano. "Trickster, Scapegoats, Champions, Savior." *History of Religions* 23 (Nov. 1983): 117–39.

Harris, Joel Chandler. *Uncle Remus: His Songs and His Sayings.* Edited by Robert Hemenway. New York: Penguin Books, 1982.

Hughes, Langston, and Arna Bontemps, eds. *The Book of Negro Folklore.* New York: Dodd, Mead and Co., 1958.

Hurston, Zora Neale. *Mules and Men.* New York: J. B. Lippincott, 1935; Rpt., Harper and Row, 1990.

———. *Tell My Horse.* New York: J. B. Lippincott, 1937; Rpt., Berkeley: Turtle Island, 1981.

Hyde, Lewis. *Trickster Makes This World: Mischief, Myth and Art.* New York: Farrar, Straus and Giroux, 1997.

Hynes, William J., and William G. Doty, eds. *Mythical Trickster Figures: Contours, Contexts, and Criticisms.* Tuscaloosa: University of Alabama Press, 1997.

Johansen, Ruthann Knechel. *The Narrative Secret of Flannery O'Connor: The Trickster as Interpreter.* Tuscaloosa: University of Alabama Press, 1994.

Johnson, Basil. *Ojibway Heritage.* New York: Columbia University Press, 1976.

Jurich, Marilyn. *Scheherazade's Sisters.* Westport, Conn.: Greenwood Press, 1998.

Landay, Lori. *Madcaps, Screwballs, and Con Women: The Female Trickster in American Culture.* Philadelphia: University of Pennsylvania Press, 1998.

Lenz, William F. *Fast Talk and Flush Times: The Confidence Man as a Literary Convention.* Columbia: University of Missouri Press, 1985.

Levine, Lawrence. *Black Culture and Black Consciousness: African American Folk Thought from Slavery to Freedom.* New York: Oxford University Press, 1977.

Lincoln, Kenneth. *Indi'n Humor: Bicultural Play in Native America.* New York: Oxford University Press, 1993.

Lopez, Barry Holstun. *Giving Birth to Thunder, Sleeping with His Daughter: Coyote Builds North America.* New York: Bard/Avon, 1990.

Makarius, Laura. "The Myth of the Trickster: The Necessary Breaker of Taboos." In *Mythical Trickster Figures: Contours, Contexts, and Criticisms,* edited by William J. Hynes and William G. Doty, 66–86. Tuscaloosa: University of Alabama Press, 1997.

Niditsch, Susan. *Underdogs and Tricksters: A Prelude to Biblical Folklore.* San Francisco: HarperCollins, 1987.

Papanikolas, Zeese. *Trickster in the Land of Dreams.* Lincoln: University of Nebraska Press, 1995.

Pelton, Robert D. *The Trickster in West Africa: A Study of Mythic Irony and Sacred Delight.* Berkeley and Los Angeles: University of California Press, 1989.

Radin, Paul. *The Trickster: A Study in American Indian Mythology.* With commentaries by Karl Kerényi and C. G. Jung. New York: Greenwood Press, 1956.

Ramsey, Jarold. *Reading the Fire.* Lincoln: University of Nebraska Press, 1983.

Ricketts, Mac Linscott. "The Shaman and the Trickster." In *Mythical Trickster Figures: Contours, Contexts, and Criticisms,* edited by William J. Hynes and William G. Doty, 83–96. Tuscaloosa: University of Alabama Press, 1997.

Roberts, John W. "The African American Animal Trickster as Hero." In *Redefining American Literary History,* edited by A. LaVonne Brown Ruoff and Jerry W. Ward Jr., 97–114. New York: Modern Language Association of America, 1990.

———. *From Trickster to Badman: The Black Folk Hero in Slavery and Freedom.* Philadelphia: University of Pennsylvania Press, 1989.

Sekoni, Ropo. *Folk Poetics.* Westport, Conn.: Greenwood Press, 1994.

Sherman, Josepha. *Trickster Tales: Forty Folk Stories from around the World,* illustrated by David Boston. New York: August House, 1996.

Smith, Jeanne Rosier. *Writing Tricksters: Mythic Gambols in American Ethnic Literature.* Berkeley and Los Angeles: University of California Press, 1997.

Swann, Brian, and Arnold Krupat, eds. *Recovering the Word: Essays on Native American Literature.* Berkeley and Los Angeles: University of California Press, 1987.

Thomas, H. Nigel. *From Folklore to Fiction: A Study of Folk Heroes and Rituals in the Black American Novel.* New York: Greenwood Press, 1988.

Thompson, Vivian L. *Hawaiian Legends of Tricksters and Riddlers.* New York: Holiday House, 1969.

Turner, Victor. *The Ritual Process.* Ithaca, N.Y.: Cornell University Press, 1977.

Vizenor, Gerald. *Manifest Manners: Postindian Warriors of Survivance.* Hanover, N.H.: Wesleyan University Press, 1994.

————, ed. *Narrative Chance: Postmodern Discourse on Native American Indian Literatures.* Norman: University of Oklahoma Press, 1989.

————. *The People Named the Chippewa: Narrative Histories.* Minneapolis: University of Minnesota Press, 1984.

————. *The Trickster of Liberty: Tribal Heirs to a Wild Baronage.* Minneapolis: University of Minnesota Press, 1988.

Wadlington, Warwick. *The Confidence Game in American Literature.* Princeton, N.J.: Princeton University Press, 1975.

Walker, Barbara G. *The Woman's Encyclopedia of Myths and Secrets.* San Francisco: Harper and Row, 1983.

Wiget, Andrew. "His Life in His Tail: The Native American Trickster and the Literature of Possibility." In *Redefining American Literary History,* edited by A. LaVonne Brown Ruoff and Jerry W. Ward Jr., 83–95. New York: Modern Language Association of America, 1990.

Notes on Contributors

Houston A. Baker Jr., professor of English at Duke University, was for many years director of the Center for the Study of Black Literature and Culture and Albert M. Greenfield Professor of English at the University of Pennsylvania. In 1992 he served as president of the Modern Language Association. He has been the recipient of a number of awards, including ten honorary doctoral degrees, poetry prizes, teaching awards, the Pennsylvania Governor's Award for Excellence in the Humanities, and grants from the Guggenheim Foundation, the National Humanities Center, the Fulbright Fellowships Program, the National Endowment for the Humanities, and the Rockefeller Research Fellowship Program. He is an internationally known lecturer and the author of dozens of books and essays on African American literature, literary theory, and related topics, including *Black Studies, Rap, and the Academy, Workings of the Spirit: A Poetics of Afro-American Women's Writing, Blues, Ideology, and Afro-American Literature,* and *Long Black Song: Essays in Black American Literature and Culture.*

Sandra K. Baringer received her Ph.D. in English from the University of California, Riverside. She has served as a postdoctoral fellow at the University of California Humanities Research Institute. Her work has been published in *American Indian Culture and Research Journal* and *Studies in American Indian Literature.*

Sacvan Bercovitch is the Charles H. Carswell Professor of English and American Literature at Harvard University. He has served as chair of the English Institute, president of the American Studies Association, and fellow of the American Academy of Arts and Sciences. He has been honored by grants from the Woodrow Wilson Foundation, the Ford Foundation, the Huntington Library, the Guggenheim Foundation, the American Council of Learned Societies, and the National Endowment for the Humanities. In 1992, he won the James Russell Lowell Prize from the Modern Language Association for best scholarly book. Bercovitch has published more than 150 books, edited collections, articles, essay-reviews, and translations, including *The Puritan Origins of the American Self, The American Jeremiad, Reconstructing American Literary History, Ideology and Classics American Literature, The Office of "The Scarlet Letter,"* and *The Rites of Assent: Transformations in the Symbolic Construction of America.*

Lawrence I. Berkove is professor of English and director of the American studies program at the University of Michigan–Dearborn. He is a specialist in American literature of the late nineteenth and early twentieth centuries. He has published extensively on Twain and is particularly interested in assessing the influence of Calvinistic thought on his literature and in studying Twain's skill with language. Berkove is also a noted scholar on Ambrose Bierce, Jack London, Dan De Quille, and other Comstock authors. He is presently editing a book of Comstock memoirs and preparing an anthology of Comstock literature.

R. Bruce Bickley Jr. is professor of English and former associate and interim Dean of Arts and Sciences and Director of the Honors Program at Florida State University. He is the author of numerous articles, reviews, and book chapters, as well as *The Method of Melville's Short Fiction, Joel Chandler Harris, Joel Chandler Harris: A Reference Guide, Critical Essays on Joel Chandler Harris,* and *Joel Chandler Harris: An Annotated Bibliography of Criticism, 1977–1996.*

María DeGuzmán received her Ph.D. in English and American literature from Harvard University where she taught Latina/o literature in the expository writing program. She is now assistant professor of Latina/o Literatures and Cultures in the Department of English at the University of North Carolina, Chapel Hill. Her current projects include a book manuscript *"American" In Dependence: Figures of Spain in Anglo-American Culture.* She is the author of essays on Floyd Salas and on the Spanish American War, and with art historian Jill H. Casid, she has coauthored and produced three photo-text essays, one published in *Art Journal* and two in *Iris.*

William G. Doty is professor of humanities and religious studies at the University of Alabama at Tusacaloosa. During the academic year 1997–98, he was Goodwin-Philpot Eminent Scholar at Auburn University. He is author, editor, or translator of some fourteen books and eighty essays, including *Mythical Trickster Figures: Contours, Contexts, and Criticisms; Mythography: The Study of Myths and Rituals;* and *Picturing Cultural Values in Postmodern America.*

Claudia Gutwirth is a Ph.D. candidate in English literature at New York University. Her areas of interest include structuralism, literary genealogy, and the intersection of art and technology. Her essay in *Trickster Lives* is the first time her work has appeared in print.

Lewis Hyde has worked as an electrician, counselor, and professor. He is the author of *Trickster Makes This World; The Gift: Imagination and the Erotic Life of Property;* and a book of poems, *This Error Is the Sign of Love.* A MacArthur Fellow and former director of creative writing at Harvard University, he is currently Luce Professor of Art and Politics at Kenyon College.

Gail Jones is lecturer in English at the University of Texas at San Antonio. She has served as assistant editor of the *Call,* the newsletter of the Jack London Society. She has authored essays on Jack London and presented papers on London at conferences sponsored by the Jack London Society, the American

Literature Association, Associated Colleges of the South, and the Texas Medieval Association. She is presently completing an edition of short stories.

Debbie López is associate professor of English at the University of Texas at San Antonio. She is the author of essays on Keats, Melville, Twain, and London, and has completed a book manuscript entitled *Taking the Fall: Lilith and Lamia in the New World Eden*. She is a regular participant in conferences of the American Literature Association and the Jack London Society.

Nancy Alpert Mower teaches writing and literature at the University of Hawai'i at Manoa. She has written extensively on Hawaiian folklore and has presented her work at the American Literature Association Symposium on the Trickster and at other national conferences.

Jeanne Campbell Reesman is interim dean of graduate studies and professor of English at the University of Texas at San Antonio. She is the author of *American Designs: The Late Novels of James and Faulkner* and *Jack London: A Study of the Short Fiction*. She is coauthor of *Jack London: Revised Edition* (with Earle Labor) and *A Handbook of Critical Approaches to Literature*, 4th ed. (with Wilfred Guerin et al.). She edited the collection *Speaking the Other Self: American Women Writers* and coedited *Rereading Jack London* (with Leonard Cassuto) and *No Mentor But Myself: Jack London on Writers and Writing* (with Dale Walker). At present, she is at work on a book manuscript entitled *In the House of Pride: Jack London and Race*.

Jay Winston teaches composition and literature at the University of Rochester. He has previously taught at Northern Arizona University. His scholarly interests include hybrid texts in twentieth-century American literature, from various "modernisms" to the "Native American Renaissance."

Index

Kingston, Maxine Hong, xx, 2, 187
Kokopelli, 7
Krishna, 190–91

Lamia, 123–24, 126
Language, trickster and, xv, xvi, xviii,
  xxvii, xxviii, xxxi (n. 41), 4, 85, 97,
  131–46, 160–62, 195, 205
Laye, Camara: *The Dark Child,* 35; *Drums
  and Shadows,* 35
Legba, xi, xv, 42
Lenz, William, 110
Leskov, Nikolai, 82 (n. 12)
Levinas, Emmanuel, 8, 79–80
Levine, Lawrence W., 39, 42
Lévi-Strauss, Claude, 3
Lewdness, xiii, 3, 7, 168
Lilith, 121–29
Literature, trickster in, xi–xii, xxii–xxiv
Loki, 185
London, Jack, xxvi, 110–18; "The Dream
  of Debs," 118; "Goliah," xxvi, 116–18;
  Martin Eden, 111; "The Master of
  Mystery," xxvi, 115; *The People of the
  Abyss,* 111; "The Priestly Prerogative,"
  xxvi, 114; "The Seed of McCoy," xxvi,
  115–17; "The Son of the Wolf," xxvi,
  114–15
Lono, 16
López, Debbie, xxvi
L'Ouverture, Toussaint, 100
Lowell, Robert, 103; *The Old Glory,* 103
Lowry, Malcolm, 174, 177

Madison, James, 197–98, 208
Makarius, Laura, xiii
La Malinche, xi
Malinowski, Bronislaw, 111
Mann, Thomas, 2
Mao Tse Tsung, 63
Mapplethorpe, Robert, xxx (n. 35)
Marx, Karl, 205
Masau'u, 9
Mason, Mrs. R. Osgood, ix
Matlacihuatl (Entangling Woman), 188

Melville, Herman, xxiii, xxvi, 78, 82
  (n. 10), 97–107, 110, 174; "Bartleby,"
  98; *Benito Cereno,* xvi, 97–107; *The
  Confidence-Man,* 99; *John Marr and
  Other Sailors,* 99; *Moby-Dick,* 99; *Omoo,*
  99; "Piazza Tale," 78, 82 (n. 10); *Pierre,*
  99; *Redburn,* 99; *Typee,* 99; *White-Jacket,*
  99
Millman, Lawrence, 11
Milton, John, 138
Mimicry, 36
Mohammed, Khallid Abdul, 202
Monkey King, xi, xix, xxiii, 187
Mookini, Esther: *He Mo'olelo Ka'ao o
  Kamapua'a,* 21
Mooney, James, 34, 36–37, 44, 45
Morrison, Toni, xxvi, 121–29
Moss, Thylias, xxvi–xxvii, 131–46; "The
  Adversary," 132, 137, 139;
  "Approaching Venus' Flytrap During a
  Hungarian Film: A Subtitle," 143–46;
  "Birmingham Brown's Turn," 143;
  "Interpretation of a Poem by Frost,"
  142; "Passover Poem," 132, 135–36,
  139, 141–42; "Running Out of
  Choices," 131–32; "Spilled Sugar," 132,
  138–42; "There Will Be Animals," 142;
  "Tribute to Jesse and Then Some," 132,
  136–37, 142; "The Wake for the Lost
  Two Hundred Miles," 132, 134, 139;
  "The Warmth of Hot Chocolate," 132,
  138–39, 140, 145
Mower, Nancy Alpert, xxiv
Multiculturalism. *See* Trickster:
  multicultural context of
Mure, 100–107

Nanabozho, xxiii, xxvii, 148–62
Nation of Islam, 202, 207
Native American Indian myth and
  religion, xvi–xvii, 27; gender in, 8–9;
  interpretations of trickster figure in, 1,
  2, 9–11; motifs in, 6–8; other cultures'
  understanding of, 3, 4–5; syncretism of,
  159. *See also* Cherokee myth and